A Year
and a Day

A Year
and a Day

HOW THE LISBON LIONS
CONQUERED EUROPE

Graham McColl

SIMON &
SCHUSTER

London · New York · Sydney · Toronto · New Delhi

A CBS COMPANY

First published in Great Britain by Simon & Schuster UK Ltd, 2017
A CBS COMPANY

1 3 5 7 9 10 8 6 4 2

Simon & Schuster UK Ltd
1st Floor
222 Gray's Inn Road
London WC1X 8HB

www.simonandschuster.co.uk

Simon & Schuster Australia, Sydney
Simon & Schuster India, New Delhi

A CIP catalogue record for this book
is available from the British Library

ISBN: 978-1-4711-5710-3
Ebook ISBN: 978-1-4711-5712-7

Typeset in Bembo by M Rules
Printed and bound by CPI Group (UK) Ltd, Croydon, CR0 4YY

MIX
Paper from
responsible sources
FSC® C020471

Ltd are committed to sourcing paper
in sustainable forests and support the Forest
international forest certification organisation.
SC logo are printed on FSC certified paper.

CONTENTS

CHAPTER 1

Made in America

It was a goal of quality to win a lusty all-British affair and it warmed those who had left the comfort of their homes and braved the iron-cold conditions. Celtic were taking on Tottenham Hotspur and Jimmy Johnstone, the Celtic outside-right, had been fielded, craftily, by Celtic manager Jock Stein in a more central role, at inside-right. Johnstone had dropped deep into the middle of the park to draw several Spurs players to him, which made especially effective his natty pass, crisp as a newly sliced apple, to Stevie Chalmers. The centre-forward had taken over Johnstone's natural beat and went whirling down the wing in his teammate's place, covering half the length of the pitch, before cutting inside to the goal-line and whipping over a cross for Bobby Lennox to come hurtling in and whisk a diving header past Bill Brown, the Tottenham goalkeeper. It made the score 2–1 and sealed a vital victory for Celtic that had been forged in the fierce heat of competition.

Celtic were far out of sight not only of Tottenham – on the day – but also of their own followers, through performing in an unseasonably frigid San Francisco as part of their close-season tour of North America in the late spring and early summer of

1966. There had been a non-partisan, neutral crowd of 12,000 looking on at the Kezar Stadium and no major trophy at stake but Celtic, in the 1960s, famously and avowedly did not play friendlies: the Glasgow club contested every match, regardless of its billing, with intensity and purpose and a desire to win. This match had proved that to be no empty motto.

The dynamic fashion in which Celtic took the game to Spurs enthused the organisers of a series of challenge matches that summer of 1966 which had the objective of popularising football – or soccer – in North America. Celtic were putting together a whole new ball game and those Americans present were being given a privileged preview of it.

The match with Tottenham arrived in the middle of a tour that had begun on 12 May 1966 with a 10–1 victory over a Bermuda Select. The trip combined hard training with sight-seeing, socialising and activities such as snorkelling, sunbathing, visits to horse-racing and receptions with local dignitaries. The players had barely finished their domestic fixtures – with a 1–0 win at Motherwell on 7 May that clinched the Scottish League title – before they were whisked on to a transatlantic flight. There were no complaints at being taken away from hearth and home for five weeks; the opposite was true. A place on the tour was prized by every player and those in and around the first team had fretted for weeks over whether Jock Stein would include them or not. Holidays to the USA were, in the mid-1960s, only for the super-rich and footballers were still far from being included in that bracket. These were young men who, as boys, had holidayed, if they were lucky, within Scotland and now they had the chance to visit the land of all-night diners and tailfinned cars, a near-fantasy land that represented post-war expansiveness and freedom, as seen in the movies. When the time came for those selected to be measured for their special suits and raincoats, the ones who missed out watched all those preparations with heavy hearts.

'It was the making of us, that tour,' Bobby Lennox, the Celtic outside-left, says. 'It got us all together. We'd fly to Toronto, train the next day, play the next night; fly to New York, train, play; it was great and everybody got so friendly and so close and it helped the team blossom; it really did. St Louis, San Francisco, Los Angeles; Vancouver; it was the trip of a lifetime. In the sixties, America felt as if it was a million miles away. We knew two or three months in advance that they were only taking a certain number of players and you were really hoping you were going; that you were actually going to San Francisco.' Although not, under Jock Stein, wearing flowers in their hair.

'It couldn't happen now,' Lennox says. 'It was glamorous at the time but it was part of the job. I was engaged to Kathryn and, even then, phoning Kathryn at her mum's house in Saltcoats – I had to phone from my hotel room to the girl downstairs [on reception] and say, "Ardrossan/Saltcoats . . . A . . . R . . . D . . ." right through . . . She'd go to New York and go through the spiel to the girl in New York, who'd go on to the girl in London, then she'd go on to the girl in Glasgow. I'll never forget the first day I did it. I sat for ages waiting to get through – and Kathryn was out . . . I couldn't believe it – you were quicker writing letters.

'It got us all so close. Bobby [Murdoch] moved into midfield and joined Bertie [Auld]. We trained hard and we had to win the games. It was a great five weeks. Jock got everybody going and found room-mates for people although Jimmy and I were always together. He might change some people but he and I always roomed together.

'Everybody loved Bermuda, obviously. So on the last day there, we were out having our photograph taken in front of the Princess Hotel, which was magnificent. Sir Robert [Kelly, the Celtic chairman] was there and he said, "If you win the European Cup, you'll be back." That was a throwaway line . . .'

Eddie Baily, the Tottenham assistant manager, who was selecting their team in place of Bill Nicholson, the manager, admitted that Celtic were on a different plane to their British friends and rivals. 'They are a better team than us,' Baily had said of Celtic prior to that friendly between the clubs in San Francisco. 'All I can hope to do against them is prevent goals. I do not have men with the ability of that little fellow Lennox to get goals close in. We must try to contain them as much as possible. I'm sorry it has to be this way but our reputation can't stand a big defeat so we'll play a very tight game.' That was quite an admission of inferiority from a representative of a club that was one of the premier forces in the British game in the 1960s. Tottenham had won the FA Cup and League Double early in the decade and had become, in 1963, the first British club to lift a European trophy, when they had beaten Atlético Madrid to win the European Cup-Winners' Cup. The London side, though, would prove to be distinctly inferior to Celtic over three matches between the clubs during a tour that would not only be the most vital in Celtic's history but one conducted almost in private. No British television station sent cameras to the matches and there was minimal interest from the North American media – and so Jock Stein could experiment in peace with the shape and set-up of his team.

'Out there,' Billy McNeill said, 'we would have meeting after meeting and you could just sense that Jock was preparing the groundwork for the following season and the European Cup. It cemented the relationship between the players and not only did that help each of us individually, it helped to galvanise the whole team.' Celtic had always had soul – an indomitable spirit was now being added to that by Stein.

The supporters at home would, in time, enjoy seeing the fruits of that North American odyssey but a fortnight into Celtic's five-week stint across the Pond, the major sporting news back in Scotland had been as expected for the time of year – the Epsom Derby, still held on a Wednesday afternoon, and the most glamorous occasion in the flat-racing season, was enjoying its annual day in the sun, although for most Britons, the panoramic splendour of the Downs would be viewed only through the narrow aperture of a black-and-white television screen – albeit a new, 23-inch one for the well-heeled among the population. Charlottown, ridden by Arthur 'Scobie' Breasley, a 52-year-old grandfather, won the race, confirming that the unlikely can – and will – happen in sport. Fanatics in Glasgow, desperately seeking a fix of football, could take in the Junior Cup final replay at Hampden Park on the evening of Derby Day, 25 May, in which Bonnyrigg Rose would defeat Whitburn 6–1.

Glasgow was undergoing one of its perennial wet spells and anyone seeking solace in television that Wednesday evening would find no sport on the schedules; the early evening bringing instead a programme that encapsulated, through its name alone, the mores of the new teenage-orientated times – *A Whole Scene Going*. The Beatles had released a new single, 'Paperback Writer', which Paul McCartney admitted was not their best but which he defended on the grounds that they could not keep writing love songs for ever and that they had to experiment if they were to move forward. It was just another day in the 1960s.

Celtic, themselves experimenting, spent 25 May 1966 in Hamilton, Ontario, Canada, where they were to face a pasta-fuelled concoction – the Hamilton Primos, who performed in front of minuscule crowds and who were limping along pitifully after having been rescued from collapse only through the sponsorship of Primo Poloniato, a local Italianate-foods magnate.

'Big Jock used the Hamilton game as a training session rather than as a competitive game,' John Clark, the sweeper in that Celtic team, says, 'as he did another game, down in St Louis, to keep us match-fit. It gave him a chance to play players in different positions, forward-wise.

'The night before the Hamilton game he made us go to see *The Sound of Music* at the cinema. Nobody wanted to go because everybody had seen it but rather than have players all out the night before, even before a game against Hamilton, he wanted us somewhere where he knew where you were. He didn't want you out before a game, even though it wasn't a key game, you know? He made sure of every detail, like that, and that you were well fed and that everything was spot on in terms of your travelling and the hotels, the flights. On that tour, we also got more in-depth closeness with him.

'Jock had a good way with him. There was always a bit of fun and laughter about the place. If you got him angry you would get the backlash. He could sometimes put it on a wee bit, then walk away and you would see Neilly [Mochan, the trainer] laughing because he knew it was a wind-up but the players maybe didn't know it was a wind-up.'

That limb-loosening exercise against the Hamilton Primos proved to be a match typical of a tour that was something of a picaresque adventure and that would see Celtic confronting giants and nipped by gnats. Covering 15,000 miles in total, Celtic would face clubs such as Bayern Munich, the West German Cup holders; Bologna, the runners-up to Internazionale in Italy's Serie A; and Atlas of Guadalajara, who had finished second in the Mexican league; as well as Tottenham Hotspur. Interspersing fixtures against such clubs, Celtic would also face local, patched-together outfits, whose quality was not so much variable as uniformly poor. Thus, on that May evening, a week before facing Spurs in California, Celtic came face to face with the Hamilton Primos, a club patched together through three Italian players and eight hard-bitten Britons.

Stein was treating every game on the tour with his habitual

seriousness and he told his men to go out and get the match won early on, so that he could make some substitutions and rest some of his men for the subsequent meeting with Bologna. The Celtic players followed their manager's instructions to the letter, going 9–0 up by half-time. Not that Stein was entirely happy with that – at the interval he could be found laying into his attacking players for faults in their performances. His team eventually won 11–0, which meant that they had now won all five of their tour matches up to that point and had scored 35 goals, conceding only one, in a 10–1 skewering of the Bermuda national side.

'The first week of that tour, in Bermuda, was supposed just to be for relaxation,' John Clark says, 'but Jock Stein didn't think like that. He arranged a game with the local people.

'On that tour, you were in the best hotels and had the best of everything. It was really professional – there was also no idea that you could just hang about, have a drink, come back when you wanted, oh no . . . he was spot on. He didn't over-train us; just enough to keep your legs moving and for sharpness because we were training, playing matches, flying all over the place. We trained enough to keep our fitness but never over-doing it because we had the travelling and America is all flights of two or three hours.

'He gave us a bit of freedom to let us enjoy the cities we were visiting. The word they use now is "bonding"; we wouldn't have known what the word means but that was what we were doing. Oh, America was the making of a lot of good things for us. Seriousness and fun, combined together, helped to make the whole thing. Things like seeing the Golden Gate Bridge . . . remember, this was a time when seeing things like that was almost unimaginable.'

The impression of Stein being a strict disciplinarian, who would afford his players little room in which to breathe, is exploded by Clark, although it is clear that there was a limit as to how far the players would be allowed to go in any given situation. The manager, a strict teetotaller, would sit up far into the night, drinking tea endlessly, and abhorred alcohol, viewing it as a bad habit, especially for professional sportsmen.

'He didn't like to see people drinking,' John Clark confirms. 'He knew people were drinking but he didn't like to see it. He never hammered people for it but when he got the players on the training field, he knew there were certain individuals he would have to pick up and get it [the alcohol] out of them. He knew the ones to do it with. He knew who to pick out and say, "Tomorrow morning we'll get you on the field . . ."'

'He mixed with you all the time and he always wanted to know where everybody was. He had his moments with players, disciplining them a wee bit, over in the States, naming no names . . . but you couldn't really step out of line with big Jock by behaving in indisciplined fashion – he'd just put you on a plane and tell you to go home.'

Stein's side Stateside had wowed seasoned observers of the game – Billy Steel, the former Dundee and Scotland great, and now an American citizen, had stood amazed at their skills and fitness. Sammy Cox, a former Rangers favourite, who had emigrated to Canada, was so enthusiastic about Celtic's style that he had mingled with the players sporting a Celtic badge in his jacket lapel. Richard Attenborough, the actor, who was in California making a film called *The Sand Pebbles*, travelled to the game with Atlas on the Celtic team bus after having been asked to the team hotel by Stein to wish them luck.

The five-week-long excursion would come to be regarded fondly by those who had been on it – a mere eighteen players – but they had little immediate nostalgia for the experience. That would take time.

'Most of the boys would be willing to take on a similar

venture in the future – but not too soon,' Billy McNeill was to say that summer of 1966 as he anticipated the squad's return to Glasgow. Players such as Ian Young, the full-back, allowed to return a week early for his wedding, expressed relief, arriving back in Scotland, to have all the travelling behind them. There were outbreaks of homesickness among the players and nor did the Celtic players have to look too far to find friction on the field despite their being nominally involved in a series of bounce games. If they were taking it seriously, so too were some of their opponents. Tottenham's tackling in the three matches between the clubs was brisk and unforgiving but within the type of parameters with which British players were familiar. Spurs players such as Pat Jennings and Terry Venables spent even more time with the Celtic players than with their own squad-mates, at the clubs' shared hotels.

Bologna were a different prospect entirely. The match between the Scots and the Italians took place on Friday 27 May 1966 at the Roosevelt Stadium in Jersey City, New York, a city whose population was beginning to drop as a result of elements such as gridlock, pollution, violence and vandalism. Into this urban maelstrom, Celtic flew, only to face their own slice of vice – Jock Stein afterwards described the game with the Italian side as a 'disgraceful exhibition: Bologna were desperate to win and when they realised they were being outplayed they were ready to stop our players in any way they could.'

Juan Carlos Morrone, the Argentinian forward featuring for Bologna, on loan from Fiorentina, was dismissed after 65 minutes by Harry Nowick, the referee, after fouls on Tommy Gemmell, Auld and Murdoch. Bottles were subsequently hurled on to the field of play, from the crowd, which was composed almost entirely of New Yorkers of Italian descent. Three times, Bologna tried, and failed, to introduce, surreptitiously, replacements for Morrone, who supposedly had to be threatened with arrest before he would finally leave the pitch. Newspaper reports back in Scotland suggested that Celtic players had been struck by stones and mud, pushed and jostled and that the police had used force to put an end to it all. John Clark suggests that that was a fabrication.

'There wasn't a riot or anything like that,' John Clark says, 'just guys that were over-enthusiastic coming on to the field. I can't remember any riot or players being struck by stones. It wasn't anything vicious although I do remember an American policeman on a horse getting guys off the park who had broken on to the field.'

The match, which ended goalless, was one that neither side had actually wished to play: Stein had baulked at the pitch, which had been marked out on a baseball diamond and which was less than the stipulated regulation-width for football, while the crossbars had been hung comically low by the organisers. The field of play was rutted in places, bare in patches. But given that the crowd had already been admitted to the stadium, both the Scottish and the Italian clubs' officials had agreed to proceed. It was possibly the sole moment in keeping with a friendly match on a night of general hostilities.

The players soon recovered. At Celtic's team hotel, Billy McNeill played a joke on one teammate and, in retaliation, the wronged party picked up the book on McNeill's bedside table and asked, 'Are you enjoying this book, Billy?' The tome was then flung out of the window high in the hotel, whence it went hurtling to the ground, along with McNeill's travel money, which he had kept within the book's pages. A posse of players went racing down the stairs, chasing the dollars.

The team 'lived out of each other's suitcases', as Bertie Auld put it. The Celtic men, as with any band of brothers, frequently borrowed each other's gear as part of the process and one evening, during their sojourn in Canada, the players were attending yet another interminable civic reception when, after quite a few drinks had been consumed, a strawberry, of all things, dropped from the buffet table on to the top of one player's shoe. He immediately sought a perpetrator. As Tommy Gemmell, the full-back, was nearest to him, he opted to blame Gemmell for planting the strawberry on his shoe and snappily exacted retribution by grabbing the back of the shirt Gemmell was wearing and ripping it in two until the collar was the only part of it remaining intact.

'How do you like your shirt now, Gemmell, eh?' he enquired, less than solicitously.

Tommy replied, 'My shirt's fine; it's in the wash – this is one I borrowed from Bertie.'

Stein's team were being hot-housed in experiences that could not be found in Scottish football: deep humidity on some match-days; pitch-invading opposition supporters; seriously hostile and expertly brutal opponents; deep and solid defences; fanatical opposing team managers; travel to matches through varying time zones; hugely unsatisfactory playing surfaces. The match against Spurs in California, for example, on 1 June, came more than halfway through the schedule, but it had been the first time on the tour that the Celtic players had really been happy with a pitch: the Kezar Stadium, more usually the home turf of the San Francisco 49ers, had a good surface with long grass.

Celtic had featured regularly in Europe since 1962 but the 1966–67 season would see them make their first attempt at winning the European Cup; Stein saw this as an advance opportunity to prepare them thoroughly for the forthcoming challenges at the club game's highest level. His players all had some experience in Europe, but they had not come across the same intensity before, in such a short space of time, with each game producing a different type of conundrum, as they did on that tour across North America. All of these varying experiences would inure the Celts against being surprised by anything that might be thrown at them in the European Cup campaign.

Stein had experimented freely. Gemmell had been used in a more attacking, midfield role at certain stages in matches as a means of pressurising the opposition. The player, the most extrovert in Stein's team, and a man not averse to posing for pictures with an airline stewardess slung across his arms, had been moved to right-back on the North American tour, from his usual position on the left side of the defence. Stevie Chalmers, too, had been fielded there, as Stein sought a player with pace to fill that role – in Chalmers' case the experiment had lasted only as long as the first attack of the opposition before his complete unsuitability as a defender was exposed and he was swiftly switched upfield.

'Many of the moves made and the player switches tried will serve us well as the season goes on,' Stein said, stressing that he was looking for 'an improvement' on the previous season, when Celtic had won the league and the League Cup. 'We were happy with last season's performance but we will be trying to step up on it, particularly in Europe.'

Other than the closeness induced by the tour, these players were bound together by a serious commitment to Celtic. This was in the era before badge-kissing became fashionable, not least because the Celtic strip did not feature a badge – and the Hoops were also, as yet, unsullied by a commercial sponsor being emblazoned across the chest or anywhere else on the team kit. Had there been a badge, though, it is unlikely that the Celts of that era would have yielded to the temptation to seize it and slobber over it or extend it from their chest or to beat it with their fist in a quasi-religious gesture as a means of establishing common ground with the supporters on the terracing or in the stands. Their commitment was deeper, ingrained in their minds, in their souls. They were all local players, all part of the community, the majority of them Celtic supporters from birth. They did not need to make superficial gestures of allegiance because their feeling for Celtic came from the heart.

As Joe McBride, the striker, put it, 'In most games that you play for Celtic, you get this feeling that you're playing for the best team in the world, and, having been a Celtic fan all my days, every time I pulled that jersey on it gave me a kick.' There were no calculated career moves from such players; no plans to remain at Celtic for two or three years – or fewer – to see if something bigger and better might come along. For most of Stein's players, there was nothing superior to taking the field in a Celtic jersey.

Bertie Auld had twice joined Celtic and twice his feeling for the club and what it offered him had won him over when he would have been rewarded better financially elsewhere, not least after having moved to England and joined Birmingham City, with whom he had achieved considerable success both domestically and in European competition.

Others of Auld's teammates had made similarly private pledges of loyalty to the club. Bobby Lennox, for one, had been courted by numerous clubs as a teenager, including Chelsea, but had resisted them all assiduously, remaining in Junior football until Celtic sought his signature. Stevie Chalmers, also in Junior football, had been offered tempting signing-on fees from other clubs but he too had resisted until Celtic came along to ask him to sign. John Clark, the sweeper, had been the first groundstaff boy in the club's history and had had to paint various fixtures and fittings inside the ground in green as part of his duties; he was stained green.

'The bulk of the players,' Billy McNeill said, 'would have wanted nothing other than to play for Celtic. We had a magnificent team spirit. We enjoyed each other's company. I'm not saying we were the greatest pals – we weren't – but we had a feeling and a pride in our achievements and we enjoyed the fact that we could take on the best on the European scene and do well.'

A third tour match with Tottenham, this time in a rainy Vancouver, at the Empire Games Stadium on 4 June, saw Bobby Lennox – who had been unearthed on this tour as a goalscorer of exceptional ability – latch on to a fine Johnstone pass in the 19th minute to notch his 18th goal in nine tour games. Celtic shared the same hotels and transport to and from the games with Tottenham and prior to that match players had ridden in the same hotel elevator. Alan Mullery, Tottenham's excellent midfielder, and Lennox had stood smiling at one another, almost nose to nose. 'This is as far away from me as you'll ever get tonight,' Mullery warned Lennox, in friendly fashion, in advance of Lennox quashing his words emphatically with his goal.

A huge furore would follow Spurs' equaliser. 'I can still see it,' Lennox says. 'There were about three minutes to go when big Gilly [Alan Gilzean, the Tottenham striker] pushed Billy and Terry Venables knocked it in.' Jimmy Johnstone complained so stridently to John Webber, the referee, that he was dismissed, for the third time in his Celtic career. Johnstone, who had been spoken to repeatedly by the referee during the match, did walk off – but only to take up his habitual position on the right wing. The referee warned that he was prepared to leave the field if Johnstone did not accept his decision. At that point, Dave Mackay, the Spurs captain, intervened as a key character witness to plead Johnstone's case to the referee, stating that the Celtic player had been such a fulsome entertainer that he should be shown leniency and allowed to remain on the field of play. The referee finally relented, albeit 'against my better judgment', and accepted that as this was an exhibition match and Johnstone had exhibited greater flair than anyone else on the field, discretion should be extended in his direction and he should be allowed to remain on show.

The amicability of the tour had been restored by the time Celtic, now in the final days of their transatlantic travels, returned to California to face Bayern Munich on Wednesday 8 June 1966. The Germans had voyaged to the USA still celebrating their 4–2 West German Cup final victory over MSV Duisburg in Frankfurt on the previous Saturday and had bounced hazily on to the Californian Tarmac on arrival, beaming broadly and collectively, and looking surprisingly refreshed for men who had just undertaken a transatlantic flight. It seemed likely that they would be in the mood to be taking it easy in a friendly to be played only hours after touching down on American soil.

Celtic, in contrast, had by this stage become drastically depleted and appeared to be limping to the conclusion of their tour – Stein even nursed the concern that they might not be able to field a full side for their final matches, against Bayern and Atlas of Guadalajara. Auld was injured, as were John Cushley and Frank McCarron, who was having intensive treatment on his injured ankle. Johnstone and Ian Young had been given special dispensation to return home on Monday 6 June to prepare for their long-planned weddings the following weekend and Stein was now considering the prospect of fielding John Fallon, the reserve goalkeeper, in an outfield position or borrowing a player from Tottenham to make up the numbers.

'I remember big Jock saying to me, because they were falling like tenpins, "Phone Agnes and put the wedding off,"' Johnstone laughed. 'I said, "You're joking." This was to be like a royal wedding, with the publicity and everything. I said, "How can I?"' Johnstone had initially agreed to relieve the pressure on Stein's squad by remaining with Celtic until after the match with Bayern but, temperamental artiste that he was, had then changed his mind following his objection to his putative dismissal during the third game with Spurs. Johnstone had begun the tour by suffering a dose of sunburn in Bermuda and was now concluding it with a dollop of pique. He departed from Canada on the Monday, a decision that would have lasting consequences for the winger, who landed at Prestwick Airport laden with gifts but also with a phobia that would haunt him for the remainder of his life.

'On the flight coming back,' Johnstone said, 'the bloody thing fell I-don't-know-how-many-thousand feet out of the sky. It was horrific. It wasn't just a wee bit of turbulence. All the meals were being put out. We were fourth from the back – Ian Young and I. We had cut the tour by a couple of games because he was getting married as well. So me and him came back together and they were serving two seats in front of us and without warning the whole thing fell and all the food was suspended in the air – there were "weans" up in the air. You should have seen the mess of everything after it. The stewardesses were all over the place. So I hated the flying because of the fright I got. It left me petrified. That's what did it for me. Before that I had been flying everywhere, which we had to do. People would always talk to me about that being only one incident but I would say to them, "If you get caught in an electrical storm, that will soon change your mind about the flying."'

It was a patched-up Celtic, then, shorn of the team's most eye-catching component, that took the field at the Kezar Stadium on Wednesday 8 June, where they ran into some serious turbulence of their own. Celtic, well ahead of their opponents in terms of skill and attacking flair, dominated Bayern to an uncanny degree but found themselves freakishly 2–0 down to a double from Rainer Ohlhauser. John Hughes, the Celtic winger, would later state that the Bayern game was particularly notable in that

Celtic were dominant to a degree he could not remember in any previous match against a top-notch side. Bobby Lennox brought a goal back with his 19th of the tour but with the game winding towards its conclusion, one incident sparked another riot.

'Late in the match,' Stevie Chalmers recalls, 'we won a corner-kick. I was standing on the goal-line, waiting for the ball to be delivered, when I was whacked, full in the face, by Gerd Müller, the striker, back helping his team defend their goal. He took to his heels, so I followed him, across the penalty area, off the field of play and away round the back of the German team's goal.'

The incident is described laconically by John Clark as 'a bit of a skirmish down in California'. It sounds, in retrospect, like a scene from a slapstick movie, although Chalmers afterwards felt severe pain from the stinging cut on the inside of his mouth that he had sustained from Müller.

'Stevie punched him,' Clark says, 'and they ran after one another and players then ran after them. We then got to a tunnel and there was no way out because the door was locked and everybody was caught in the one place. In an instant, it was all over. It was just a case of the German hit our player and our players hit him back. That was Gerd Müller; so it wasn't dud teams you were playing.'

Hundreds of supporters subsequently invaded the pitch. The game was held up for five minutes, with Stein intervening to calm things down as fights involving the invading fans erupted. Zlatko Čajkovski, Bayern's dangerously driven Croatian coach, had spent the second half behind the Bayern goal and his presence would seem directly to have inflamed the situation.

Once everyone had calmed down and the match had resumed, Joe McBride got the equaliser for Celtic. Fred Reynders, the local referee, said afterwards that he had intended to send off Chalmers and his German assailant. 'I made for the goalmouth where it all started,' Reynders said, 'but before I reached the trouble there were eight or more players brawling there and then others began to fight behind the goal. I would have had to send off eight players and that was out of the question.' Čajkovski had wished to take his team off the field ten minutes from time but Stein had intervened to keep the game going.

'We were so much on top,' Stein said, 'that I would never have allowed our lads to leave the field when the Germans wanted to chuck it. They started the trouble because Chalmers was clearly assaulted and no man can take that stuff without hitting back. The Germans introduced a new dimension to the game – eleven-man defence.'

The storm soon blew over. 'We were fine with the Germans after that,' John Clark says. 'It was just frustration. It fizzled out quickly.' The following day, though, as Celtic left the hotel that Bayern had shared with the Scots, Müller stood outside the building impassively, smugly, provocatively, enjoying immensely the shouts and abuse he received from Celtic players as they boarded their team bus.

The temperature soared too during Celtic's meeting with Atlas of Mexico in the Coliseum Stadium, Los Angeles, reaching the nineties, but while Atlas rotated their team through the use of substitutions, Celtic, by force of necessity, had to keep their starting eleven unchanged throughout. Willie O'Neill and Joe McBride were both carrying injuries but Stein had no alternative other than to field them.

'When we played Atlas, the Mexican champions, down in the Coliseum,' John Clark says, 'that was really burning hot that day. That was the last game, us finishing off, but they were just after their season that week. Technically, they were really good.'

Even against Atlas, with the homeward journey at the forefront of their minds and at the conclusion of a lengthy tour, the Celtic players had strained every nerve, muscle and sinew to secure the win; and it made no difference to them that the game was played in baking heat. They were, as Stein demanded of them, unflagging in their efforts, relentless to the last, and Charlie Gallagher scored the only goal of the game two minutes from the end. Gemmell broke forward and hit the ball hard and low into the penalty area for Gallagher to slip it into the net from the edge of the six-yard box.

It was, then, a weary, depleted but largely happy Celtic party that touched down in Scotland early in the morning of Wednesday 15 June 1966, with players having fitted in a visit to Disneyland to watch a film being shot; a trip to Grauman's Chinese Theatre where foot- and handprints of the famous are in the cement of the sidewalk; horse-racing at Hollywood Park; before flying into Prestwick on a VC-10 from New York.

On tour, Celtic had secured eight victories and three draws in their eleven games, scoring 47 goals and conceding only six. Kurt Lamm, President of the American Soccer League and the tour organiser, told Celtic at the end of the tour that he wanted them back. 'Write your own tour schedule,' he said. 'Celtic are the greatest team we have ever brought over here.'

Stein and his players were considerably less keen, at the time, to return even though Stein described the tour as having been 'a great thing for the club in so many ways. We have played against different types of teams in different conditions and we have met rough teams, just as we might in European Cup games. The trip has been tough but it has strengthened the spirit among the players. We have been almost able to see that spirit grow.

'We've had tiring moments, difficult times here and there but on the whole nothing but good can come out of this tour for us. The players know each other as they have never done before. They have become a much closer-knit team and team spirit has improved as a result. They have shirked nothing – but a future tour would have to be shorter, with fewer games. We have found five weeks just over-much.'

Fast cars and glitzy holidays always appealed greatly to Stein and a stylish vehicle was ready to speed Stein away from Prestwick for a quick break before he got down to plotting a way forward for Celtic that would take them on an even greater and more memorable journey.

CHAPTER 2

New Ball Games

It was almost as if Jock Stein saw the staging of the 1966 World Cup as something of a personal affront. His punchy comments after his visit to the tournament suggested that it had been little more than an enormous waste of this busy man's time. He stated that he had not seen a single thing that he might incorporate in Celtic's play for the new season.

'The big difference between the 1966 World Cup and the first World Cup tournament I saw,' he said, on arriving back in Glasgow from the North East of England in the mid-July of 1966, 'was that in Switzerland twelve years ago there were entertaining, attacking ideas galore. Celtic took their players to that 1954 World Cup in order that they should learn.' Stein had at that time been a solid, stolid centre-half who had just captained Celtic to their sole league title in an arid twenty-seven-year period that would end only with his accession to the post of Celtic manager in 1965. He had been captivated by the flexibility of the Hungary team, whose whirling football, flexible, non-fixed forward line, swift interchanging of position and precise passing game took them to the final, only for them to be overwhelmed by the physical force and pragmatism of West

Germany. It was a memory that would inspire him as to what might be possible for a well-organised, well-coached football team from a modest-sized nation. The Hungarians, for all their skill and style, had paid for a lack of a hard edge, a flaw that could never be laid at the door of any of Stein's teams.

'Not a single thing practised by any of the teams in Group Four will be copied at Celtic Park,' Stein said of the 1966 versions of Italy, the Soviet Union, Chile and North Korea, adding that he had felt a sense of disappointment at the 'grave lack of entertainment provided by the majority of World Cup games so far. Strictly speaking, something can be learned from any game but there was nothing in the North East to copy because there was nothing on show there that I had never seen before,' Stein stated firmly. 'Our style won't be changed and nor will the endeavour to play attacking football that pleases the public.'

It is unlikely that Stein was shamming when making such statements but, with his memory for detail, his witnessing of the international encounter between Italy and the Soviet Union would have been added to the bank of information that the manager stored in his vast vault of a mind, which held treasures of footballing knowledge. An Italian side featuring three players from Internazionale of Milan had sat back with a stacked-up defence while the Soviet Union players sought victory from first to last, plugging away patiently until Igor Chislenko streaked away from Giacinto Facchetti, Inter's left-back, to score the game's only goal in the 57th minute. A packed, massed Italian defence could be beaten, Stein had seen, through patience, perseverance and a steady, unwavering commitment to attack.

The World Cup was still in progress, its quarter-finals in prospect, when Celtic returned to training on 21 July 1966, a Thursday, although some players had returned early for extra work – John Hughes, Billy McNeill, Joe McBride, Ian Young,

Tommy Gemmell, John Cushley and Bent Martin. These players, the post-honeymooning Young apart, were characterised humorously by Stein as his 'heavy team' – the more powerfully built members of his side – and he duly provided them with extra conditioning work to keep them in trim.

'In those days, your manager didn't often come out and take part in the training, but Jock did,' Billy McNeill said. 'He made sure he was there and what he did was put the emphasis on positive football. The ball wasn't usually seen in training sessions back then but with big Jock it was an intrinsic part of it all. We never did anything without a ball. That was forward thinking.'

It was unusual for the loquacious Billy McNeill to come up with a one-word answer to any question but that was his response when asked what it was that drove Jock Stein to achieve things for Celtic. 'Success.' That was the only word McNeill felt it necessary to use; that was really all there was to it. Stein had been in professional football for quarter of a century and had been a working man for thirty years by the time he arrived at Celtic as manager and although he had enjoyed a couple of trophy-winning years at Celtic Park during the tail end of his career, that was counterbalanced by many more unsuccessful years as a player with Albion Rovers and Llanelli. It left him hungry to make much more of his managerial career – and of his life – now that he had the opportunity.

Stein had spent too long in obscurity to relinquish easily his chance in management. There would, consequently, be nothing half-hearted about his approach to his job of improving his players and his team. This was serious stuff. Stein had to be the focal point at the club; he had to have total responsibility for all team matters and that way he could be sure that everything was done the way he wished it to be. Delegation did not come easily to him. Everything went through him. His own special governance was essential.

When the players were at Seamill, their training base on the Ayrshire coast, Stein would amble into the lounge and seek a place to sit that would allow him to watch the door and see everyone within the room. If someone was already sitting in such a spot he would be told to shove up by the manager to make space for Stein. He feared anything escaping his attention. Seamill had been used by Celtic for decades prior to Stein's arrival, as a place of preparation for major matches; the unspoken reason as to why the club would decamp from Glasgow was to keep all of the players in one place and to ensure that they refrained from over-indulgence in alcohol in advance of kick-off time for a big game. That remained important to Stein but he did more with the place, using it as a haven, where for a few days the players could relax into the right frame of mind for a match and could rid themselves of pre-match tensions. It also enabled him to read them closely, to gauge their moods, to see how they interacted over an extended period of time. The traditional purpose of the resort was also important to Stein as it allowed him to underline his hatred of his players indulging in alcohol. If a player was nursing what appeared to be a soft drink, Stein would express a degree of thirst and ask for a taste. If he found that the concoction contained some surreptitious vodka or rum, the offender might find the contents of the glass being tipped over his head.

Stein would mow the grass on the pitch at Celtic Park; he would answer the telephone at the club to random outside callers. He alone would deal with the press and if players had a problem, they would tend to go straight to Stein with it, bypassing Sean Fallon, the assistant manager, even though it took a great deal more bravery to confront Stein in his office. Going to anyone other than Stein was pointless.

His bulk made him an intimidating figure. Stein was around six feet tall and his love of sweets and heavy food – the types of stews and puddings that fuelled industrial Scotland – had increased his weight to around 15 stones by the mid-1960s. He would tower over players and, if giving them a dressing down, he would seem to become bigger and bigger and ever more intimidating.

At training too, Stein was the focal point. The ankle injury that had ended his playing career in the late 1950s would bother him for the remainder of his life and prevented him participating in full-scale practice matches but that made him even more dominant on the training ground. His bear-like figure – and growl – and his dark tracksuit made him a distinctive presence. He would be among his players and yet slightly distanced from them. He could stand back and observe, in his watchful way, how his men were performing. He was not averse to a joke in training and he could join in with any laugh that was going but he could be all smiles one day and then, when the players arrived for training the following morning, he would be glowering over them and ready to put them through the mill in a tough, two-hour session. Through such unpredictability and the exercising of it, Stein maintained his power and control over the players. There was always a degree of distance between him and them, which was something he worked hard to maintain. They were not allowed to get close to him. Just when they thought they could spy a chink in his armour, just when they thought they were broaching the invisible shield that prevented them getting close to him, he would shut himself off again.

Fear underpinned everything Stein did as a manager but he did not succeed because his players were terrified of him. It was a special kind of fear that he instilled in them – a fear of failure, a fear of being omitted from the team and from his plans; not only because that would hit them hard financially but because, as soon as he arrived at Celtic, it had become clear that things were starting to happen for the club. Anyone who was not fearful of missing out on being part of Stein fulfilling his promise would have been of no use to the manager.

'He never asked you to do something you weren't capable of doing,' Tommy Gemmell said. 'He had a great saying, "Play to your strengths and disguise your weaknesses." He made us very tactically aware, we were extremely fit, he was good at motivating. He was always experimenting – he tried a lot of things in training that sometimes we would never use in matches because he thought they wouldn't work. Everyone played to their strengths.'

Fun could quite as easily be to the fore in much of Stein's dealings with his players. He enjoyed bustling around the training ground, setting up drills, joshing with players such as Jimmy Johnstone, but if a training drill was not carried out properly, he would soon explode into anger. Stein's thinking was that training should be carried out with the same intensity as a match because, he felt, if it was not, then how could players suddenly find a higher level of play on a matchday?

Jock Stein's playing career had schooled him in the necessity of taking nothing good for granted in football. He had been a doughty centre-half: big, bulky, good in the air but a player who would get through a game without exhibiting any particular flair on the ball. People did not pay at the turnstile to see Jock Stein perform and, as with so many managers, the playing style of his teams was in contrast to that which he had exhibited as a player. He was determined to produce teams that exhibited flair and were attractive to watch.

Stein's lack of outstanding playing talent had seemed destined to ensure he would spend his career in some of the quieter backwaters of British football, never even enjoying reflected glory among the game's gilded performers. Stein was born on 6 October 1922, in Lanarkshire, and made his debut for Albion Rovers, the tiniest and least successful of his native county's senior clubs, during the Second World War. For the next eight years, he combined playing football in the bleak surroundings of Cliftonhill with work as a miner, before switching, in 1950, to non-league Llanelli in Wales. A year later, his first big break arrived out of nowhere.

At the beginning of December, Celtic had been stricken by injuries to their central defenders and were scrambling around, looking for emergency cover, when Jimmy Gribben, a trainer and a scout on the club's backroom staff, dredged his memory and recalled a player whom he thought might be able to fit the bill. Stein was duly signed for Celtic for a fee of £1,200 from Llanelli on 4 December 1951. When his name was announced over the Tannoy at Celtic Park as part of the line-up for the match with St Mirren four days later, a loud murmur of surprise rippled round the ground. It was the last time in his life that Stein would suffer from obscurity. One year later, having established himself in the Celtic team, he was made captain. They swiftly won the Coronation Cup in 1953, and a League and Cup Double in 1954.

'A lot of that was down to him,' Billy McNeill said in remembering Stein the player. 'Not that he was the greatest player in the world but he was a good captain and a good leader. Those things left a big impression on me, a young Celtic supporter at the time. The fact that he would sometimes knee the ball rather than kick it was quite interesting. That's not a skill that many people perfect but the big fellow did.'

As Celtic took the field in another Scottish Cup final, in the spring of 1955, against Clyde, Stein, the captain, looking severe and serious, wore a glowering frown, while behind him Charlie Tully grinned broadly. Tully was the team's star forward but he was also a serious drinker with an aversion to training and a propensity to go AWOL. Stein could not afford to treat the game so lightly but he learned from such wayward characters that not all footballers ticked away like him. Stein's wary outlook was justified when he picked up an ankle injury in a game against Rangers in August 1955. After several unsuccessful attempts at a comeback, he was advised to retire, in 1957, by a London specialist and it was then that Robert Kelly, the Celtic chairman, intervened in a fashion almost as vital to Stein's career as that of Gribben six years earlier.

'We like the Stein influence at Celtic Park,' Kelly said, 'and have offered Jock a scouting appointment. He will also learn the managerial side of the business from Jimmy McGrory. This will stand him in good stead for the future.' Stein was soon coaching the reserve team and revolutionising that stratum of the club. The players had used fishermen's jerseys as training tops and the rough material would brush against their skin. Those jerseys would then remain unwashed from one training session to the next. Stein ensured that the players were given more appropriate kit and that it was washed regularly and he also made a point of getting to know his teenage players as people, taking time to talk to them and make them feel appreciated and important rather than merely the second-string, back-up boys. Those off-field methods, together with some advanced coaching, worked, most notably when Celtic won the Scottish Second-Eleven Cup final in 1958, with Stein's boyish Celtic side defeating an experienced Rangers 8–2 on aggregate. A total of 40,000 people had watched the two legs. Stein was on his way.

Dunfermline Athletic offered him his first managerial post in March 1960. He pulled off a win over Celtic in his first game as a manager and saved the Fife club from what had seemed certain relegation. The following year Stein's Dunfermline lifted the Scottish Cup, the club's first major trophy. European football came to Fife, bringing some unforgettable floodlit nights to the regulars of East End Park. Stein followed that with a sustained league-title challenge at Hibernian, whom he joined in 1964, and so, when he returned to Celtic at the beginning of 1965, he had accumulated more than a decade of experience relating to displaying leadership skills as player, coach and manager. That grounding ensured that Stein's right to respect when taking over at Celtic could not be disputed. As his players got down to training in the July of 1966, Stein had every right to look relaxed in the role as the central figure at Celtic.

In his 1966 pre-season training sessions, Stein focused heavily on shooting practice, with players constantly taking shots at either end of the field. Amazing that, even half a century later, such things are not always prioritised by managers. Bent Martin, a Danish goalkeeper signed in January 1966 after performing well for Aarhus against Celtic in the European Cup-Winners' Cup, and John Fallon, Ronnie Simpson's predecessor as first-choice goalkeeper, were at one end trying to keep the shots out and Simpson and John Ferguson, another reserve goalkeeper, were at the other.

'It was really demanding over the season to play on the pitches we had here in the Scottish League,' John Clark says. 'Now, there is more thought put into fitness and sports science – our sports science was Jock Stein. That was it – end of story. He knew what to do – he was away ahead of his time. He didn't overstep the training and if he thought people needed a wee rest he would let them walk about and do their own thing. All of the training methods that you can see nowadays, Jock was doing back then.'

Intriguingly and imaginatively, another addition to a 1966 pre-season Stein session was a match in which two teams of fourteen faced each other, using two balls. Workers constructing the new Jungle enclosure looked on agog as Stein put his players through a futuristic footballing session on the pitch during an intense two-and-a-half-hour stint.

'We worked with the ball all the time,' Jimmy Johnstone said. 'Big Jock was a great believer in that. As soon as the training started, the first day, all the balls were out. That is the secret: work with the ball all the time. Maybe seven or eight exercises with it; volleying it from both sides, crossing it, heading it. That meant we could concentrate on moving the ball at speed, and moving position at speed, because we were all so comfortable with the ball. We made it look awfully easy at times, we really did.'

Few players had needed the change of manager from Jimmy McGrory to Jock Stein more than Jimmy Johnstone. His talent had never been in doubt but he had been affected even more than most of the Celtic players by the whimsical workings of Jimmy McGrory, the manager, and Sean Fallon, his assistant, both of whom were heavily influenced by Robert Kelly in his role as chairman. Most notably, Johnstone had been dropped for the replay of the 1963 Scottish Cup final with Rangers to make way for Bobby Craig, one of a series of eccentric – and expensive – Fallon-Kelly-McGrory signings. Celtic lost 3–0. That was an inauspicious ending to Johnstone's first season in the first team. His debut had also been symptomatic of those mismanaged times – a 6–0 defeat at Kilmarnock. During the first half of the 1964–65 season, prior to Stein's arrival as manager, Johnstone had played regularly for Celtic but, alone among the Celtic forwards, he had failed to score a league goal. Not only that but, as Stein took charge, Johnstone had been demoted to the reserves and it was at half-time in a second-eleven match with Hibernian that he visited the toilet only to find the fearsome figure of the Celtic manager following him in and rapping out a ready riposte to the player's willingness to allow his talent to fizzle away in mediocre fashion.

'What the hell are you doing here?' Stein asked Johnstone rhetorically. 'You should be in that first team. You get out there now and show me what you can do.' A bemused Johnstone would respond immediately.

'See that man for motivation . . .' Johnstone said. 'He was unbelievable. Nobody had ever said anything like this to me before. I went out in the second half and scored a hat-trick, didn't I? See that wee gee-up, what a difference that made! That was the man's greatest strength. He just knew exactly the right thing to say to every player to get them motivated. Not just with me; with everybody. He knew me better than anybody in the world. He knew all my moods and habits. I don't know how. I think he should have been a doctor, a psychiatrist! He knew people and because he knew what made us tick, he made us feel we were the best team in the world. He knew how to make us believe in ourselves.'

There would be little further reserve football for a player who was transformed by Stein and whose potential had been spotted by no less a figure than Alfredo Di Stéfano, the world's most distinguished footballer. 'This little man is a magnificent player,' Di Stéfano said after Celtic's match in Barcelona in late 1964, 'and one I would be proud to have in any side in which I was too.'

Yet it had been beyond Fallon and Kelly and McGrory to get the best out of the headstrong, often wayward 'Jinky' Johnstone. His was a mercurial talent, one that, until that point, would shine only when it took his fancy, as Stein had suggested during that toilet talk. Johnstone's abilities would subsequently be harnessed and channelled by the imposing Stein, who tamed him – as far as anyone might – while simultaneously freeing him from the shackles of the traditional winger's role. Johnstone, under Stein, evolved into something new, the man with the free role, the 'out' ball for his teammates. British wingers, traditionally, had been light and quick and designed to go to the goal-line and, from close to the corner flag, whip in a cross for a centre-forward, muscles bulging, to beat off defenders' challenges and plant the ball in the net. Under Stein, Johnstone had the scope to rove inside, outside or through the middle, turning the role of the winger into something new. He also became a reliably regular goalscorer and, alone among his teammates, assured of being the only forward who could feel secure of his place in the Celtic side every week while the others were interchanged at will by Stein. Insecurity had been replaced by certitude but Johnstone could still fall foul of the manager if he failed to obey instructions and work his magic within Stein's well-defined parameters.

Johnstone and his teammates had returned from holiday that summer of 1966 to find a ground that had been radicalised for the new season. The old, dilapidated barrel roof that had stood over the north terracing for decades, and which had run parallel to the touchline, had been stripped away and replaced by one that, innovatively, did not leak, unlike its predecessor, and which stretched the length of the touchline and covered the terracing known as 'The Jungle' – always the most raucous and uproarious section of the ground. That old roof had looked as dated as the 2-3-5 formation of previous decades and the terracing below it had now been elevated for a new and heightened Celtic era; resurfaced, streamlined and smartened up – in keeping with the sudden arrival of a team that bore only the most tenuous connection with its predecessors.

While the Celtic players, fresh from holiday, were limbering up for the new season, training in 83-degree heat in Glasgow, news arrived that some of Europe's more gilded names were having a less pleasant summer. Sandro Mazzola, Italy's star striker, was shielding his face upon being driven away from the airport in Genoa, where the Italian team was pelted with rotten tomatoes after Italy's elimination from the World Cup, following defeat by North Korea. Fans in a furious crowd of

700 banged Mazzola's car windows and kicked the vehicle, just in case he was not fully aware of their displeasure. The Italian team, most displeasingly for the fans, had appeared resigned to their fate long before the end of the game against North Korea, lacking in spirit against a side that took the game to them with an overwhelming degree of drive and passion. What lessons might the onlooking Stein have taken from that one?

Quietly, unobtrusively, amidst all the World Cup hoopla, the draw for the first round of the European Cup had been made in London on 10 July, the date of the World Cup's opening match. It paired Celtic with FC Zurich, the Swiss champions.

'I'm happy enough with the draw,' Stein said, with his habitual care and caution, 'but you can't treat anyone with disdain in this class of competition.' The news provided a tingling of anticipation that would not leave Celtic supporters even through an unprecedented, gluttonous feast of televised World Cup matches and even though, at the time of the draw, the tie was a whole ten weeks away.

CHAPTER 3

Full Control

'Celtic will do well in the European Cup,' Matt Busby, the Manchester United manager, said in the August of 1966. 'They have a good, all-round side and the way they go about their work is bound to bring success. I was impressed by their half-back line of Murdoch, McNeill and Clark. Gemmell was an outstanding full-back. And that support . . . I thought I had seen and heard everything from Everton and Liverpool supporters but the Celtic fans beat the lot. Their enthusiasm seems to give the players additional energy and they never stop running.'

It was all beautifully diplomatic on the part of Busby, a softly spoken, genial and seemingly avuncular individual, not least because his team had just suffered a 4–1 pre-season defeat to Celtic. Privately, though, Busby questioned whether Celtic would be found wanting if they were to reach the fiercely contested, latter stages of the European Cup. He had gone close to winning the trophy several times and so he understood the perils that lay ahead. Jock Stein did too and he was aware that the weeks leading up to Celtic's first participation in the tournament would be vital if his side were to make a credible and concerted attempt at winning it.

There are few more delicate living organisms than that of a football team. This is a game that demands finely tuned individualism – when the ball arrives in the vicinity of a player he may head it, pass it, hold on to it, get rid of it, dither over it ... He can apply artistry to what he does, perform his task in a basic, functional manner or do something in between but whatever he does must be carried out with precision. He can direct the ball to any point within 360 degrees of him; short or long. The player also, almost contradictorily, has to balance the urgent requirement for individual initiative and improvisation with an awareness of their responsibilities to the team. The game is about self-expression from the first minute to the last. At the same time, again almost contradictorily, the player who deviates from the team ethos has the potential to poison everything.

It was bearing all of that in mind that Jock Stein described his Celtic side as a team without any stars. Stein could coax and cajole players into following his demand for selfless invention; equally, he could be hard – it was unusual but not unknown for him to whack a player around the head if the manager felt that was required to maintain discipline.

Football is such, though, that even in sides constructed on steely teamwork, such as Stein's Celtic, sustained success will still see certain players exalted more than others. It has to happen. Supporters require points of attraction and football journalists, many of them more akin to showbusiness columnists than experts on the game, need individuals upon whom they can hang their hat. Such players are not always the best or most important to the team but simply the most eye-catching.

Jimmy Johnstone was the undoubted star of Stein's Celtic side. His inimitable close control, springy red hair, diminutive frame and penchant for the unexpected, all combined to make him stand out. The other player whose style caught the eye was John Hughes, a player, unlike Johnstone, who could veer between pantomime villain and silky virtuoso, very often in the same game. Even Jock Stein, a man certain of his mind and of his opinions, appeared unable to categorise the player. When Stevie Chalmers became only the third Celt to score a hat-trick against Rangers in a league match, in January 1966, he was told by Stein, in the minutes post-match, that Hughes had outshone and out-performed him. Yet in other matches Stein, on the bench, could see the ball hurtling out of play, often in his direction, with Hughes standing stork-like on the touchline, having been unable to control it. Stein would mutter to those around him on the bench, 'I've got no idea why I keep playing him.'

A boy athlete, Hughes would stand out as soon as he stepped on to the football field principally because of his powerful physique. Tall and strong and sleekly built, he had been per-forming as centre-forward when Jock Stein arrived at the club but the manager switched him to the left wing, where his pace, control and power would, Stein thought, be more effective — and at those moments when he harnessed all of those assets, it was. Alternatively, that physique would draw extra attention to him when he failed to prosper. Nicknamed 'Yogi', seemingly after the American cartoon bear who was 'smarter than the average ranger', Hughes would eventually find his image less than cartoonish, would come to see himself as a performing bear and tire of being enchained by the club and exalted, berated and baited in almost equal measure. He also had developed a dislike of Jock Stein, the person. His great friend John Divers had been unceremoniously ejected from the club in the summer of 1966, after having been made to train on his own by Stein during the previous season. Divers had discovered only via the newspaper that he was to be leaving Celtic, whom he had served for the previous decade.

'Stein used to say, "I'll put you in the stand for six weeks." If he did that, you lost your bonuses,' Hughes says. 'It was him

[Stein] who decided who was in the squad and if he dropped you, you missed out on bonuses. So that's how much control he had over things. Nowadays, if a player is earning thousands of pounds a week and the manager threatens to put them in the stand, they'll go and sit there quite happily. He was very good at his job but he ruled by fear.'

Stein was not scary enough, though, to prevent Hughes, on his return from holiday in the July of 1966, seeking a confrontation with the manager. The player had turned down Celtic's contractual offer prior to taking his annual break one month earlier and Hughes's restlessness was so well known inside the game that Joe Harvey, the Newcastle United manager, had approached Stein at the World Cup and asked about taking Hughes to St James' Park.

'I have tried to get him before,' Harvey said of Hughes, 'and now that he is unsigned I thought it was worthwhile making an approach on a friendly basis to Jock Stein while he was in this area. Jock, naturally, wants to keep him and, for the time being, the matter rests there but I have left him in no doubt as to our interest.'

The situation involving Hughes reflected a restlessness in Scottish football during the summer of 1966.

Several prominent players had made public their desire to leave their clubs because of dissatisfaction with their level of pay. The most luminous rebel who felt he had a cause was Denis Law, the Scotland and Manchester United striker, who had asked to be placed on the transfer list because he had believed there should be a signing fee due to him when he agreed a new contract with United. His contract had expired on 30 June 1966 but in the 1960s this did not make him a free agent, able to negotiate his price with a series of clubs desirous of his services; a situation of huge advantage to a footballer. No – if Law or any other player, including those at Celtic, failed to sign a new contract, the club retained their registration, preventing them moving anywhere at all. That could leave a player out of the team, excluded from training and, as Hughes suggests, on pitifully basic wages if they were unable to come to terms with their employer.

It was a situation deeply disadvantageous to the game's performers and one against which independently minded individuals, such as Hughes, were bound to chafe as they felt the leash that bound them to their club to be uncomfortably tight. Hughes resented the power that a manager could have over his earnings and thus his welfare. Yet the situation was of enormous benefit not only to the manager but also to Celtic and to the supporters of the club. The control that a football club could exert upon its players meant that a manager really could build a team, really could plan as long term as the vagaries of a contact sport will allow, rather than simply talk about it for public relations purposes and to keep the fans at bay. The manager really did have a pronounced influence on his players and on their lives in general, which, in turn, ensured he had the authority and the power to maximise from them a high quality of performance. Call it fear, call it coercion, call it anything you wish, it worked when a manager such as Stein knew how to exploit the terms under which players were tied to their club.

'I believe that we are capable of losing the next game we play,' Stein would say. 'And I try to gear the players up to that fact. We make changes to the line-up frequently. That way, no-one becomes complacent.'

Stein had been given an open-ended amount of time to stamp his imprint on Celtic; he would have been amazed at an era in which the average timespan for a manager in, for example, the English top flight would be a mere nine months. The contractual situation for footballers also meant that there was no annual, or biannual, 'churn' of players exiting a club at the conclusion of their contracts – and there was certainly no question of Celtic signing any player on loan as a quick fix. As Celtic prepared for the 1966–67 season, no-one moved into or out of the club. The players could feel that they were, to a large extent, owned by the clubs but it made for a precious stability across the game of football. 'There's no point in being told you've got full control,' Stein would say, 'unless you really have full control.'

Stein blended a progressive approach to football with a traditional approach to players' pay. Celtic's players, that 1966–67 season, were, on average, earning £40 per week: with Billy McNeill, the captain, on £50 – unbeknown to his teammates. Jim Craig, in the final year of his dentistry degree at the University of Glasgow, and who had consequently missed the tour of the USA, was on £30 a week, and glad of it.

'Football would just give you a living at that time,' John Clark says. 'I started on a fiver a week, then I got seven pounds a week, then it went to ten then to fourteen then to eighteen – the highest wage I got was about sixty pounds a week – and you got bonuses as well. Other people could earn the same as us, maybe through working a lot of hours with a lot more effort. It gave us a good enough living back then but you weren't making enough money to put away plenty for the future – no way could you do that. I wouldn't change my life – in my time I was happy and I enjoyed playing and we got a lot of success, a lot of honours, won everything that was going in football and got capped by my country. What more could you ask for?'

As in life, so in football. The perception of Stein among his players depended on the individual concerned. To the brooding Hughes, Stein came across as vindictive. To the more naturally ebullient among his players, he was a source of inspiration.

'I thought Jock was great,' Bobby Lennox says. 'He made us all players. We were going nowhere until he arrived and said, "We could maybe do this and maybe do that." He knew when to have a laugh with you and when to show he was the gaffer. After European Cup ties we would all come in at eleven o'clock and there were a couple of massage tables and him and Sean and all the boys would be lying having massages or be in soapy baths and Jock would have a wee sing-song with us. Once he walked out of the dressing room, though, he was the gaffer again. He knew when to give you a pat on the back and when to come down on top of you. He was great – he read things so well. He liked a laugh and a sing-song but he was the gaffer and you always knew he was the gaffer. You always watched what you were saying in front of him.

'He knew his football inside out but big Jock ruled by fear a lot – although you admired him, you were frightened of him. In those days you were tied to that club and that manager as long as they said, "We're retaining you." His man-to-man motivation was great. He never missed a thing. He knew everything that was going on.'

For his part Stein, the tough, hard, former miner, spoke almost movingly of how he saw the players as being like family – 'because I spend more time with them than I do with my own family'. As in all the best families, discipline was to the fore. The manager admitted that he would feel 'a sag' some mornings on his way into Celtic Park but that he would find his spirits pick up on sight of the players and that he would revive fully once in among them. Simultaneously, and this is perhaps what Billy McNeill means in describing Stein as a complex character, the manager would freely admit to being something of a loner. The two elements in Stein's character are not contradictory. His working background had made him aware of the dangerous vagaries of life, leaving him wary and watchful, and it was through a detached but close, studied understanding of people that he understood how they worked. That, in turn, made him a successful communicator and motivator.

Stein dealt with the press in summary but not summery fashion in the July of 1966, when he made it clear to them that he had no inclination to discuss any player's contractual situation, including that of John Hughes. 'There's nothing to say on that,' he commented shortly after Celtic had returned to training. Stein stated that there had been no offers made for Hughes but Harvey and Newcastle soon submitted to Celtic a bid of £72,000 for the player.

It was a tempting piece of bait for Celtic, who, to put the matter in perspective, had made a profit of almost £10,000 in winning the league and the League Cup in the 1965–66 season. Entry to the ground on a league matchday would be four shillings for the terracing and seven shillings for the stands so it would take an awful lot of shillings, to equate to £72,000, a figure only slightly short of the record transfer fee between British clubs.

Hughes had proved to be the only Celtic player unwilling to accept terms for the following season. The others watched and wondered what the outcome would be. Stein knew that a slip in his handling of the situation could result in a mass outbreak of contractual discontentment among his players. That would be disastrous for any attempt at making progress in the European Cup.

'The fact that John Hughes is for sale does not mean that we are planning to follow the Alf Ramsey line of discarding orthodox wingers,' Stein said, noting the success of the England manager in doing so at the World Cup. 'We still have Johnstone, Auld, Chalmers, Lennox and Gallagher, who can play the old-fashioned wing game and while Hughes may go, we are still looking for other forwards. The accent for us will still be on prudent, attacking football.' It was a wily statement from Stein; neat, pointed and precise. It showed Hughes that he was dispensable. It showed that Stein would not be held to ransom over pay. It showed the other players named that he prized them as highly as Hughes, regardless of the price Newcastle would be prepared to pay for the winger. Simultaneously, it showed them that with such a depth of competition, none of them could be sure of their places in this Celtic team. It underlined that Celtic were a team without stars.

One day later, Hughes had re-signed, but Stein was unforgiving of anyone who crossed him and Hughes's jutting out of his chin had the potential, long term, to have a bruising effect on his relationship with the manager. Stein forgot nothing.

With individualism and self-expression coming powerfully to the fore in society in the mid-1960s, football managers were wary of individuals such as John Hughes, who were discontented at the manner in which they would be tied to contracts that afforded them as much wriggle room as a worm on the end of a hook. Stanley Matthews, one of the highest-earning footballers in the post-war years, had spoken of 'the blind alley' that was the footballer's career and Hughes, a sentient, intelligent individual, was equally engaged by the idea that the restricted wages and short lifespan of the footballer, together with the lack of preparation for the eventual intrusion of the outside world, post-football, made for a despotic financial situation.

Most of the Celtic players, though, rather than quibbling over contracts, were simply grateful for the opportunity to play a game in return for earning a living. They knew the realities of the day-to-day grind outside football. Stevie Chalmers had spent time in a dull job assembling furniture and had done his National Service; Tommy Gemmell had been an apprentice electrician at the Ravenscraig steelworks. Such occupations were not gilded by huge and endless rewards. Even Jimmy Johnstone, coveted as a youngster by Celtic and Manchester United, had trained for a working life that might materialise if football were not to work out for him even if, typically, he had not done so in complete seriousness. Both Benny Rooney, son of Bob Rooney, Stein's physiotherapist, and Johnstone went to the Burnbank School of Engineering for an apprenticeship. Johnstone was in a different class but one day the lecturer came along to ask Rooney for help 'as Mr Johnstone is misbehaving', Rooney recalls. 'He was sitting on a girder below the roof throwing paper at the teacher. Just in good fun – crazy but good fun.'

Down in Ayrshire, Bobby Lennox, to please his parents, took on a job at an ICI factory before Celtic signed him and he believes that that helped him vitally in his own football career. 'Working in the ICI, which I did for almost a year,' Lennox says, 'helped me become a footballer. A lot of guys now go from school to football and think life's easy. I was working shifts, making boxes, a dreadful job, in ICI and when I went full time in football, I thought, "I'm not going back to work in a factory if I can help it." I think it helped all us guys that we had worked – and playing Junior football helped us as well. Most of our guys worked before they came to Celtic Park and you don't want to go back to that kind of thing.'

Professional footballers at Celtic and elsewhere could earn relatively well during their playing days from a game that was sustained largely through the weekly income from the turnstiles, which admitted the type of grey grafters who could not escape workaday lives by playing football but who did so through watching it. Entry was easily affordable for the working man and woman and the money raised was not enough for any player in Britain to contemplate early retirement once their playing days were over. George Best was talking in 1966 of becoming the first millionaire footballer but he was smart enough to understand that if this were to happen it would be through trading on his special name in the game by opening boutiques and through other external sources of income. Bobby Moore, England's World Cup-winning captain, would be on £100 a week with his newly signed contract at West Ham United in 1966, but only a tiny number of British players could expect such wages. At Celtic the players' £40 a week were still handsome earnings in relation to the working man – and while a switch to England might find them increasing that basic amount of pay, it would not necessarily be a sizeable enough increase to compensate for the upheaval involved in moving. Moreover, Celtic players had the incentive of hefty bonuses for doing well in cup and league – and for winning European Cup ties.

'On a European night,' Jim Craig says, 'there were fourteen bonuses up for grabs. Everybody who played got a bonus. The figures were always the same: 125 pounds for the first round; 250 pounds for the second round; 500 pounds for the quarter-finals; 750 pounds for the semi-finals; 1,500 pounds for the final.' It made European competition, for the players, extra enticing, raised the pleasure involved in winning through.

A question of cash had Celtic supporters threatening to boycott the season's opening fixture of the competitive season – a tricky-looking League Cup tie at Tynecastle against Heart of Midlothian. The Celtic Supporters Association suggested that those who did attend were going 'under protest'. Entry to the ground was up by 25 per cent – to five shillings. The stand was an impressive four shillings more than its usual six shillings and that was only for the wings; anyone wishing to cast a disdainful gaze over the rest of the support, in the centre stand, would have to pay fifteen shillings, double the previous season's price. It was a compliment to Celtic, amidst the financial pain felt by the fans, that they should be seen as such a lucrative attraction.

Bill Lindsay, the Hearts chairman, showed that marketing-type sophistry was not entirely alien to the game of football in the 1960s. 'The increase is because the police insist that this game be all-ticket,' he said, 'and this means extra police charges, the printing of tickets and their distribution – all very expensive.'

Nor was this match a precious, prized one-off, for which it might be worth digging deep; it was merely the first of six games in an opening, four-club, League Cup group stage. Still, a Scottish Cup tie at Tynecastle in March 1966 had seen a crowd of 46,000 crammed in and the police's concern stemmed from the manner in which the match had been halted for ten minutes after the crowd had spilled on to the pitch.

Hearts' anticipated slew of cash failed to materialise and they suffered for their increased prices. After all the hoo-ha from Mr Lindsay, the slow sale of tickets forced Hearts to put into operation six cash turnstiles on the day but the club, who habitually increased prices for the visits of Celtic and Rangers, were still left embarrassedly clutching more than 15,000 expensively unsold tickets. It was also a less-than-profitable day on the field of play for the Edinburgh side, Celtic emerging from rainswept Tynecastle with an efficient 2–0 victory, achieved minus John Hughes, who, despite all the palaver over the prospect of him becoming one of Britain's most expensive players, had not been selected for the match – not even named as the substitute. Stein's decision to exclude Hughes altogether once more emphasised his full control over all team-related matters and showed the others in his squad their potential, uncertain fate if they were ever to challenge the manager's authority.

Hughes would be kept aside for all but one of the six League Cup group-stage matches that August. The tournament was in a slightly odd format, with the draw loaded so that clubs of a similar ilk would face each other in their groups – thus Celtic were in with fellow First Division clubs Clyde, Hearts and St Mirren, while other sections would comprise clubs from the nether regions of the Scottish game; with the winner of each section proceeding to the quarter-finals. It mattered little to Celtic: by late August they had defeated each of their rivals comprehensively, in turn, en route to fixing for themselves a place in the quarter-finals.

Hughes did enjoy an outing in a simple 3–0 stroll against Hearts, in the return League Cup tie at Celtic Park, with Celtic already securely through to the next round, but by the beginning of September 1966, this potentially pricey show-pony was trotting out in the reserves once again, finding himself debarred from the first-team squad. He would appear sporadically over the remainder of the season, partially through Stein's capricious team selections, partially through a mid-season injury, and would never quite shake off his reputation for inconsistency.

Hughes would later look back on that time and admit that it had given him a necessary and welcome jolt. 'I had to learn,' he said, 'that I was only part of a team at Parkhead and I would never get anywhere as an unpredictable individualist; brilliant one week, deplorable the next. It is the eleven men out on the field that matter and I wasn't part of things. I hated being on the sidelines, sometimes twelfth man, sometimes in the reserves, sometimes wondering if there was a place for me at all. The glory and glamour went, rightly, to the boys in the team who were winning games.' The experience of being omitted had, he said, made him use 'the ball better, being less selfish with it' and employing his 'physique to advantage where before it was never any real help to me'. It had also made him 'more determined than ever before'.

Stein would always get through in the end. 'He could bomb you out for six weeks and then come and ask you to "do it" for him – and you would do it,' Hughes says.

There had been no ceaseless roll of pre-season friendlies for Celtic before the season was launched; just that one game, with Manchester United on 6 August 1966, one week prior to the Hearts match: a seven-star encounter given that United included, among their ten internationals, Pat Crerand, the former Celtic player, Denis Law and George Best, along with Bobby Charlton, one of the principal drivers of England's World Cup triumph, which had culminated only seven days previously with the 4–2 victory over West Germany in the final at Wembley Stadium. Charlton's visit to Celtic Park was as uncomfortable for him as the previous Saturday afternoon had been enjoyable, as Celtic carefully prised apart United.

The presence of John Connelly and Nobby Stiles, also World Cup winners with Alf Ramsey's England team, added weight to the victory over Manchester United but Jock Stein reiterated his view that the World Cup had been one that had lacked innovations of a sort that he might incorporate at Celtic. 'Tactically, the World Cup threw up nothing completely new,' Stein said. 'It was more of an emotional affair, won on team spirit and enthusiasm in the end. We have never been short of those things at Parkhead. Fast, attacking football is what the fans want to see and I think we provided that last season. It's better the others chasing us than the other way around.'

Evidence of that was shown when Celtic faced Rangers in a Glasgow Cup tie on 23 August. The Ibrox club had desperately spent £100,000 in signing Alex Smith from Dunfermline Athletic and Dave Smith from Aberdeen, days before the season began, in a nouveau-riche-type attempt to catch up with Celtic. But the idea that there was any sort of parity between the two great Glasgow clubs was exploded with a resounding boom, through a 4–0 victory that was Celtic's biggest winning margin at Ibrox since 1897.

'He announced the team at the start of the game and I was named at outside-left,' Charlie Gallagher recalls. 'I never played at outside-left and big Yogi [Hughes], who usually played there, looked at me as if to say, "What are you doing playing there?" Jock Stein came up to me and said, "For the first half-hour you're not going to get a kick of the ball but you'll be our best man out there." In those days, the Rangers full-backs followed their wingers and after a bit he shouted to me, "Start wandering." I did and every ball was going out to big [Tommy] Gemmell [at left-back] and he was just running on to them all, freely, up the left wing. We were 1–0 up at half-time and Jock told us that Rangers would change their set-up for the second half – and they did. They tried to combat Gemmell running riot down the left and they left me and Bobby Murdoch free to hit our forwards and, with them short of cover, Bobby Lennox sped in to get a hat-trick and we won 4–0. It was a clever, clever ploy.'

Tommy Gemmell was one of the players most enjoying a personal regeneration under Stein's renaissance of Celtic. Sean Fallon, who had been running team matters prior to Stein's arrival, had told the player, 'If you cross that halfway line again, Son, you'll not be in the team.' This was Fallon's response to Gemmell's desire to get forward and support his forwards. The player had privately wondered what was so wrong with bringing a degree of exuberance to his game and had duly delighted in it being unlocked by Jock Stein upon the new manager's arrival at Celtic Park. Suddenly, Celtic had a goalscoring full-back of a kind never previously seen in Scotland.

Attacking came naturally to Gemmell. It was as a winger that he had begun life at Coltness United, the Lanarkshire Junior club, close to his Craigneuk home, from whom he joined Celtic for a fee of £75. His attacking instincts had been curbed by Fallon and, at a stroke, that diminished the player's value to Celtic by approximately 50 per cent, restricting his talents to only one half of the field.

'Our instructions were very simple,' Gemmell said of those dim and dark days prior to Stein's arrival. 'If you were a full-back, you were expected to punt the ball the length of the park in the direction of the winger. If you could mark your opponent, get the ball off him and hump it 60 or 70 yards from the back to the front, you were termed a good player. If you wanted to play in the first team, you had to conform to their basic ideas about football. Dunky MacKay was a footballing full-back so he was left out of the team because he was playing too much football.' MacKay, a right-back who liked the overlap to a fatal degree to his long-term prospects at Celtic, would be transferred to Third Lanark in November 1964, missing Stein's arrival at Celtic – and the prospect of glory – by the narrowest of margins.

Tommy Gemmell, who had been the Dux (head boy) of his primary school, was canny enough to adapt to Fallon's demands and had made the left-back spot his own during the two seasons prior to Stein's arrival. He would soon be transformed into a world-class overlapping full-back and would also happily take on the mantle of Stein's team's most socially outgoing player.

'The quiff in my ginger hair made me look a bit colourful and the press guys started calling me flamboyant,' Gemmell said. 'I had actually been quite reserved as a youngster but once I read those words, I started trying to live up to them.' How different it might have been if Gemmell had continued to have his talent stifled by the pre-Stein management.

A key theme in those early stages of the 1966–67 season was the unselfishness of the Celtic team; not only in their play but in their desire to see each other do well, shown by the way they joined in unison to celebrate a goal. Another was how Celtic overwhelmed opponents – if one Celtic player was beaten, someone else would pop up in his place. Another theme was how often Jimmy Johnstone was proving to be the match winner, either by softening up opposing defences or by scoring or laying on goals himself.

There was also a growing familiarity about the Celtic team as the summer of 1966 neared its conclusion. Ronnie Simpson, in goal, had not missed a match since October 1965; Tommy Gemmell since Boxing Day 1964; John Clark had last been absent from the Celtic line-up in April 1965. The forwards could not count on such unbroken runs but Bobby Lennox, Joe McBride, Stevie Chalmers, Bertie Auld and Jimmy Johnstone had all been involved on a regular, ongoing basis since Stein's arrival at the club. One man, though, distrusted the idea of seamless continuity. For Jock Stein, there was always the fear that a settled team might create complacency.

'I don't want to go through the season with a recognised first team going on unchanged week after week,' Stein said. 'I want to build up a first-team pool and I want to be able to use that pool. My teams will be chosen for the job in hand. A team will be picked for specific games. I think this is the best way to work, especially when you have a crowded programme with a lot of important games.' Stein was stronger than ever after the tests he had faced and come through during the close-season. He was now ready to flex his muscles.

CHAPTER 4

Domestic Bliss

The very thought had Jimmy Johnstone gurgling with joy. 'Oh, I loved to beat the Rangers,' he would giggle. 'I loved to stick it to them,' he would say, shuddering with laughter that convulsed his chunky body in almost uncontrollable fashion.

There would be several opportunities for Jimmy to indulge in that particular pleasure during the 1966–67 season. The Glasgow Cup tie victory over Rangers had been a huge fillip for all involved with Celtic but a win in the first league match of the season between Glasgow's great rivals, scheduled for mid-September 1966, would help further to establish that the Old Firm were planted firmly in a new era in which Celtic would bloom and Rangers would wither. Johnstone and several of his teammates could remember vividly the 1963–64 season when Rangers and Celtic had met on five occasions in league and cup and Celtic had lost every single time. That bitter memory was making their new and sudden success against their old rivals all the more sweet.

If evidence were required as to the importance of an Old Firm game, it had been supplied in the aftermath of Celtic's terrific 4–0 victory at Ibrox in August 1966. Subsequent to their defeat, Rangers had opened an investigation into why the club had suddenly gone into reverse.

'If the Celtic game had gone on longer we would have lost more goals,' John Lawrence, the highly opinionated 71-year-old chairman of Rangers, went so far as to admit. Lawrence also castigated the fitness of his club's players. 'An alteration must be made in our training schedules,' he said. 'What was good enough twenty years ago is not good enough today. We are tiring far more than other top teams in Scotland today and that is something we intend to put right forthwith.'

The crisis had been considered grave enough for Lawrence to convene an emergency board meeting at a Glasgow hotel. Given the severity of his words in public, it is not difficult to imagine that Lawrence and his fellow board members may have been even more harsh and direct in private when considering the Grand-Canyon-like gulf now developing between Scotland's two football superpowers.

Heart of Midlothian, meanwhile, announced that Tommy Walker, the longest-serving manager in Scotland, would be giving up the administrative side of his post to become a new, fully fledged 'tracksuit manager' and to devote more time to tactics and training. It is possible to imagine the accompanying groans, creaks, harrumphing and looks of disgust and disbelief from Walker on his being asked to haul himself away from his hidden lair underneath the Tynecastle stand and out on to the training field that he had thought he had left behind at the end of his playing days. Walker had enjoyed a successful, fifteen-year spell in which Hearts had won the league and competed in the European Cup but his particular breaking point had been the Edinburgh club's 3–0 League Cup defeat to Celtic in Glasgow.

The common factor in all this turbulence was, of course, Jock Stein. His emphasis on his players attaining an exemplary level of fitness meant that they had the speed and stamina to match their talents while Stein could be seen on the training ground, in the thick of it, tackling players or clutching cross balls while enacting the role of goalkeeper; always he could be seen goading, cajoling, pushing and prodding, making his players feel his hot breath on the backs of their necks and going crazy whenever a drill was not carried out to his full satisfaction.

Given the evidence, how could other clubs remain satisfied with their old-style managers keeping a distance from their players? Such managers regarded their offices as their natural domain and a reflection of their elevated status in being promoted from former-player to managerial level. The idea of mingling regularly with the players would, they had always thought, sully that status, reduce their standing, and now Jock Stein had turned that entire concept on its head.

'With Jock Stein at training,' John Clark says, 'you had to do everything sharply. It didn't matter if it was a wee loosening-off exercise; you had to do it sharply and if you did it properly you would have no problems with him but if you slackened off he would punish you all right.

'He was a stickler for timekeeping. If you were a minute late, he would crack up, go mental. He'd say, "I told you eleven o'clock and you were a minute late." It helped you with your discipline and it helped you with your life. You had to be there, to the minute, and if some players were a few minutes late for training, it would trigger a harder, more tricky session. That way, the other players would feel their pals had let them down.

'He [Stein] was our fitness coach, he was our chef, he was everything; he was the boss. He was always thinking about the game; always thinking about different formations.'

Clark was a fixture in Stein's teams but always at the back of his mind was the memory of Stein as reserve team coach prior to leaving to establish himself as a manager. Clark recalled one occasion when Celtic were to play a reserve match at

Dumbarton and he and Billy McNeill arrived early at St Enoch railway station in central Glasgow to meet Jock Stein. The two young players decided to go for a walk to use up the time, rather than waiting around, and returned to the scheduled meeting place one minute late to discover a furious Stein who proceeded to give them a serious blast as a reprimand for their lateness. He dismissed their protests about being only fractionally tardy by stressing that there were no degrees of lateness; only the unacceptable offence itself.

For Clark, this was a salutary lesson. As a conscientious pro, he had felt some insecurity over his place in the team during his early days at the club and anything that might hamper his hard-fought right to be a Celtic player would play on his mind and push him to be even more dedicated than before.

Before Stein's arrival, Celtic had been something of a zany institution in terms of its management and Robert Kelly, the chairman, had, during the first half of the 1960s, been carefully grooming Sean Fallon to become only the fourth manager in Celtic's history. Jimmy McGrory had been manager since 1945 but he was never seen on the training ground and his period in charge had been, to put it mildly, less than successful. During two decades, Celtic had won the league title only once and that had been in 1954, when Jock Stein, as team captain, had exerted an influence on his fellow players that compensated for McGrory's lack of aptitude for managing a football team. Not only did Stein help Celtic to the league title but they had also won the League and Cup Double for the first time since 1914. Stein had also guided Celtic to the Coronation Cup in 1953, when they defeated Arsenal, Manchester United and Hibernian to land a trophy that was contested by eight of Britain's major clubs to mark the accession to the throne of Queen Elizabeth II. That was quite a spurt of success in the midst of two largely barren decades.

It was not Stein, though, but Sean Fallon whom Kelly had kept close from that team, retaining his services at Celtic even while allowing Stein, who had proved himself a successful reserve team coach in the late 1950s, to leave for the post of manager at Dunfermline Athletic. Fallon, a rugged full-back whose career at Celtic had spanned the 1950s, was quickly brought on to the coaching staff following his retirement as a player in 1959 and, as the mid-1960s approached, the Irishman was becoming ever more prominent as the face of Celtic management, both to the players and to the press.

Kelly, Fallon and McGrory would often present themselves as running Celtic like a triumvirate, almost as if each had equal status. The chairman had a habit of entering the Celtic dressing room pre-match and slapping his leather glove into the palm of his hand while inanely, in footballing terms, exhorting the players to go out and do their best. Fallon liked to smack his fist into the palm of his hand while emphasising work-rate, fight and other characteristics that he would stress as part of his budding managerial role.

To provide a flavour of the wackiness of the Fallon-Kelly-McGrory management team, they were, by late 1964, publicly pondering whether to field Billy McNeill as a forward, in the '[Alfredo] Di Stéfano style' – a reference to Real Madrid's gloriously gifted Argentinian, a five-times-in-succession European Cup winner, scorer of 49 goals in that tournament, and the smoothest and most stylish of footballers. McNeill was a gritty, powerful centre-half, quite brilliant at winning the ball in the air, but he was no sublime ball-player. The idea was ludicrous.

On the day after a rare victory over Rangers, in September 1964, Fallon, Kelly and McGrory, in unison, had triumphantly explained to the press how the game had been won. This was the same trio that had presided over five defeats out of five against Rangers the previous season. The victory over Rangers was also their first win in fifteen consecutive Old Firm matches. It had to happen sometime – although this was stretching the law of averages to breaking point – and so to claim it as being part of a concerted plan was daft. Rumours of a miracle cure to Celtic's ongoing malaise were greatly exaggerated by Kelly and Fallon and, within weeks, the club was in distress again, following a demoralising 3–1 aggregate defeat to Barcelona in the Inter-Cities Fairs Cup.

It was still always going to be hard to dislodge the managerial structure that Kelly had put in place, not least because it suited perfectly the stiff, patriarchal, 63-year-old Celtic chairman. As a player, Fallon had ingratiated himself with Kelly by driving Kelly and his wife home from matches, sometimes staying over at the chairman's house, dining with him, even walking his dog. According to Alec Boden, a centre-half in the same team as Fallon during the 1950s, the players would clam up in Fallon's presence in the knowledge that anything they said might be taken down and used in evidence against them once Fallon reported back to the chairman.

With Fallon as manager-elect, Kelly's grip on the playing side of Celtic remained immensely strong, as it had been since he had become chairman in 1947, after which he had quickly begun interfering in transfer business and team matters, with the genial Jimmy McGrory the next best thing to a puppet manager. Kelly, a stockbroker, would, of a morning, pay a brief visit to Celtic Park and stroll out to the top of the players' tunnel, where he would light up a cigarette and stand for ten minutes observing the players training, taking a break from his professional calculations to assess the value of the football club's assets. It would take a lot for him to let go of all this, not least because it was widely known that, almost throughout McGrory's tenure as manager, it was Kelly and not McGrory who had been selecting the Celtic team.

'Bob Kelly had a regular Friday-night gathering at his house,' one player who spent the entire 1960s at Celtic recalls, 'and he would invite Jimmy Steele, the masseur, and any of his few pals, not his fellow board members, and they would go over the team and decide what it should be, with Jimmy McGrory noting down the team. We managed to extract as much humour from the situation as we could.'

Steele would be the butt of jokes from the players the following morning about his role in team selection and the players would kid him on, asking him for the line-up or whether they were in the team. On matchdays, the boots for the starting eleven would be laid out underneath each player's kit. It was a frequent occurrence for a selected player to head off to relax in the snooker room for a while only to return to the dressing room to discover that his boots had been removed owing to a late change of mind from Kelly with regard to the team for that day's match.

Fallon's inept management also became a running joke among the players. He had been installed as assistant to the manager in 1962 and on New Year's Day 1963 at Ibrox, Celtic went down 4–0. At half-time a stand-up confrontation between Fallon and Pat Crerand, the fiery half-back, over how to retrieve the match made it Crerand's final game for Celtic, on Kelly's instructions. The player swiftly departed for Manchester United. Matt Busby, the Manchester United manager, had been pondering whether to recruit Crerand or Jim Baxter, his talented counterpart at Rangers. Fallon's intervention meant Rangers retained the jewel in their crown while Celtic lost theirs, handicapping the club still further.

Legendarily, among the Celtic players of the 1960s, Fallon was not only incapable of inspiring the Celtic players – to the point of alienating those such as Crerand – but he was equally ham-fisted in the transfer market. Upon making moves to sign a player from a medium-sized Scottish club – a player not rated by the footballers at Celtic Park at the time – Fallon met the smaller club's directors and told them in firm and decisive terms that he would pay them no more than £15,000 for the player and that that was his limit – take it or leave it. The club's directors, not believing their luck, proceeded to go into a huddle as if they were considering whether to succumb to Fallon's supposed hard bargaining when they were actually desperate to snap his hand off for the inflated fee. The player in question was, subsequently, barely seen in a Celtic shirt.

Even Kelly, then, after several years of all this, could not be blind to the fact that making Fallon manager of Celtic would have enormous inherent risks attached and would probably prolong the club's unprecedented run of mediocrity. Attendances were plummeting and matters came to a head with the second leg of the 3–1 aggregate defeat to Barcelona in early December 1964. Afterwards, Fallon fulminated publicly, heartily condemning Celtic players for a 'lazy' attitude, while Kelly, seeing the light, began to consider seriously an approach to bring back Stein to the club. Yet Kelly, used to exerting an influence on the club that was in inverse proportion to his footballing knowledge, was still unwilling to relinquish power entirely. His marriage having proven childless, Celtic was his family, his greatest preoccupation, and although he wished to bring Stein into the management circle at Celtic Park, Kelly decided, initially, that it would be very much on his own terms.

'Celtic treated Jock badly at the start,' Len Murray, a young Glasgow lawyer who would represent Stein during the 1960s, said. 'They offered him [the job of] assistant manager to Sean Fallon. God forgive me if I'm wrong but basically I think [that was] because Jock was not Catholic and then, when he made it clear that he wasn't interested in that, they offered him joint-managership with Sean and he said no to that as well, before they appointed him manager.'

Kelly's intention had been to retain power while simultaneously feeding off Stein's knowledge and ability. The set-up
would, consequently, have been similar to that which had
preceded it, with Stein simply replacing McGrory in the trio
running footballing matters at Celtic. That was never going to
tempt Stein away from Hibernian, still a major name in Scottish
football, and where his 'full control' of the club, in his own
well-loved phrase, had propelled them from mid-table to the
highest echelons of the league. Once it had been established that
he would not compromise in his desire to be solely responsible
for team management at Celtic, Kelly had to back down and
offer Stein the job on Stein's own terms. It had benefited Stein
to have had that hurdle placed in front of him – by clearing it,
he had established fully the manner in which he would operate.
He had made it clear that interference from Kelly – or Fallon –
would not now be brooked.

It also, strangely, helped Stein that he was non-Catholic.
All of Celtic's managers and directors had been Catholic until
that point and while Kelly was not a bigot, he realised he was
altering club tradition through appointing the best man for the
job, regardless of his background. Having pondered such a step
deeply and having done the right thing in appointing Stein,
the chairman would have to give his new manager full and
unequivocal backing to ensure that the venture proved a success.

This was an era in which football managers did not insist
upon hauling an entire backroom staff with them whenever
they moved to a new club. Stein arrived alone and co-opted
the backroom staff who were already there. Fallon had been put
in his place and would support Stein very much as an assistant.
Neilly Mochan, another teammate of Stein's from the 1950s,
was the trainer, whose role was to supervise fitness routines and
to run on to the park with 'treatment' for any player who might
need help with a knock during a match. Bob Rooney was the

physiotherapist. They would all prove supportive to Stein and would form a bulwark around him, carrying out any orders he delegated. As with the players, they had little choice but to bend to Stein's will. Such was the enormousness of the manager's personality and knowledge that there was no need for him to consult with anyone else or to lean heavily on another person's presence to fill any weaknesses or flaws in his managerial style. For all that anyone could see, Stein was as close to flawless as it was humanly possible for a football manager to be.

This was the dawn of the golden era of football management. It was becoming a truly recognised profession in the 1960s. Before the Second World War, it had been a role often classified as secretary-manager, a title that accurately reflected the largely administrative nature of the post. Those wealthy enough to be on the boards of football clubs had to attend on a daily basis to the professions and businesses that had enriched them in the first place and so needed someone to keep the club ticking over in their absence, in similar fashion to a foreman on a building site, dealing with everyday financial matters and corralling the players into some sort of order. After the war, the football manager became more influential than ever before. As the 1960s took shape, players were using lighter boots, strips and footballs, enabling freer movement and allowing managers to shape tactics, to put their own stamp on training methods, transfers and discipline. With the best of them, such as Stein, that influence was evident on the field and, like an image taking shape when rubbed through tracing paper by a coin, Stein's imprint soon materialised in everything Celtic did.

Managers were unencumbered by football recruitment officers poring over computerised data that provided appearances, goals, assists, age and potential resale value of a player. Those such as Stein and Busby dealt instead in the type of intangible assets in a player that will be prized by a manager who really knows the game. Stein prioritised the footballer who was willing to put in spade-loads of work off the ball; the type of quality, along with desire and indomitability, that fails to show up in more clinical assessments of players' values.

'Before Stein, you didn't really take a lot of notice of managers,' John Hughes says. 'You wouldn't have known who the manager of Aberdeen was, for example; it didn't seem to matter that much.'

When alarmed opposition clubs began seeking to mimic Stein's ways it was, to some degree, rather insulting to him. It might be possible to take a manager such as Symon or Walker out of the sanctuary of their office, tip the soft hat off their head and replace their heavy overcoat with training gear but that would not, Superman-like, suddenly provide them with Stein's vigour, nous, knowledge or the ability to understand players better than they understood themselves.

'Jock instilled within us a real belief in ourselves,' Billy McNeill said. 'That belief was so strong that, because you were one of his players, there was no need for him to gee you up. You were a Celtic player, you were playing for Jock Stein, and that meant that every trophy you were seeking and every game you played and every single result, were all immense. So it was not as though he would have to get us built up for any particular match – he had ensured that we had, built into us, the standards that he required and we were expected to carry that into every game. Any player who displayed any sort of a lackadaisical attitude was no good as far as Jock was concerned. He wanted his players to show real determination and hunger. The last thing Jock would ever have said to us would have been, "Just go out and enjoy yourselves." We heard of other managers saying that but Jock would never have countenanced such a thing. He would tell you that the time to enjoy yourself would be after the match or, even better, after the season.' When all was said and won.

While Celtic's rivals were all in a flurry, strutting and fretting over how to get even with Stein at domestic level, the Celtic manager was, by the early September of 1966, streaking even further ahead of them, by beginning to look more and more towards the European Cup for professional satisfaction. Stein had been receiving regular reports from Switzerland on FC Zurich, Celtic's European Cup opponents, but on Sunday 4 September, three-and-a-half weeks before the first leg with the Swiss champions, he flew to Zurich and back in a day to watch the Swiss team face FC Biel-Bienne and duly defeat them 5–0.

'The Zurich defence were good – very good – but I expected that,' said Stein, 'and it is something we have to deal with very seriously. This team has a great home record. They held Real Madrid to a draw and beat Wolves only four weeks ago and they have scored 14 goals in three league games without losing one. I was impressed by their fitness and I liked [Rosario] Martinelli and [Kobi] Kuhn in the attack.' These were diplomatic words, clever and respectful. It seems unlikely that someone as expert as Stein was at reading the small print in relation to a game of football would have failed to notice some weaknesses in the Swiss champions, but he was careful not to offer Zurich any outlet for a grudge or a feeling that they were being underestimated – or to let them know how he intended to exploit any deficiencies that they might possess. Stein was the master of saying the right thing publicly while telling his players, in private, something else. Surely, for example, it was a little odd that he should be praising the Zurich defence when it had clearly not been tested by lowly opposition, while their attack, which had notched five goals in this match, received only a cursory mention from Stein. 'Jock was the ultimate fox,' Billy McNeill said. 'When Jock ran into the woods, all the other foxes ran out.'

Stein was also the ultimate observer of football. When scrutinising a match, such as that one at Zurich's Letzigrund Stadium, that involved future opponents, he would not sit passively, motionless, in a stadium's stand, blithely watching a match in much the same way as a fan. Instead, he had to be active and would sit with a pad and pen, mocking up a recreation of the pitch with players dotted in position, and then inking in every pass made in a game to show, ultimately, by scoring and over-scoring his notes, those players to whom the ball would go most often and thus uncovering the key individuals in any opposition team. As with so much of what Stein did, this was a simple idea – its genius was that he was the one to think of it and to carry it out. He embodied genius driven by common sense.

'For big games,' Bobby Lennox says, 'he would have his team talk at Seamill. Then we'd go to Glasgow and we'd start getting organised. He'd keep away [from the players] a bit. I don't think he kept in and around the dressing room, on top of people. He'd come in, make sure everything was all right and then maybe go away out of the dressing room and then come back in before the kick-off and provide a wee reminder here and a wee reminder there, a few words here, a few words there but he wasn't in your face, in the dressing room, the whole time. He was excellent tactically.'

Lennox had, in early 1965, been among the minority of Celtic players who had been less than rapturously enthusiastic about the appointment of Jock Stein as Celtic manager.

'It was not a development that particularly pleased me,' he says. 'At that point I had, at last, started to establish myself in the first team. On instructions from the management, I had begun to play further forward and to use my speed and quickness of thought and it had worked.' Unlike others, who had become disillusioned by the manner in which the team was being guided, Lennox was now scoring regularly and freely after three years at the club.

'When I heard the news that Jock Stein would be the new

manager of Celtic, I didn't take it well. I fretted that the new man, whom I did not know at all, might not fancy me as a player and that my hard-won place in the team could be in jeopardy. My future as a Celtic player seemed more uncertain than ever before.

'During the six weeks when we were waiting for Jock [to fulfil his commitments to Hibernian before joining Celtic in March 1965] I scored five goals in five games but the thought that had entered my mind when his appointment was announced could not be dislodged. With a new manager, anything can happen. Instead, Jock not only changed my career but changed my life. He brought out qualities in us all that we hadn't known were there.'

Stein's desire to make the trip to Switzerland swift and short was characteristic of a man who behaved as if time was his dedicated foe. He would often motor down to Liverpool or Manchester to take in an evening match at one of the colosseums of the English game but he would be back in Glasgow in the early hours of the following morning to ensure that he would not miss a single day out on the training field with his players. If stuck in the car park at Anfield or Old Trafford when trying to get away sharply before the supporters emerged, he would roar in frustration, 'Who put all these cars here?'

The Celtic manager's increasing reputation for excellence was throwing up intriguing conundrums. Clyde, the nearest club geographically to Celtic, in a League Cup tie on the final day of August, had reacted to Celtic's fearsome reputation by keeping every player behind the ball as if to admit that possession of it was something better suited to Celtic.

At one point Bertie Auld, tiring of the tedium, sat on the ball in a swathe of conceded space and invited the Clyde players to come and have a look at this memento of their previous existences as ball players. Auld's bold gesture had come about after he had passed the ball back and forth between him and Ronnie Simpson several times without drawing a challenge from a Clyde player.

'I do remember Bertie doing that,' Joe Gilroy, the Clyde forward, says. 'It angered me intensely. He was just rubbing it in. You knew he did that. That was his nature. Nobody retaliated but you thought, "How good are these people?" Of course, it was disrespectful but that's Bertie; you can't help loving him.'

Auld, who actually sat on the ball three times that afternoon at Clyde, was a roguish individual on and off the park but a person with an enormous spirit, great heart and a subtle wit. John Divers had been transferred to Partick Thistle by Stein in 1966 and shortly afterwards, when facing his former team, he suddenly found himself hit by a driving tackle that sent him up into the air and left him sprawled in a heap on the ground. 'Oh, JD, I didn't know it was you,' Divers' assailant, Bertie Auld, told him, all innocence, as he helped Divers to his feet, as if to clatter an old friend and teammate in such a way would have been the last thing on his mind. It was a moment typical of Auld's winning combination of charm and cheekiness but it had been that very thing, that very essence of his character that had seen him eased out of Celtic in 1961. Indeed, his initial spell at the club had seen him living almost permanently with the threat of leaving hanging over his head.

'I was actually transferred to Dumbarton because there was no loan system at that time,' Auld says of his first departure from Celtic Park, as an eighteen-year-old, in 1956. 'Jim "Peem" Docherty went to Alloa [Athletic] at the same time but was not brought back.' Such was the erratic, chaotic management of Celtic in the late 1950s that Auld too might have been forgotten or dismissed and left to languish in the Second Division but, fortunately for him, he was recalled. Even so, his furiously competitive style was not to the liking of Robert Kelly, who had almost puritanical ideas on how his players ought to conduct themselves on the field of play. Kelly, as a result, would attempt to send Auld to Everton along with Bobby Collins, another vigorous competitor, in 1958, but Auld refused the move.

'They were wanting me to go to Everton in a double transfer with Bobby Collins,' Auld says, 'and I didn't want to leave because I was a homebird with a great attachment to Panmure Street [in Maryhill, Glasgow]. No way was I going just whenever they clapped their hands but when Collins was leaving I was disappointed because he was one you looked up to and learned from.' When Birmingham City came calling in 1961 and Celtic again made it clear they wanted him to go, Auld decided he had to make the switch for the sake of his career. It says much about those mismanaging Celtic in that era that they were willing to allow not only the talented Auld but Collins, a future Footballer of the Year in England, to leave so readily.

Life in Birmingham was good to Auld. He played in an Inter-Cities Fairs Cup final against Roma and he helped Birmingham City to a momentous victory in 1963 when they defeated Aston Villa, their fiercest rivals, in the League Cup final. Yet he always pined for a return to Celtic, despite enjoying life in plush Solihull. When the call came to return, he was even willing to take a cut in wages – a hefty five pounds a week – to facilitate the move.

'I had a nice lifestyle in Birmingham,' Auld says, 'but one of Jock Stein's friends phoned me and asked if I wanted to come back. The phone rang and who was it but a friend of Jock and he told me Jock was coming back as manager and that Jock was wondering if I would come back. Birmingham wanted me to stay and I wouldn't have come back to anybody else but Celtic but I'd actually have come back even if Jock hadn't been there.' A fortnight after Auld's return, Stein was officially announced as the new manager of Celtic and the signing of the fiery Auld symbolised, more than anything, that this would be a new, professional, winning Celtic, not one guided by false and idealised principles, as under Kelly.

The gulf between Celtic and their opponents was becoming, sometimes, as Auld's gesture underlined, circus-like in its freakishness – Clyde had conceded a shocking 12 goals to Celtic in three games during the opening month of the season – but a contest with Rangers could still stir the blood.

The first league encounter between the two great Glasgow sides would prove to be a towsy one. At Ibrox, in August, Rangers had enjoyed a sprightly opening five minutes before being swept away, like a tent in a storm, in the face of Celtic's superiority. At Celtic Park, on 17 September, the opening five minutes would also be vital.

Once again, Rangers looked arthritically slow in comparison to Celtic – and less than a minute had passed when Auld, hovering on the edge of the Rangers penalty area, whipped a low shot past John Greig, his closest challenger, and narrowly inside the left-hand post of Billy Ritchie, the goalkeeper, who stood comically, legs splayed, stranded on the wrong side of goal, his sharp features drawn to the ball hurtling into his net, a great hulking symbol of the gulf in speed, reactions and know-how that was growing, exponentially, between the clubs. Two minutes later, Murdoch, from 22 yards, picked out the same spot and although this time Ritchie did dive in the right direction, he was, as with his teammates throughout the afternoon, just that fraction too slow to be in any way effective.

Celtic were fast, precise and accurate; Rangers slow, slack and imprecise. In the face of the speed and slick passing style of Celtic, the visiting team's response was to sling high crosses into the box, hopeful of a forward getting a head to the ball, but as Willie O'Neill, Tommy Gemmell and Billy McNeill dwarfed the Rangers forwards, this basic, unimaginative tactic was rendered impotent by Celtic's aerial power. The other flailing variation put forward by Rangers was to hoick a long ball down the middle, hitting and hoping for the best. Neither course of action yielded results.

'Apart from losing the two early goals,' John Greig said of that first Old Firm league encounter of the season, 'we were very close to Celtic.' As a statement this was undeniably, blisteringly true, utterly valid, scrupulously fair and piercingly accurate. If those goals had not gone in, Celtic would not have won the match.

'The tempo of the game would be higher against Rangers,' John Clark remembers. 'You'd be quicker to the ball and in parting with the ball; your concentration had to be higher. The atmosphere was great, especially when you consider the grounds weren't covered. It was a noise – you couldn't distinguish singing or anything – it was just a noise; one big noise. Good games to play in; I used to love them. Anyone will tell you, you are more switched on when it comes to a big game.'

After twelve competitive fixtures of the 1966–67 season, Celtic had won every time and had scored 43 goals and conceded 8. It was clear that this was a club whose players needed to be thrown ever-meatier challenges to feed their ravenous hunger for competition. For that, they would have to look to Europe and a chance to test their abilities against opponents who would offer a different dimension to the teams they faced in Scotland. The local clubs were already receding fast in Celtic's rear-view mirror as they sped sleekly away from the cobbled streets of domestic football for the new and fresh vistas offered by the European Cup.

CHAPTER 5

An Alpine Expedition

Ah, the European Cup, that rarefied competition that would surely provide for Celtic some respite from the crudities induced by the wintry, muddy, blurred entity that is Scottish football. The memory of Real Madrid sashaying their way around Hampden Park in the spring of 1960 while gracefully picking apart Eintracht Frankfurt 7–3 in an exemplary European Cup final still sustained both the dreams and daytime thoughts of thousands of Scots. They would never forget Alfredo Di Stéfano and Ferenc Puskás lighting up Scotland's national stadium, their all-white strips symbolising the purity of their game, while notching their fifth successive European Cup in front of the largest crowd of appreciative neutrals ever to assemble for a football match anywhere on the planet.

That Real–Eintracht match remained a hot topic of conversation in Glasgow even six years later but Celtic's first foray into the competition would be rather different and would expose them to an evening that made the average Scottish match look like taking tea in the park. It all looked so innocent beforehand – the draw had provided them with a tie against FC Zurich, to be played in the late September of 1966, and the

Swiss were expected to melt as easily as fine Alpine chocolate in the clutches of a toddler. Such an analysis was for the fans – it was different for the Celtic players and management. Zurich were a club that had to be taken seriously and with considerable justification – Zurich would make the encounter the most sparky Swiss–Scots encounter since Ursula Andress had emerged from the sea to leave Sean Connery both shaken and stirred in *Doctor No.*

Onlookers might regard the tie with Zurich as a formality but Stein knew that anything can happen in football at any time. Football supporters often choose to ignore that. As a reminder of that, it was necessary for Celtic to look back only six months or so, to when they had been hauled to a surprise defeat, early in 1966, away to tiny Stirling Albion, then struggling frantically against drowning in the relegation whirlpool at the foot of the First Division. Celtic had lost 1–0 on a day when the Stirling players' fight and determination had erased the skills gap between them and their superior opponents, bashing a dent in Celtic's hopes of winning the league title at a vital time of the season.

It was inevitable that Zurich would be of a far higher calibre than Stirling and while the press and punters might make a hullabaloo about Swiss football not being the best in Europe, the players knew they would have two tough games to negotiate – determined opponents; high stakes; expectant crowds; variable refereeing that might frown on the type of robust challenges that are woven into any British domestic football match.

'We thought it could be possible for us to play a similar season like in 1963–1964, as we had then reached the semi-final,' Jakob 'Kobi' Kuhn, the Zurich captain, says of his side's embarkation on their own European voyage that season. 'We saw ourselves pretty much on the same level. In the 1965–66 season we had won the championship and lifted the cup at national level. In an international perspective we definitely weren't ranked as favourite for the winning of the European Champion Clubs' Cup. Nevertheless we were at a strong European level.'

Zurich were truly exotic at a time when few people ventured abroad on any regular basis. A spicy part of European football, something that provided it with its special tang, was that no-one really knew what to expect from any team until they saw them perform in front of their eyes on their own club's home turf. People could speculate as madly as they wished about Swiss football and its relative strength but it was impossible to be sure of what might materialise and what hazards might be thrown up until FCZ actually trotted out on the famous turf at Celtic Park.

Stein was warily diplomatic beforehand. 'It is quite obvious that Ladislav Kubala [the Zurich manager] has done a lot with his team,' he said. 'A lot of people think this will be easy for Celtic because we beat Basle a few years ago but it won't be. I have always said that you can't treat any team lightly in the European Cup.'

For Othmar 'Omi' Iten, the Zurich goalkeeper, football was a combination of finance, friendship and frolics. His eventful evening at Celtic Park would have severe consequences that would signal the beginning of the end of the 23-year-old's football career.

'I was a student at the University of Zurich,' Iten, a cheery, outgoing individual, says, 'where I studied economics – I would end my studies in 1969. At that time I was very lucky to be able to finance my life with the money I got from FCZ; on average 2,000 Swiss francs per month. With the exception of two pro-fessional players in the team, all the others were ... working during the day. Playing football was our hobby, we had a lot of fun, we were good friends and usually, when we played at home, we had, with our wives or girlfriends, a dinner in the evening, which usually ended in a bar with live music and a lot of singing. So football was for us not work but amusement and comradeship.'

All the more reason for Stein to view Zurich, free to relax and enjoy their evening at Celtic Park, as being dangerous and unpredictable – but unlike the Stirling Albions of this world, Zurich were no star-crossed losers. Only two years previously, as Kuhn notes, they had reached the semi-finals of the European Cup and although they had then suffered a regal defeat from Real Madrid, it showed that they might be as good at performing the role of party-poopers as they were at partying.

'In 1966, Zurich was a very good team,' Iten says. 'Half of the team played in the national team during the world championship in England and in the season 1965–66 Zurich was the winner of both the Swiss Championship and the Swiss Cup for the first time in its history.' Swiss football was also beginning to embrace professionalism and the footballers of Zurich followed a regime that approximated in outline that of any set of professional players. 'Four times a week there was a training in the evening,' Iten confirms, 'usually two hours, starting at 18.30.' So Zurich's footballing burghers missed out on the delights of a couple of hours of morning training followed by a free afternoon to hit the pool halls, bars and betting shops. How, then, could they possibly call themselves professional footballers? They were, though, very well-prepared physically, indeed better than the players at British part-time clubs who got by on two evenings of training per week – and you did not come up against World Cup footballers every day; especially at a time when it was harder to qualify for the World Cup finals than to miss out on them. Rene Brodman and Xavier Stierli, the full-backs, Fritz Kunzli, the striker, Heinz Bani and Werner Leimgruber, the midfielders, and Kobi Kuhn had all been in Switzerland's World Cup squad.

'We intended not to return empty-handed [from Celtic Park]

in any case,' Kobi Kuhn says. Even so, Iten, Kuhn and their jolly teammates were wary of an evening out at the cavernous Glasgow ground.

'After the draw for the first round placed us with Celtic,' Iten says, 'we knew that it was going to be very difficult to defeat Celtic but, of course, one has always to believe and to have the will to win a match, even if the other team is much better. At that time, our coach was Kubala, a former international player of Hungary and Spain. He said to us before the match at Celtic, "Indians do not have any pains!"'

It would prove a wounding evening for Iten and the other braves of Zurich – in a game that Fred Hansen, the referee, from Denmark, would describe as 'the most difficult match I have had to handle in European football – and I have refereed 25 of them. I am reporting three players – Stierli and [Ernst] Meyer of Zurich and [Bobby] Murdoch of Celtic [all of whom had been booked – in an era when a booking was as rare as a Fabergé egg]. I could have booked more. It was a very hard game to control. There was so much anger on the pitch that at one moment I thought of stopping the match and speaking to both captains but that might have caused even more trouble. I did my best in a very difficult time.'

Nor did Hansen himself escape criticism. 'This is proof that a referee from an amateur country will not do,' Robert Kelly, the Celtic chairman, snapped. 'What should have been a great game was spoiled.'

It had, as Kelly implied, initially been a match replete with promise. 'We are not a defensive team,' Kubala had insisted, upon Zurich's arrival in Glasgow. 'We will be going out to make goals. I like to go for goals.' There was little reason to believe that this was a bluff. Rosario Martinelli and Fritz Kunzli each had scored eight goals already in the Swiss league and Zurich had scored 24 in total in their six league games until that point. Both strikers had scored two goals apiece in the 4–1 victory over Lugano the previous weekend.

True, almost, to Kubala's words, Zurich nearly slipped into the lead in the opening minute at Celtic Park. Kunzli fed Martinelli and his powerful shot zipped through the air in the direction of goal. It looked a certain opener – the ball swerved deceptively and looked to have caught out Ronnie Simpson, who was scampering across goal to intercept it before its likely trajectory was altered drastically, catching him on the hop by its sudden and unexpected change of direction. Simpson, though, quickly pinged back in the direction from which he had come and fisted the ball away.

For Simpson to be on the field for Celtic at all was a contortion to match any of his on-field flips and twists. He was the only member of the Celtic side to have been managed previously by Jock Stein and it had not gone well. Simpson had been on the staff of Hibernian for almost four years when Stein had bowled into Easter Road as the Edinburgh club's new manager in the spring of 1964 and Simpson had not lasted long under the new man. Stein's arrival at Hibs had even left Simpson pondering whether, as he approached his mid-thirties, it might be time to quit the game altogether.

Life after football had already been in Simpson's mind even before Stein had arrived. Footballers in that era would earn well while they were playing but it was never enough for any of them to contemplate full and feather-bedded retirement once they were past playing. Simpson, being a canny, careful individual, had, thus, already begun planning for his future by going part-time at Hibs and combining the game with work as a salesman. Stein was always suspicious of goalkeepers, seeing them as a fickle bunch, and so objected to what he saw as a lack of commitment, demanding that Simpson become full time again. When Simpson refused to budge, it was only a matter of time before he would be hurtling out of the main door of the Edinburgh club. A step down to Berwick Rangers of the Second Division looked a natural coda to a lengthy career that had seen Simpson win FA-Cup winner's medals at Newcastle United. That was until one of the most notorious figures in Scottish football paved the way for a slightly more distinguished conclusion to Simpson's life in football.

Frank Haffey had been in goal at Wembley in 1961 when Scotland had lost 9–3 to England but had remained Celtic's first-choice goalkeeper until losing his place to John Fallon in late 1963. When it became clear at the beginning of the 1964–65 season that there was no way back into the team for Haffey, he demanded a transfer but Celtic would not allow him to leave until they had signed a reserve as cover for Fallon. Simpson's predicament at Hibs being known in the game, Celtic offered £3,000, which Stein accepted with alacrity, and Ronnie Simpson became a Celt.

It was something of a step downwards. Hibs were several places higher than Celtic in the league and already soaring under Stein. Simpson's role as an unwanted outcast was emphasised heavily in that his move to Celtic took place on the day when Hibs travelled to Pittodrie to defeat Aberdeen 3–1 in some style and win the Scottish Summer Cup, the Edinburgh club's first cup triumph since the Second World War and a victory that caused a major stir in the game. It provided further evidence of Stein being a manager with the gift of winning, coming, as it did, only weeks after he had taken over at Hibs.

It would not be long until Simpson's talents brought him into the Celtic team – and not long either until Stein forced him out of it again. When Fallon lost his edge, Simpson made his debut in November 1964 at no less a venue than the Camp Nou, facing players such as Jesús Garay and Sándor Kocsis of Barcelona in a Fairs Cup tie. That was a mere two months after his signing for Celtic but the defeat to Barcelona also prompted Celtic's recruitment of Jock Stein as replacement for Jimmy McGrory and two months further on, in January 1965, the month in which Stein agreed to take the post of Celtic manager, Simpson was summarily returned to the reserves. The goalkeeper had anticipated exactly such a scenario – when he had heard Stein was coming to Celtic Park he had said to John Fallon, 'I might as well clear out my locker now.' It seemed that Simpson, as the final signing of Jimmy McGrory's twenty years as manager, was now likely to be plunged into his much-anticipated retirement.

Instead, in September 1965, after a shaky performance from Fallon in a 2–1 defeat to Rangers, Simpson was brought in from the cold after eight months on the sidelines. He soon convinced Stein of his worth and mutual respect replaced mutual suspicion.

Simpson's early save proved a rare piece of inventiveness from a Celtic player in the first half of the match with Zurich. Celtic toiled, failing to find, with any regularity, the fluidity, the intricacy that had served them so well up until that point in the season. There was a real sense of optimism coursing through the Celtic support at this time. Jock Stein had revived their spirits and during the agonisingly drawn-out, three-month-long close-season, excitement and anticipation for the European Cup had been building, an excitement that had been heightened by the tremendous friendly victory over Manchester United and by Celtic's imperious domestic form. That excitement had been reflected in the sizeable midweek, pay-at-the-gate crowd for the Zurich match and it was channelled into ever more frenzied support for the team in their efforts to overwhelm the most demanding opponents Celtic had yet met that season. The electrifying effect of the crowd gave Celtic an energy to keep pounding away at the Swiss while Zurich, inspired by the occasion, redoubled their efforts to hold out and hold on to a rewarding draw.

Zurich appeared a strong match for the home side: purposeful, determined and organised. Celtic had huffed and puffed but had been unable to blow Zurich's Alpine chalet down, leaving the home side looking almost stumped. Nothing prevailed until Gemmell pounded into an advanced position midway through the second half and found John Clark supplying him with the ball. Gemmell, fielded at right-back, went coursing forward into space ceded by the Swiss in the heart of their midfield, gathering the ball in his hulking stride before whacking in a shot that flew over Iten's head and dipped below the crossbar to leave Switzerland's goalkeeper of the year flailing around as if trying to swat a zig-zagging fly with his hands. Stein always encouraged Gemmell to shoot from distance and the manager's encouragement and belief in one of his players had once more been converted into a goal.

'The goal which I had to take from Tommy Gemmell, with a shot from 30 yards,' Iten says, 'was, of course, especially disappointing for me. It was an extremely hard and speedy shot, coming not straightly flying but making curves to the left and right and finally landing in the goal. But already before that goal it was for our team a real battle and we had also much luck that Celtic had not scored before Tommy did because we were more or less during the whole game forced on to the defensive. Corners: Celtic 17, FCZ 0!' Iten's words reflect how, while it may have looked as though Zurich were comfortably holding their own, they were actually expending enormous effort, unseen to onlookers, just to maintain parity. This happens often in the game of football. Iten is backed up as blameless by Kobi Kuhn, his teammate, in respect of teams being simply defenceless when disarmed by Gemmell's exceptional shooting from distance. 'I remember well – Gemmell was famous for such shots,' Kuhn says. 'He has scored goals from this distance also in the league. That's why we weren't unprepared for these situations. It would have been essential to disrupt Tommy Gemmell early on [as he advanced forward]. Unfortunately we haven't been able to do so in this situation.' Zurich appeared to have allowed Gemmell to fly forward as if waiting to get down to business only when the player approached the heavily manned penalty area.

Iten also confirms the intensity of the physical battle to which Hansen, the referee, had alluded. 'By the way,' Iten adds, 'I got hit on my shinbone from [Jimmy] Johnstone with the consequence that it was operated on a year later and eventually it caused my football career to end at the age of 28 years. I already had the ball in my hands when Jimmy Johnstone hurt my leg – he hit my left shinbone, which was really naughty of him. The reaction of Ernst Meyer was that he hit Jimmy in his backside – the referee did not see it – [and Johnstone] wanted to do the same to Meyer but he ran away behind the goal, always pursued by Jimmy, and ended his escape near the referee, where Meyer felt it to be safe. It was really a unique scene and, after the game, we all laughed about it.'

Five minutes after Gemmell's goal, Joe McBride struck a left-footed shot that took a minor deflection on its way past Iten. On a turbulent, testing night for Celtic, potentially the most severe blow was that of Mr Hansen blowing his whistle for full-time just as McBride was climbing into the air to head the ball past Iten to make it 3–0. Instead, the two-goal margin made things feel uncomfortably tight for the players as they zeroed in on Zurich for the second leg.

'Personally, the match against Celtic was a highlight in my football career, especially concerning the atmosphere during the game,' Omi Iten says. 'There was such a noise coming from the singing 60,000 fans that on the field we did not understand any word from each other. And after the game when we looked around the places where the fans had been standing, the ground was covered with a lot of small and empty whisky bottles. So we understood why it was such a terrible noise during the game!'

The more modest Letzigrund would be a different prospect for the return and Stein saw the game itself as being a quite different one to that which had been witnessed in Glasgow. 'Zurich will have to change their style for this match,' Stein said. 'They were defensive but now they have to come out and try to get three goals if they are to beat us. They must attack and so that will leave more space for our forwards. At Celtic Park, they always had an extra man in defence. If Jimmy Johnstone got past Stierli, the left-back, there was always an extra man behind. It was the same on the other wing with John Hughes. They also seemed always to have an extra two players in the middle. Our players had to keep possession because of their packed defence and that made passing difficult. The pattern changes naturally when they come at us. It is unlikely we will be caught in possession as often. We can try to find the space that will be behind their more open defence.

'If we were to go to Zurich and lose a two-goal lead, we would deserve to go out of the competition. They came over to play all-out defence and to stop us scoring. They didn't succeed. Now they have got to expose themselves more and that will change the game.'

Prior to flying out to Zurich at midday on the Monday, Stein had five of his 'heavy team' report for a morning training session at Celtic Park, in the belief that 'a day off could be harmful to them'. It made sense, given that the journey to Switzerland would take seven hours and the team would then have only a light, limbering-up session on the day before the match.

The Swiss, Orson Welles expounded in his impromptu speech in *The Third Man*, had espoused 'democracy, peace and brotherly love' but had come up with little more than 'the cuckoo clock'. Well, Switzerland could provide Celtic with access to the next round of the European Cup and the cuckoo clock was a curio imported from Bavaria, but it had been in Switzerland that *catenaccio* – a fashionable and effective form of defensive foot-ball – had been invented and, for all Stein's positive words, the players were concerned that Zurich, an 'excellent side' according to Stevie Chalmers, might prove able exponents in hitting Celtic hard on the break in front of their own supporters.

This led to a degree of apprehension on the part of the Celtic players as they settled into the luxurious Dolder Grand Hotel, described by Tommy Gemmell as 'a seven-star job'; a hotel that boasted a nine-hole golf course and its own heated swimming pool, Bond-style luxuries in the mid-1960s.

'I had no thoughts of us winning the European Cup,' Bobby Lennox says of being at the outset of Celtic's continental jaunt that year. 'You just wanted to go to Zurich and play in this stadium you had never played in before. It was a big thrill to be going to Zurich and playing; I'd never been there. That's how we approached it.

'A number of us were actually quite concerned about Zurich. We felt that, given that they were at home, they would drive at us in the same way we had attacked them in Glasgow. So Jock sat us down before the match, in one of the Dolder Grand's hotel rooms. It wasn't a big room and people were crammed in, sitting on plush, ornate armchairs. Jock then surprised us all when he told us to expect Zurich to play in exactly the same way as they had in Glasgow.

'"They're not good enough to change," he said. "We'll beat them here. We'll get at them." One or two of the lads still weren't sure and so they questioned him. I think Billy McNeill suggested that Zurich would come out aggressively and try to defeat us. Jock was emphatic. "They've not got the players to come out and beat us," he said. "They're not good enough. We'll beat them here tonight."'

The Celtic players had visited the Letzigrund on the evening prior to the match to find joggers, walking-race competitors and high jumpers using the facilities at this multi-purpose stadium. None of those athletic activities would have any effect on the pitch, which was perfect, lush, green, not the muddied heaps that were becoming prevalent in Scotland as autumn rolled into winter. The Letzigrund looked eminently suitable for Celtic to get the ball down and play. Sir Stanley Rous, president of FIFA, based in the city, would be watching and that, together with the onus being on Zurich to find inventive means of breaking down Celtic, promised a less fractious contest.

A late decision would be made by Stein on whether Chalmers or McBride were to be in the team – and he opted for Stevie. Jimmy Johnstone and John Hughes had suddenly found excellent form – Hughes had played a key role in three of the goals against St Johnstone on the previous Saturday and Johnstone had been at his twisting, winding best. Stein insisted before the match that his team would attack, playing to their strengths, but then Kubala had said much the same on arrival in Glasgow. It was then the accepted norm in European football that the home team had a duty to attack, in front of their own supporters, and that the away team must defend. This game bucked that particular trend.

With 22 minutes gone, the tie was as good as over. Gemmell collected the ball in the vicinity of the halfway line, rumbled forward, picking up speed over the whole ten yards in front of him, and then sent a screaming shell of a shot high into the net behind Iten.

'I scored a 35-yarder at Celtic Park and then scored an identical goal over there, in Zurich,' Gemmell said. 'You would have thought the goalkeeper would have been clued-up from the first match. The one in Zurich was from the same distance and the same angle as at Celtic Park and still he wasn't ready for it.'

A sound defence is provided by Iten to the charges levelled against him by Gemmell. 'It was really hard to save the hard shots of Tommy Gemmell,' Iten says. 'At that time I did not know another player with a harder shot than Tommy had.' Of some consolation to Iten was the assessment of Switzerland's *Sport* magazine, 'This was an outstanding match from Iten, one that was, for him, the most difficult of his career.'

The second goal was more of a close thing. Bobby Lennox's shot was blocked, Chalmers, alert and agile as ever, collected the rebound, turned and slipped a low shot past Iten. Three minutes into the second half, Lennox was felled by Herbert Neumann, the German. Concetto Lo Bello, the Italian referee, awarded a penalty and Gemmell whacked his kick past Iten and low into the corner of the Swiss net.

'I don't remember anybody really doubting Jock Stein's word again after that,' Bobby Lennox says.

Kubala, before the first leg, had said, 'I am 39 now so I play no more. I leave that to younger men.' In Zurich, his side's resources had been stretched to the point where he had had to field himself for the first time since early 1965 – and, sadly, for the great man, he was as anonymous as it was possible for such a great footballing name to be, flickering, shadow-like, on the left wing. The Hungarian, in exile from his communist-run country, had won 11 Czechoslovak caps while playing for Slovan Bratislava; nine Hungarian caps playing for Vasas of Budapest; and 19 Spain caps playing with Barcelona. He was deserving of considerable respect and he and his team now conceded defeat graciously.

'We had thought it could be possible for us to play a similar season like in 1963–1964 when we reached the semi-final,' Kobi Kuhn says, 'but things turned out differently. The duel didn't go our way and it was a tough one to lose.'

Now Stein, impatient to test his team against thoroughly

demanding opposition, wanted, he said, to face Internazionale of Milan or Real Madrid in the next round, a sure sign of his confidence in his players.

'We won easily,' Stein said 'because we were allowed to play football tonight. It would now be better to get our strength tested. We would prefer at this stage to have a club of the standing of Real or Inter. I feel that such a draw now would be to the benefit of Celtic. If we have any hopes of winning the tournament, and we most certainly have, then these teams have to be beaten at one time or another. We must be just as good as anyone and I feel we can beat the big shots. We have a relatively quiet programme ahead of December and so that would give us time to concentrate on matches of such high rating.'

Instead, the draw in Florence, on 13 October 1966, set Celtic the task of defeating Nantes, the champions of France. 'I am completely happy with the draw,' Stein said, changing, chameleon-like, his outlook. 'There are no easy games in this competition but I feel we could have got it much tougher than this.'

Gemmell, the leading goalscorer over those two legs, would reflect carefully on Jock Stein's central role in the exceptional and swift transformation of Celtic. 'It was all about guidance and leadership,' Gemmell said. 'The players were there when Stein arrived at the club. They just needed to be moulded into a team. And that's basically what he did. We were one big, happy family with players that could play and that makes a big difference. You get a lot of players of good ability in different sides but the actual players don't play as a team. They play as individual units. You've got to get the whole team playing as one single unit before you can get success and that's what hap-pened with us.'

It was not only through strength of personality that Jock Stein developed the magnetism that made him the centre of everything at Celtic. His restructuring of the team had revealed to the players that his judgment was impeccable. On his arrival at the club, Celtic, in common with almost every other team in Britain, fielded a five-man forward line, typically with Stevie Chalmers at outside-right; Bobby Murdoch inside-right; John Hughes centre-forward; Bobby Lennox inside-left; and Bertie Auld outside-left. Every one of those mercurial attacking players would be retained by Stein but each one would have their position in the team altered so that they could be more effective. Chalmers was switched to centre-forward; Murdoch to midfield; Hughes to the left wing, where he would compete for a place in the team with Lennox; and Auld would join Murdoch in midfield. Soon, all of those players could see that the manager knew their strengths better than they did themselves, which served to consolidate his power and prestige inside the club. There is no point in a manager being hard all the time – you've got to show you're human. That understanding of how to get the best out of people would all have been natural on Stein's part. That's what made it so good.

Len Murray, a lawyer who represented Stein during the late 1960s, confirms that Stein's rugged exterior often hid a different, more surprising side to him.

'He was a very sensitive man,' Murray says. 'The thing that hurt him most of all was that one of his closest friends, indeed there are some who said he was his closest friend, was very much a Rangers man, and he came to visit Jock [on one occasion in the mid-1960s]. They were going out together and Jock was in his bedroom getting ready and Jean [Stein's wife] told the friend that Jock was going to Celtic as manager. The guy got up and walked out [of Stein's life] and that really hurt Jock.

'Jock, as I knew him, was a highly intelligent individual. I always got the impression that he never ever pretended to be anything other than an ex-miner but he would have succeeded at anything he turned his hand to. He was kind of rough in some ways but very gentle in others. Rough in that he didn't suffer fools gladly. I thought he was an admirable individual. He had a weakness for the horses, of course. None of us is perfect and he fell into the majority in that respect.'

That snub by his friend provided Stein with extra motivation for his Celtic team to defeat their great rivals on a regular basis. 'I've seen so many people,' Billy McNeill said, 'in the main, people who didn't know the man as well as they might have done, saying that to big Jock the Rangers game was no more important than any other game. That is absolute nonsense. It was the most important game in the calendar for big Jock. I think it was down to the fact that that gave him the opportunity to show the Celtic support that he could beat Rangers. Nothing delighted him more than doing so. He may well have said differently publicly – but he didn't mean it, I can assure you. There was no doubt in Jock's mind which game was the most important one.

'Big Jock was never the big, hard man I've seen him described as. He had a hard side to him and he could hurt you when he felt like it – he had a tongue that could cut you in bits. He could shout too. But there was a right soft side to him. He could get really bad-tempered, which, as far as I'm concerned, is an endearing factor. I hate people who have no passion and big Jock certainly had plenty of passion. He could be sympathetic and, indeed, quite a soft man at times. He'd maybe punish people and think, later on, "Maybe I shouldn't have done that." He could be a good counsel and a good father figure. He was a man of great contradictions, a very complex individual.'

Domestic life was much more uncomplicated for Celtic than the fascinating challenge that had been thrown at them by FC Zurich; confronting local opposition was routine in comparison to all this continental gadding about. Queen's Park and

Airdrieonians were comfortably eliminated in the semi-finals of, respectively, the Glasgow Cup and the League Cup, and the early autumn brought a string of league victories that consolidated Celtic's position at the top of the First Division. A victory at Dundee, along with a subsequent 5–3 demolition of Hibernian at Easter Road and thumping defeats of St Johnstone, Airdrieonians and Ayr United saw Celtic ease into a three-point lead over Kilmarnock at the top of the league in late October 1966 and the players enjoyed a three-day training and golfing break at Seamill, Ayrshire, as a special 'reward' for the defeats of Zurich and Hibernian.

Not that Stein was content with domestic bliss. Santos, the club for whom Pelé performed, had been approached in September 1966 and invited to play at Celtic Park in a friendly on 12 October – one week after the second leg with Zurich. The Glasgow club negotiated with Santos for weeks to try to bring them to Scotland but in late September the Brazilian club sent a telegraph to say that the Brazilian Football Federation had barred them from participating in such a match at such a time. If the greats would not face Celtic voluntarily . . . Celtic would have to make it compulsory. A win over Nantes would bring Inter and Real back within Stein's range.

CHAPTER 6

Pressing the Point

The golden sound of silence was one of the finest aspects of sport in the 1960s. Footballers, as with Victorian schoolchildren, tended to be seen and not heard. Few players were dissatisfied with that. Pre- and post-match press conferences involving a guarded, docile, non-committal player – fearful of saying anything offensive in case they upset the manager or the board of directors – had yet to be invented and newspaper reporters at a match were expected to entertain their readers by making intelligent comment and analysis based on what they had been privileged to see rather than taking down screeds of functional comment from a player emerging from the showers twenty minutes after a match. Footballers were not protected from objective analysis through having been 'helpful' to the press by sitting through a press conference and providing a quote-happy claque of stenographers masquerading as reporters with enough meaningless bilge to fill a double spread in their papers.

Only very rarely were players asked for their opinion at all – the idea, revolutionary in retrospect, was that these young men could communicate best by playing football to a high standard. Managers tended to speak through the press only in the most perfunctory fashion, giving out team line-ups, commenting on injuries and players' fitness and occasionally, although not always, providing some insight into a match after it had been played, for the benefit of the Sunday or Monday newspapers. Even then, they would usually do so only in the briefest of terms.

Radio silence, too, was bliss. The airwaves had yet to be polluted with hours of 'phone-ins', of 'pundits' endlessly debating the merits of this or that player, manager, owner, benefactor or other football-club-associated individual and manufacturing squabbles among themselves to drag the entire thing out for a couple of hours. Tweeting, of course, was confined entirely to the birds.

Not that all was entirely hunky dory. Newspaper reporters would still attempt to spark some goblin-like mischief now and then – and nor was Jock Stein exempt from their jaundiced, withering eye. First of all, during the 1966–67 season, Stein had been taken to task by some elements in the press for having said that he had found little or nothing to learn when attending the World Cup finals held in England during the summer of 1966. This instance of press outrage seemed to be, as so often, manufactured for its own admiration and benefit. A World Cup may be enjoyable and entertaining but not every single one will throw up radical ideas in terms of how to approach and play the game.

Celtic's manager would again find himself the object of press scrutiny in late 1966, and this time it was for the more serious accusation that Stein had attempted to interfere with the free functioning of the press itself. When Bobby Murdoch was sent off in a league match against St Mirren at Celtic Park on 5 November, Stein hurried from his dugout to harry the press photographers and usher them away as they took pictures of the midfielder leaving the field of play. Images of Murdoch trotting off the field would still appear alongside match reports of a flat afternoon for Celtic that had petered out in a 1–1 draw – the first time Celtic had failed to win a match in any competition in the three months since the start of the season.

During the subsequent days, a flustered press accused Stein of interfering with their freedoms because of his suggestion that photographers ought to have a designated, allocated space, possibly in a marked-out area behind one of the goals, from which they would not be allowed to stray during the match. Radical stuff indeed. Stein suggested that it was no longer tenable that they should be allowed to move around anywhere they might wish outside the perimeter of the pitch. His ire had been drawn, during the Murdoch incident, by photographers hurrying down the touchline to harry a player who was already suffering the major and unusual disgrace of being officially banished from the game.

The matter was complicated by the nature of Murdoch's dismissal. With less than ten minutes remaining against St Mirren, and Celtic drawing 1–1 with a team second-bottom of the First Division, Murdoch had, in frustration, reputedly challenged the referee in relation to a throw-in that had been awarded to the Paisley team. For his troubles, the midfielder had been booked and, then, within seconds, dismissed, supposedly for making further comments to referee Bert Henderson. Stein was perhaps sympathetic to a player who was reserved by nature off the field but a competitor on it and whose dismissal looked dubious, not least because there was some doubt as to whether it had been Murdoch or another player – Joe McBride was in the vicinity – who had made the disparaging comments to the official.

The issue was brought to the boil by the press and it resulted in a 'stakeout' a few days later, when press reporters did as is their wont and hung around awaiting comment on this particular issue. The venue was Celtic Park, where a board meeting was taking place, with, the press surmised, the Murdoch matter, and the club's attitude to photographers, on the agenda. After several hours, Stein emerged alone, into the heavy air of the winter's night. The dozing reporters stirred into life, hoping for their vigil finally to be rewarded.

'There is nothing to be discussed,' Stein told the gaggle of pressmen. 'There is no issue.' And that was that – there was nowhere for the matter to go. It was beautifully simple. No player managed by Stein would, the press knew, be commenting anonymously and nor would anyone in authority at the club. Stein was exerting the 'full control' that was so vital to him, and with the Celtic manager unwilling to muck in and join the debate, to play the game, the entire issue would be left to fizzle out soggily until early December, when Murdoch would appear in front of the Scottish Football Association's disciplinary officials to discover whether he were to receive additional punishment. His dismissal was upheld, he was reprimanded for his particular choice of language during the incident in question and fined £30 by the SFA's Referees' Committee but, crucially, not suspended, which hinted at a degree of sympathy, for whatever reason, from those hearing his case.

The episode showed that Stein was still regarded in some parts of the press as something of an upstart even though, only a week before, Rangers had been on the end of yet another defeat to Celtic, one that was quite different in form to the previous two but which had proved, for the Ibrox club, equally bitter in taste.

Bobby Murdoch, who would be to the fore in that victory over Rangers, had been a half-back – a defensive midfield player – at St Modan's school in Lanarkshire alongside Benny Rooney and John Cushley, both of whom would also be signed for Celtic. Yet Murdoch was being played as an inside-forward when Jock Stein became Celtic manager. His place had appeared in some danger as there was something of a cull of inside-forwards upon Stein's arrival at the club. Hugh Maxwell and John Divers were a couple of early casualties, their swift departures marking a change in style on the part of the manager. With the ruthless reconstruction that Stein was carrying out, Murdoch's inside-forward role was also redundant.

Stein wanted pacier play and, as part of that, he was intent on reshaping his team. Five forwards was the norm at the time, with two inside-forwards as link men, each fixed between the wingers and the centre-forward. Stein wished for greater flexibility in his players and for his forwards to be able to revolve at speed rather than remaining in one particular position. Maxwell and Divers were too deliberate on the ball for Stein's new system. Divers was a fine technical footballer but, hampered by poor circulation, he lacked pace. There would be no place either for the bulky Murdoch, who was never the quickest of players, in Stein's attack. Instead, he became one of the two fulcrums for attacking play in the Celtic midfield, alongside Bertie Auld. There, Murdoch's vision and precision on the ball became a prime element in making Stein's team tick. With the game spread out in front of him, he could win the ball, open up play and shoot from long-range.

Mild-mannered, gentle and unassuming off the field of play, it says much for Murdoch's popularity with his teammates that, despite his reticent nature, he accumulated not one but two nicknames – 'Chopper' and 'Sam'. Both were related to his tendency to go into the tackle with considerable enthusiasm; the latter name was a reference to Samuel B. Allison, a Glasgow demolition man. Those monikers reflected only one side to a man who had a delicate-as-a-fairy-cake touch on the ball but they did accurately represent his enthusiasm for battle: Murdoch was a Scottish footballer of a type that was prized by clubs throughout Great Britain in the post-war years. Such players could marry, in one being, sensitive artistry on the ball with shuddering, industrial-strength tackles and controlled aggression that stretched the laws of the game to the very limit.

'He could play,' John Clark says, 'but he could do you in a minute as well, him and Bertie. They were two good midfield players and look at the pace we had with Bobby Lennox, Stevie, Jinky, the two full-backs. You couldn't get any better, could you? If you were looking to build a team just now and you had all those players, you'd be thinking, "I'm lucky."'

Rangers had spent much of the first three months of the season smarting from the two major humiliations dealt out to them by Celtic and, as autumn turned to winter, that uneasy feeling would continue to plague them. They faced Celtic in the League Cup final at Hampden Park on the last Saturday of October 1966 and although this game did not result in the efficient and comprehensive scuttling of a Rangers team that had been witnessed in the two previous Old Firm encounters that season, it was perhaps even more unsettling for the Ibrox club. This time, Rangers managed to get close to Celtic and even matched them for much of the game – but they still suffered another dispiriting defeat.

'We have often played better against Rangers and lost,' Stein said, hardly hiding his glee, in celebration of lifting the League Cup through his side's 1–0 victory, Stein's fourth trophy since taking over as Celtic manager twenty months previously. Rangers had even gone so far as to have had the ball in the net, which would have been a major advance into undiscovered territory for them, but it proved to be a hoax. Bobby Watson had volleyed the ball home from the edge of the six-yard box after Ronnie Simpson had uncharacteristically punched Kai Johansen's cross only partially clear. The cause of Simpson's error, though, had been a foul by Alex Smith. The Rangers player had made a back for Simpson as he went to meet the ball.

The referee, Tom 'Tiny' Wharton, was alive to the Rangers man's piece of sharp practice and correctly disallowed the goal.

For all that Rangers had got closer to Celtic than before, they were still far from being on the same level. Bobby Lennox was sharp and agile and alive in a way that no Rangers midfield player or attacker could match when, in the 18th minute, Bertie Auld's beautifully flighted, left-footed, diagonal ball deep into Rangers' half was headed down, back in the direction from which it had come, by Joe McBride, into the path of Lennox, who was expertly positioned to volley from ten yards and the ball went streaking past Norrie Martin in the Rangers goal.

Once again, a Celtic victory provoked panic at Ibrox, with Rangers, within three days, offering Eddie Turnbull, the Aberdeen manager, the position of coach alongside Scot Symon, the manager. This provoked yet another defeat for the Ibrox club, with Turnbull turning down the opportunity, after due consideration – he was unwilling to defer to Symon over the selection and recruitment of the team. John Lawrence, the Rangers chairman, failed to seize the day and appoint Turnbull as manager; as Robert Kelly had done when appointing Stein after he had turned down the suggestion that he join Celtic as assistant to Sean Fallon. Turnbull, like Stein, was one of the new 'tracksuit managers' and would have been a fresh and vibrant rival to Stein.

'It's hard for somebody to realise the sheer charisma or the sheer presence of Jock,' Jim Craig says. 'He wasn't a particularly tall man, but he was very good at making his presence felt and you always knew who was boss. He had a certain presence. Certain people come into a room and you look at them automatically. He was an amazing man and it was an amazing time. We were very, very privileged to have been there at that time.'

Rangers had lacked the nerve to remove Symon altogether

and replace him with as close to an equivalent to Stein as they might have found in Scotland. Bobby Seith would soon be named as Rangers' first ever coach – previously coach at Dundee, he was a far less threatening figure for Stein than Turnbull might have been.

'He was an amazing professional,' Jimmy Gordon says of Stein. Gordon had been given access to the Celtic manager when making a film about the club that season. 'Jock Stein was a man who could have managed anything, an imposing character. Physical presence for a start – he was a bulky individual. He would stand in the corner of a room where he could see everything. He also, I felt, had a kind of slow-burning fuse. Sometimes it was as though he paused and decided to lose his temper, as it were. It wasn't an immediate reaction. It was premeditated – cool anger rather than hot. It was as though there was a slight delay and then he erupted. It only happened a couple of times as I recall but it was the same sort of pattern. He would lose the rag if he felt like losing the rag. So you felt that it was premeditated – with journalists or with other people involved in football.

'He kept dealings with players between himself and the players although I do recall [once] he was annoyed when Celtic were playing Partick Thistle at Parkhead and Celtic were really showboating – and Bertie Auld was showboating a bit too much. Jock said, after the event, "I put him in his place. These are fellow professionals. You don't make a fool of them."

'I remember there was one referee – Celtic had been nearly robbed of a game – and he gradually lost his temper with him. Journalists say, "Oh, I always stood up to him, you know." Did they hell! He was a very intimidating presence – by and large they did what he told them to do. He was simply an imposing figure with great personal charisma.

'I also remember we would be going over to Barrowfield to

film training and the players would be turning up in their cars and he would say to me, "You know, this is all new to football people." Only five years or so before, the players would not have had cars – and these were only small cars compared to what the players have nowadays. Already he felt there was a big change. It was not that he didn't like it – just that he was observing a change.

'I remember once saying to Jock, "I don't think the opponents were that good." And he said [with a gruff growl], "That's because we didn't allow them to be good." And, of course, he's right and I'm wrong. He knows the game and I don't. If you're a non-footballer, you're as well leaving the judgement to people who know.

'Jock was very happy to let you get on with it. I found him perfectly straight and I was probably slightly in awe of him as he was an imposing and distinguished figure in Scottish life. John McPhail, who had played with Stein at Celtic in the 1950s, told me, "Everybody knew he had a weak side. The trouble was nobody went past him on that side. He bluffed them into going by on the other side." People with limitations make great coaches. People with great natural ability can't understand anybody who doesn't have great natural ability. It's working with material that is less than perfect and making it gel together.

'The players all teamed together very well. The spirit on the bus was very good and that, to a large extent, must be down to the manager. I don't think there were any egos in the Celtic team, when I think of it. They all pulled for each other.'

There was much more to Jock Stein than being prepared to muck in on the training ground. One of Stein's greatest strengths was that he was never predictable. A dismissal in 1960s football was a true rarity and thus a matter of disgrace, given the lengths to which a player had to go to be ejected from the continuing fray. Yet despite Bobby Murdoch's sending-off against

St Mirren, he would not be disciplined by Stein. Another player would, though, be disciplined internally and would suffer a fortnight's suspension for his actions during the match with St Mirren, even though his offence, in contrast to Murdoch's, had gone unseen by the referee and almost everyone else present at Celtic Park. Not by Stein, though, the only man that mattered in such instances.

Stein had been moved to state after the St Mirren match that, 'Some of our players have been warned in the past that trouble awaits them if they do not adhere to what they are told in pre-match planning. Yet they persist in going their own way. There are going to be no more warnings about this type of mistake. I don't think there is any doubt that some of our forwards' play against St Mirren was plain stupid. Real steps are going to be taken to ensure Celtic come first and individual players come second.'

The clear and true target of Stein's ire and the player principally alluded to in those words was none other than Jimmy Johnstone, who, despite being uninjured, was not only missing from the starting line-up for the Glasgow Cup final with Partick Thistle the following Monday but also for the game with Falkirk at Brockville five days later. Johnstone also, presumably on Stein's word, was omitted from the Scotland team to play Northern Ireland in the midweek.

For all Stein's tough reputation, Billy McNeill recalls that he also had a softer side, too: 'I remember he once suspended Jimmy Johnstone. He sent him away and said, 'I don't want to see you near the place. Three days later, Jock said to me, 'The wee man's been on the phone. I've not spoken to him but I'm thinking I'll maybe just phone him up and tell him it's all right to come back in.'

The draw with St Mirren was similar to an enforced pause

for breath on a journey towards the title that was never going to be entirely unhampered. 'We did not play as well as we can,' Stein had said of the St Mirren game. 'No-one should be in any doubt about that but after such a winning streak as we have had – 23 unbroken victories – it could be the best thing. The strain of winning continually is intense.'

That had been demonstrated three days before the St Mirren match, in Celtic's victory over Stirling Albion, another low-flying First Division club. Stirling had been beaten 7–3 but the performance had still not satisfied fully those of the club's supporters who had been attended the game at Celtic Park. That October of 1966, the club had newly opened a father-and-son gate at which entry could be gained for a combined six shillings – for children of school age – with Celtic happy to allow parents to lift children under school age over the turn-stile and gain entry for free. Yet many still felt that the match with Albion had not represented full value for money. Celtic had been 6–1 ahead at half-time before relaxing through the remainder of the game and allowing Albion to come back into it, something for which the Celtic players were 'ticked off', according to Stein. The supporters could be as severe and scathing as a gaggle of art critics and, in the match with Stirling, they had grown restless as they had witnessed Celtic muddle through the latter stages of a match that they had begun decisively and crisply.

'We used to go to supporters' functions,' Tommy Gemmell said, 'and the rapport we had with the supporters was unbeliev-able. Big Jock encouraged that. We had a rota system at Celtic Park. Everybody had their dinner dances or supporters' nights or quizzes and there was always a minimum of three players at these functions. Now, you start to build up a rapport with these supporters. I always tried to put myself out to get on with them because supporters can be fickle. If you're having a bad time, they can get on your back and give you a hard time. They would be a bit easier on me because I was popular among them.

'Additionally, the players were so close it was as if we were related. We used to have big parties in each others' houses and go for the odd pint together. And with Celtic being a family club, all these things helped to engender this team spirit.'

The waters remained choppy as Celtic voyaged east to Dunfermline in mid-November 1966. Johnstone was restored to the team and eager to restore his reputation with the manager. He got a goal, scurrying into the penalty area to get to a loose ball and squirt it over the line, but that moment was almost lost in a match that saw nine goals scored and Celtic gasping for air at times, not least when Dunfermline three times took a two-goal lead, with the Glasgow side only winning at the very death and then only thanks to a handball from Roy Barry, the Dunfermline centre-half, which gave Joe McBride the opportunity to score from the penalty spot with seconds remaining, and seal a 5–4 win.

At Dunfermline, the defence had looked shaky – most glaringly and obviously when the Fife side went 4–2 ahead shortly before half-time through a throw-in that seeped all the way into the Celtic six-yard box, where Alex Ferguson, a scourge of Celtic on the day, was left free and easy to slip the ball easily into the net.

It had been a mixed period – one that had included the lifting of the League Cup and consolidation of Celtic's place at the top of the league at the same time as the team's form had begun to fluctuate, often going up and down wildly within the 90 minutes of a match. Yet Stein liked turbulence, in the belief that it banished complacency. He liked to control the storm but with Nantes, the French champions, on the horizon, Stein would now have to find a way to spread calm among his group of often over-exuberant players.

CHAPTER 7

Refreshing Changes

Rotation was an idea alien to Scottish football during the 1960s – something for farmers and their crops not for football managers and their teams. Its use at Celtic Park would continue to confuse and irritate Jock Stein's players long after they had finished their careers. For Stein, rotating his players was carried out routinely, long before the concept was given its name and even as the swarm of managers around him sought a rock-solid, regular starting eleven week after week.

It was done, Stein stated, to guard against 'complacency' on the part of his players but it was also a means of maintaining managerial authority – Stein was the only person fully assured of involvement on a Saturday. That reinforced his power over his players by emphasising on a weekly basis, through the team sheet, that he was the central figure at the club. It provided him with the ability to vary his team from game to game, and to prevent players becoming jaded or tired. Stein always stressed the importance of his sixteen-man 'pool', or squad, of players as providing him with the versatility to manipulate his team selections.

'Jock chopped and changed his forward line much more than his defence,' Stevie Chalmers says. 'I didn't like that very much; it made me feel that he wasn't happy with what he saw. Sometimes it worked for him; sometimes it didn't.'

Stevie Chalmers was one player who was never likely to grow complacent about his place at Celtic. He was, after all, lucky to be alive at all, never mind fortunate to be playing football. He had been diagnosed with tuberculosis meningitis at the age of twenty, when beginning to make his way in football with Kirkintilloch Rob Roy, the Junior club. Mild symptoms of feeling unwell had led to a house call from a doctor who insisted Chalmers was whisked immediately from his Balornock home into the Belvidere Hospital, close to Celtic Park, where he had been placed immediately, and ominously, in Ward 13, for the terminally ill. For the following six months, he was confined to that ward as he fought hard for his life. The regular sight of the lifeless corpses of fellow patients being wheeled to the mortuary was a sobering one for Chalmers. It says much about his character that such a sight encouraged him to fight even harder to make sure he left the hospital alive and well.

'I never thought I was in the same danger as those other people,' Chalmers says, 'though clearly I was. I am convinced that my positive mental attitude and refusal to give in to the seemingly inevitable, together with my well-developed physical strength, helped me through the entire experience.' He made it out alive but it had been a near thing and the closeness of his brush with mortality was brought home to him when Dr Peter McKenzie, the head consultant at the Belvidere and a man who specialised in infectious diseases, picked him out to be filmed as his star patient, the one who had recovered from a normally fatal condition. McKenzie was going to take the film with him on a professional visit to North America to show to student doctors as a display of a unique case – the only one of his patients, who, until that point, had managed to walk out of the Belvidere Hospital alive.

Those who did recover from TB Meningitis tended to be hampered by the after-effects of the illness and so it was another minor miracle that Chalmers could return to football and move freely and flexibly, joining Ashfield Juniors in Glasgow.

'Rob Roy didn't seem to want me,' Chalmers says. 'Perhaps they were concerned about what I would be like as a player after such a debilitating illness, or even concerned about the effects on my health of playing football.' A Scotland Junior cap in January 1959 finally brought Stevie to Celtic's attention, 'after a long and tortuous journey', as he puts it, one that had also included two years of National Service in the RAF. Twelve days after facing Ireland at Firhill, at the advanced footballing age of 23, Chalmers signed for Celtic at Green's Playhouse on Renfield Street in Glasgow. Jock Stein, the reserve team coach, was present alongside Jimmy McGrory, the manager. 'He didn't say an awful lot on the day,' Chalmers says of Stein. 'I got the feeling he was sizing me up as a person very carefully.'

St Johnstone had offered Chalmers a signing-on fee of £100, serious money in the late 1950s, especially compared to the £20 he received upon signing for Celtic to go with his pay of £10 a week. Nottingham Forest and Newcastle United had also been interested in him but the lure of Celtic Park proved too great. He 'wandered around in something of a state of amazement and wonder' during his early days at the club but by the mid-1960s, after six years under directionless management, Chalmers 'was a bit concerned about my future at the club', where 'the situation was unstable'. When he at last made the first team, Stevie had been played on the wing, at inside-forward and at centre-forward but he had never had a settled position in the team even though he had proved to be a proficient goalscorer. Stein, on his arrival as Celtic manager, immediately made Chalmers his centre-forward.

'I had always been quite happy to play on the wing or at inside-forward,' Chalmers says, 'and although I had sometimes played at centre-forward for Celtic I had never settled there – the following week I was very likely to be switched to the wing or back to inside-forward. Jock found my best position and established me there. I suppose that's what makes the difference between a player and a manager.'

There was no player at Celtic Park more professional than Chalmers. A great family man, quiet, polite, always well turned-out, he was the perfect person to have around the club, as his teammates testify. Yet the threat of losing everything that he had built for himself at the club always hung over him. In his entire career at Celtic, he was never given a contract lasting more than one year and when Stein arrived at Celtic, Chalmers, owing to his late start in the game, was already 29, an ominous age given that Stein would state that the ideal age of a player was 25, as that provided a good blend of age and maturity. Chalmers, always extremely dedicated and fit, would make sure he would be out in front, light and lean, on training runs. No accusation of slug-gishness through age could ever be levelled at him.

One of Stein's favourite phrases was to tell his players that he was going to 'freshen up' his team. It was a phrase that was wonderfully vague, deliberately so on the manager's part, and a chilling one for his players at a time when being in the team was the only means of guaranteeing a win bonus. Sitting in the stand was damaging to a player's financial health and only one substitute was allowed; an innovation for that 1966–67 season. It ensured that everyone sweated during a match to ensure Stein did not suspect them of a lack of fragrance.

A magisterial display of this peerless command and control that Stein exercised through player selection arrived in the shape of some wonderful reverse psychology after the narrow-as-a-Venetian-back-alley victory over Dunfermline Athletic in mid-November 1966, which had raised mutterings and mur-murings in the press and among the support as to the strength of the Celtic defence. Certain players were seen – by those looking on from outside the club – as being in need of a rest. So, with a babble of voices telling Stein that it was time to freshen up his defence, the manager, in inimitable fashion, responded to the situation by naming, an unusual two days in advance of the subsequent fixture, with Heart of Midlothian, an entirely unchanged and unrefreshed team. It was a deliberate demonstration of how far Stein would be affected by external pressure – not at all. The players now had the chance to prove that they were not as disjointed and dilatory as their critics had suggested. That provided, in itself, Stein's selection with fresh motivation – something that he felt they required for every match. Celtic duly went out and trounced Hearts 3–0, with the defence performing without a hint of an offensive odour emanating from them.

Building on that triumph, Stein announced immediately that the Celtic team would again remain unchanged, this time for the first leg of the European Cup second round tie with Nantes the following midweek. So it was a happy, confident squad, the starting eleven certain of their places in the side, that flew out to western France from Glasgow at lunchtime on Monday 28 November, two days after the Hearts match, having undergone a full, pre-flight training session in the morning.

Out in France, Stein exacted a stinging revenge upon the press who had been critical of his team. He suggested to them that it was ludicrous that they should be so critical of footballers' play without demonstrating any aptitude for the game. So he invited them, at the conclusion of a training session, to show their capabilities by hitting the net from the penalty spot out on a muddy training pitch. A barrage of stray footballs were soon flying in all directions as the journalists, in suits, shirts and shoes, showed that their skills with a ball were as weak as their words of criticism had been strong.

If the Celtic players were feeling secure in a sense of

permanence through Stein fielding an unchanged team for the third successive game, the fickle nature of football was to be highlighted in the boldest terms by the fate of Joe McBride during what remained of 1966.

McBride had notched two goals against Hearts – his 32nd and 33rd of the season – and had now scored more than a third of Celtic's quite amazing total of 85 up to that point. He had relaxed contentedly at his home in Bishopbriggs the day after the encounter with the Edinburgh side, feeling certain that he was beginning to glitter as a genuine star in the Celtic firmament. His goalscoring had been almost as notable in the 1965–66 season, his first at the club. It was even better now, he explained, because he had suffered a toe injury and a hamstring strain early the previous season, which had hampered him and restricted him to a mere 43 goals overall. Now that he was in robust good health, the goals had begun to flow like tapwater and if he were to continue scoring at the same rate he would blast, as with dynamite, all the seemingly unassailable Celtic scoring records that had been set during the 1930s by Jimmy McGrory, the centre-forward. McBride had, he said, 'never had a season begin as well as this one in my career before. I'm usually struggling for several weeks before I start getting goals.'

Even before the Nantes tie, McBride was utterly certain that Celtic could win the European Cup while, domestically, he was seeking to go past McGrory's league record of 50 in a season and the First Division record set by Willie McFadyen of Motherwell of 54. Life was good for the chunky, resilient McBride, 28 years of age, who believed Celtic to be 'the greatest team in the world'. He had turned down the offer of a hefty signing fee from Dunfermline Athletic to join Celtic in 1965. McBride had been negotiating simultaneously with Celtic and when he informed Stein by telephone of his rivals' offer, enough to buy a house, a surprised Stein blurted out, 'I'd take it if I were you . . .' before catching himself and seeking to persuade McBride that joining Celtic would be a much better decision.

Confirmation of McBride's blossoming reputation came with Celtic's arrival in Nantes. Autograph hunters flocked to have McBride pen his signature and shake hands. José Arribas, Nantes' Basque manager, lamented, 'Our fans are too sporting. They want to see goals – and they don't seem to care whether we score them or our opponents do. They have heard a great deal about McBride and the goals he has scored for Celtic so he becomes a big hero, even though he will be playing against us.'

Still, under Stein, egos were punctured with regularity and minutes before the match with the French champions at the Marcel-Saupin Stadium, those enthusiasts might have been surprised to see McBride having his status as a star being questioned fiercely by Stein to the point at which the Celtic manager even went so far as to demand why McBride might even consider himself worthy of pursuing football as a career.

'We were in the dressing room at Nantes,' McBride said, 'and I went to Sean [Fallon, Celtic's assistant manager] and said, "One of my boots has fallen out of my bag." Jock said to us to get a taxi back to the hotel and it was lying on the floor of the hotel room so we got the boot, came back and Jock was still prancing up and down the dressing room. "Professional footballer, eh?" he said to me over and over again. My head was down but I don't think we were on the park ten minutes before I scored and I turned and looked at him and he said, "Aye, all right, all right . . ." It was "You're forgiven" sort of thing but before the match I had thought he was going to strangle me.'

Jock Stein had stated ahead of the Nantes tie that he was convinced 'we can win but we won't allow our confidence to lead us into anything foolish. We will play it tight until we know what it is all about. We are prepared for anything because anything can happen in a European Cup tie.'

The plan was to settle into the game and then scuttle a Nantes side who were supposedly clever but not particularly quick; they were so concerned about Celtic's pace in attack that they opted to play with two centre-backs – an unusual idea for the time but an understandable one given that Nantes had gone four games in domestic football without a victory. Yet, as with Celtic, Nantes had settled into a steady system of management under Arribas that had allowed for the careful construction of a side that Jean-Claude Suaudeau, their midfielder, believes had similarities with the modern Barcelona.

'Take the idea that we developed along the same lines as Barcelona,' he says. 'We had the same thing in place at Nantes between 1960 and 1970, thirty years or more in advance. The difference is that Barcelona found half-a-dozen players of superior footballing intelligence who pulled the others along behind them. At Nantes we only had two or three players of that profile ... For me, the essential parameters of the game have always been movement. Adaptation with movement is essential.'

Stein, as always, was prepared to jump – but only if he could see where he was going to land. 'We're not going to be daft about this game,' Stein said. 'We'll play as we did in Zurich. We'll give them twenty minutes to show what they can do. We'll have found out by that time just how good they are – and we'll take it from there. We may have to defend but it won't be rigid defence. A team like ours can never really be defensively minded. So we may be able to attack vigorously or we may find we'll be putting the accent on defence. It all depends on what Nantes reveal.'

Poor domestic form can prove deceptive in European football, which offers talented teams the chance to perform in a freer environment – and Nantes had won the French championship twice in succession and did field several French internationals who had participated in the 1966 World Cup, in which France had been unfortunate, not least when Jacky Simon, the Nantes midfielder, had been Nobbled by a Stiles tackle directly in front of the Royal Box at Wembley, leading to an international incident.

If Nantes were seeking a cheerleader, they would not find it in Simon himself, who came over all gloomily philosophical on the dark eve of the first leg. 'We are worried,' the Nantes forward, said. 'Everything is against us. We are a light team who like the ground to be firm and the ground is heavy. We like to play pretty, clever football and I am worried about Celtic's speed and strength. The hard, Scottish type of play may be too much for us. We have been playing too much football. We are tired.'

So when Nantes, who had beaten Reykjavik in the opening round, opened the scoring in the 16th minute, Celtic looked as though they might have been victims of a bluff. They had been caught out after Francis Magny had stolen possession from Billy McNeill and had swiftly sent a shot whirring past Ronnie Simpson. Nantes had begun the match like a tornado, whirling at Celtic, and their going ahead early on in the match was due reward for their diligently enterprising approach.

Eventually the variation in Celtic's play, and their strength, fitness and determination, allied to superb work in defence and a magnificent performance by Jimmy Johnstone, brought victory. Arribas had noted particularly Bobby Murdoch, Joe McBride and Bobby Lennox as the players most impressive to him when he had watched the League Cup final with Rangers in late October and those three had a great deal to do with the craftsmanlike dismantling of Arribas' team over the 90 minutes. McBride equalised midway through the first half, from a Lennox cross, and then goals from Stevie Chalmers and Lennox secured a 3–1 victory.

'In that match,' McBride remembered, 'wee Jimmy Johnstone had hardly kicked a ball in the first half; he had hardly touched a ball. Jock laid into him at half-time and you've never seen a performance like his in the second half. He wasn't letting anybody else touch the ball; us as well. He was getting the ball and going off across the park, beating one, two, three, four of them. It wasn't great football, we weren't getting goals from it, but we were in front by then so he would just take the ball for a run and hold them off that way. He was something else.'

An appreciative French crowd, living up to Arribas' words, had made clear their enjoyment of Jimmy Johnstone overpowering their own players. They delighted artistically in the spectacle of it, as only a French crowd might, and that and the more direct style of Lennox had seen Nantes unravel.

'This is the best result we could have hoped for,' Stein said. 'It was a wonderful effort, particularly after losing the first goal. We won't defend or try to hang on to our lead at Celtic Park now. We are an attacking side and we feel we can score more goals – but we'll attack sensibly.' Arribas lamented that his team had not been at their best and promised that they could – and would – do better in the second leg.

Augmenting positively his manager's comments, Robert Budzynski, the captain, said before the return, 'We cannot have great hopes of winning but we cannot accept defeat. What have we got to lose by having a go? It's a game of football. Anything can happen. We don't despair. We must attack and shoot, shoot, shoot.'

A defeat at Marseille, on the weekend in between Nantes' two legs of their tie with Celtic, relieved Nantes of their position at the top of the French league and the atmosphere among the French club's players might best have been described as resigned defiance: clearly the first-leg defeat would be a heavy burden on their backs as they trotted out for the second leg but the talent in their team convinced them that they could make the ground shake when they took to the stage at Celtic Park.

Gabriel De Michèle, Nantes' attacking left-back, struggling

with an ankle injury, joked, 'I could be lucky and not make it in time. Then I can watch [Georges] Grabowski try to tame "The Little One" [Jimmy Johnstone].' No-one, really, could tame Johnstone when he was in the mood and on a night when the 90 minutes was one long encore to his scene-stealing performance in Nantes, he again went weaving, dashing and darting among the French defenders and it was he who opened the scoring, veering into the penalty area and shooting across André Castel, the goalkeeper, from right to left.

It was not a one-man or even a one-team show. Nantes prodded and probed at Celtic like a doctor determined to find a weakness in a seemingly healthy body. Vladica Kovačević, a European Cup finalist seven months earlier with Partizan Belgrade and top scorer in the competition two years previously, hurtled through the Celtic defence and struck the inside of Simpson's post with a well-taken shot; then Gérard Géorgin did level for Nantes. Once again Chalmers and Lennox augmented the score to make it a repeat of the 3–1 with which Celtic had won the first leg.

The alacrity with which the forwards had combined and had taken their chances may have owed much to a dramatic move enacted by Stein little more than twenty-four hours before the game began, when he had 'freshened up' his squad by paying a club-record fee of approximately £30,000 to Heart of Midlothian to obtain the signature of Willie Wallace.

'I have signed for myself a whole forward line,' Stein stated in self-congratulatory mode. Given that many of his public pro-nouncements were made for the eyes and ears of his players, this was a particularly spiky one. It transmitted to them the notion that Wallace threatened each man's position in the team.

One man, Joe Gilroy, the Clyde forward, noted the signing of Wallace and thought to himself, 'It could have been me!' Gilroy had been watching a friend play for Third Lanark, the club on Glasgow's south side, when he felt a heavy hand tap him on the shoulder. 'You can guess who this was,' Gilroy says of an approach from Stein. '"There might be an offer in for you tomorrow," he said.

'This would be about November 1966 but nothing came of it. Jock was like that. He would put in an offer and if it was not accepted, he would go and get somebody else. It was a disappointment, of course it was, but as players you knew that these things happen. I must say, though, that Willie was a better player than I was – stronger, more direct. I was a bit lightweight in comparison. Willie Wallace complemented the speed and control of all the others in that Celtic team.'

Stein had, for months, been happy with his batch of defenders but had simultaneously felt that he was short of options in attack. For all that he liked to freshen up his team, he seemed to have a deliberate policy of stagnation for his defence. Clark, McNeill, Gemmell, O'Neill and Simpson were the most regular performers for Celtic by early December. When Celtic played Nantes, that quintet had missed only one match between them – and even then, McNeill had missed the game with St Mirren in early November only through having sustained a heavy cold. Willie O'Neill, who had impressed on the tour of North America, was the new regular at left-back in the first half of that season, starting all of Celtic's matches but one, at St Mirren in early September, when he had become the first Celtic substitute to be used in a competitive match.

Before Stein had signed Wallace, on 6 December 1966, the manager had intimated for days in advance that he was seeking to recruit a Scottish player based in English football. Stein denied that this had been a fake story designed to disguise his actual intentions and insisted that he had indeed spoken to a player over the border but had had to withdraw because of that player's demand that he be assured of a place in the first team.

'There is no player at Parkhead guaranteed that,' Stein growled, in another statement that burned into the attention of his charges. 'Anyway, I have got the player I wanted most of all,' Stein continued. 'I have the "pool" I want now. Defensively, I'm well covered all the way through and Wallace rounds off the forward requirements.'

With a simplicity that matched the times, all of the negotiations for Wallace's signing had been completed within half an hour of the player's arrival at Celtic Park, following a brief telephone call summoning him there. The player had been seeking a move from Hearts for months and he posed for his picture in the Celtic dressing room underneath the numbers 8, 9 and 10 shorts; yet another reminder of his versatility if anyone still needed one.

Now, with Nantes eliminated, the latest bout of European Cup pressure relieved and Celtic having steadied themselves in the league, Stein abandoned his commitment to unchanged line-ups as swiftly and radically as he had adopted it. He reverted to toying with his team – and with his players' minds.

'I'll see what the ground is like before deciding the line-up,' Stein said in advance of the match with Motherwell at Celtic Park on the Saturday after the return with Nantes. 'Wallace and McBride will play to give some of the others "a breather".' Rarely can the prospect of a hard-earned rest have been less welcome to an employee. Celtic players wanted to be involved in this team all the time; to feel part of a side in which it was a joy to play and that had its compass magnetically fixed in the direction of victory.

Amidst all the cleverly selected words on Stein's part and the excellent front he put on when discussing his signing of Wallace, the manager's move indicates a degree of unease on his part. The Hearts man had long been available, having agitated for a transfer from Tynecastle since May 1966, prior to playing for

Scotland against Holland at Hampden Park. Shortly afterwards, Stein had made a point of being in the stand at Tynecastle to see Wallace notch a hat-trick in Hearts' 4–2 win against Maccabi Tel-Aviv in a friendly. Stein had witnessed numerous fine performances from him, against Celtic. So why the delay in signing him, not least as Stein had been bemoaning, since the summer of 1966, his lack of a striker to provide him with all the options he required?

Perhaps the thing that really concentrated the Celtic manager's mind was a persistent knee problem that had now been quietly troubling Joe McBride for some time and that had caused him to be omitted from the return match with Nantes. 'We are not worried about it now,' Stein bluffed after Wallace's debut in the match against Motherwell, which McBride also missed because of said injury, despite Stein's promise, in advance, that he would play. 'We know what caused the trouble and the ten days' rest has cleared it up. Joe is now fit to play. Joe could have played [against Motherwell] but since we had Willie Wallace available I left him out to give him another week to make a full recovery.'

It has long been suggested that Wallace was brought in as a replacement for Stevie Chalmers, who would turn 31 on Boxing Day 1966, but this would seem patently odd, given how often Chalmers was scoring for Celtic and how often helping to create goals for others. The striker had been central to the goals that had eliminated Zurich and Nantes. And players were not exactly replaced, one for one, under Stein's flexible approach to team selection. Yet even one of Chalmers' teammates from the time is willing to go so far as to suggest this. 'The one that would have missed out from then on would have been Stevie. McBride had been knocking in the goals and Wallace would have been in the team as a player purchased by Stein. Managers always have to justify their purchases.'

In truth, if Wallace was being brought in as a replacement

figure for anyone then it would have to have been for McBride. The player's knee injury was now beginning to plague him seriously, as Stein knew, even if the public did not, and the arrival of Wallace on the day before the match with Nantes distracted attention from McBride not being included in the team to face the French club.

Through delaying the introduction of Wallace to Celtic, it would appear that the surefooted Stein had finally made a major slip, a blunder that was potentially costly to Celtic. A three-month qualification rule meant that Wallace would be ineligible for the European Cup quarter-finals, due in early 1967. UEFA rules stated that for a player to play in any of the rounds of the European Cup he had to have been signed for at least three months before the round was scheduled to begin. The starting date for the semi-finals was 20 March and so Wallace was eligible, only just, for that – if Celtic got through without him.

Wallace would be unlucky in missing the quarter-finals but he could also be said to have been a mite fortunate to have made it to Celtic. If Clyde had been more amenable over Stein's bid for Joe Gilroy, that man might have been the replacement for McBride. If McBride had not been injured, Stein might have decided he had enough forwards to suit his purposes.

McBride had actually first felt his knee problem on the Wednesday prior to the match with Hearts on 26 November. A painkilling injection had enabled him to perform in that match but he had missed several subsequent matches, including the one with Motherwell because of the ground conditions, which were hard and for which, as Stein put it, 'We decided to take no chances.' He was included, though, for a more significant challenge, against Aberdeen, even though the playing surface was another testing one. That match, at Pittodrie, on Christmas Eve 1966, would see McBride receive a blow that would be fatal to his participation in the rest of the season.

'I do remember that,' Bobby Clark, the Aberdeen goalkeeper, says. 'It was at the King Street End – it was a scramble in the six-yard box. I came for the ball and I dived on the ball and Joe McBride went down. Something happened to him; I don't know if I hit him or whether he jarred his knee on the hard ground. It was pretty innocent – a loose ball that I dived on.' The knee injury McBride suffered at that moment would be the final significant action involving McBride in the 1966–67 season. He had scored 35 goals in 26 games.

The tussle with Aberdeen had also been notable as the latest sign of a slight slowing for Celtic as they approached the midpoint of the league season. The pre-Christmas month had brought victories over Hearts, Motherwell and Partick Thistle but a goalless draw at Kilmarnock, in between the two legs with Nantes, had given their Scottish rivals a glimmer of hope as, on Christmas Eve, they headed north to the Granite City, where there had been some serious sabre-rattling from Eddie Turnbull, the Aberdeen manager, and some of his players. Aberdeen were banging the big drum in advance of this match, as is often their wont, with Harry Melrose, the captain, stating, 'Celtic should be afraid of us and not us afraid of them.'

The Pittodrie club, six points behind Celtic in third position, were then unbeaten at home all season, prompting Turnbull, Aberdeen's fiery, pugilistic figurehead, to be no less cautious than his captain. 'We care nothing about their reputation,' he said of Celtic. 'Every game is different. They think they are the tops. We think we are. I don't go along with all this business about Celtic's reputation. That doesn't bother Aberdeen one bit. Why should we be scared? To us, this is just another game.'

Clark, Aberdeen's exuberant young goalkeeper, recalls the game well. 'I remember it was a good game,' he says, 'played on a solid surface in the days before undersoil heating. The ground was hard and there was a big crowd, as we were pushing for the league. It was a fun game. Nobody really likes playing on a frosted surface but they sanded it so it was a good-quality game. If they don't put a lot of sand down, it's bumpy but they had and it was pretty even. If a surface was sanded unevenly there was always the chance of an unlucky bounce.

'We had a good, young team with some really good, young players, like Frannie Munro, Jens Petersen and Tom McMillan. We were right up there in the league. Celtic were a very attack-minded team with a lot of good players: Bobby Lennox, Willie Wallace, Jimmy Johnstone, Joe McBride, John Hughes, a lot of really good attacking players. Then you had big Tommy Gemmell thundering up the left side. They also had a solid defence. Billy McNeill and John Clark had a great understanding. They played 4-2-4 generally. Then there was "the old man" at the back – Ronnie Simpson. I think they had so much faith in him. He was the ideal goalkeeper – good concentration and he made great decisions.'

The playing surface helped to level the difference in quality between the sides but Bobby Lennox put Celtic ahead midway through the first half after McMillan had slipped up to allow the Celtic man a sliver of space – and that was all that Lennox ever required.

'For our goal,' Bobby Clark says, 'the ball was knocked into the far post from 40 yards and big Frannie Munro headed it down to Harry [Melrose] and Harry knocked it in. I remember also that Ronnie had one great save late in the game where he tipped it over the bar. We thought we had a pretty good team. Celtic had a very good team.' The game finished all-square.

If competition in the Scottish League was beginning to stiffen for Celtic, European club football's great tournament was now also beginning to generate more heat and light. Ajax of Amsterdam had reached the last eight of the European Cup, truly astounding every corner of the continent by thrashing

Liverpool 5–1 in the Netherlands. The Dutch were now ready for all comers and became the latest club to state how much they fancied taking on Stein's team.

'I should like to be drawn against Celtic,' Rinus Michels, the Ajax manager, stated boldly, minutes after a 2–2 draw at Anfield had secured his side their berth in the quarter-finals. 'I am convinced we would find them great opponents.' Michels had also wanted to be drawn with Celtic back in October, for the second round. Potential last-eight opponents for Celtic also included Real Madrid, the holders, and Internazionale of Milan, winners in 1964 and 1965 and already the favourites for that season's trophy. Eastern Europe was well represented through Dukla Prague of Czechoslovakia and CSKA Sofia of Bulgaria, who would present their own particular Iron Curtain problems. So too would Vojvodina Novi Sad, of Yugoslavia, if they were to defeat Atlético Madrid in a play-off after their tie had concluded in a 3–3 aggregate. With the decider to be held in Madrid and Atlético having brought the tie level by winning the second leg 2–0 at home, the Spaniards looked favourites to reach the quarter-finals, whose numbers were completed by Linfield of Northern Ireland.

'We have no need to fear any team left in the competition,' Stein said after scrutinising Ajax in their match at Anfield, 'but I don't think we have been given enough credit, sometimes, for our performances in the European Cup this season. We have played four games and we have won all four. There aren't many teams who can boast a record like that.' This was true – only Dukla Prague, of the thirty-four clubs who had participated in that season's European Cup, had won home and away in the first and second rounds, with the Czechs scoring 12 goals, one more than Celtic, and conceding two, the same as the Glasgow club, in matches with Esbjerg of Denmark and Anderlecht of Belgium.

'In European Cup football,' Stein continued, 'no matter how good the team are, they tend to win only at home. We have won away from home as well and that takes some doing in this class of football.'

The draw for the quarter-finals was made in Geneva on the afternoon of Thursday 15 December 1966 and it paired Celtic with the winners of the Atlético–Vojvodina tie, a perfect outcome for Stein as he would now be able to look over both sides in a match of the highest competitive value, when they met at the Estadio Manzanares. Vojvodina had lost the toss of the coin to determine the venue for the replay but their seriousness of intent was shown by their having spent the week between the second leg and the play-off camped in Madrid rather than returning home. They then enjoyed their turn to surprise the continent by winning 3–2 in a tough match, watched by Stein, in which Vojvodina's Dobrivoje Trivić, the inside-left, and Vasa Pušibrk, the outside-left, were sent off in the closing stages, to ensure that they would automatically be suspended for the first leg against Celtic. Additionally, Silvester Takač, Vojvodina's centre-forward, was due to be transferred to French club Rennes.

This was, though, a resilient Vojvodina team – Atlético had gone 2–0 up in the opening five minutes of the play-off but Takač got one back in 25 minutes, Dimitrije Radović had equalised on 65 and Takač got the winner 12 minutes into extra-time. Celtic might not be playing a name when the European Cup quarter-finals came around but they would be facing quite a game.

CHAPTER 8

A New Direction

It was fitting that route-closing roadworks around St Johnstone's Muirton Park should delay the start of the Perth club's league fixture with Celtic on 14 January 1967. A series of diversions, after all, had led Jock Stein to that day, one on which he finally fielded, for the first time together: Ronnie Simpson, Jim Craig, Tommy Gemmell, Bobby Murdoch, Billy McNeill, John Clark, Jimmy Johnstone, Willie Wallace, Stevie Chalmers, Bertie Auld and Bobby Lennox; the most perfect Scottish team of all.

One of the main roads to the ground had been closed for repairs and the kick-off was delayed for eight minutes to allow the queues at the turnstiles to dissipate. Eventually, there were 19,000 inside the tight confines of the Perth club's ground – around as much as Muirton might comfortably hold – and they would witness, unknowingly, history being made. It proved to be a slow-burner of a debut for this Stein team, with the final outcome remaining in doubt for some time as St Johnstone held Celtic at bay until early in the second half, when the goals began to roll in for the away side to coast home on a 4–0 victory. Stein may have stressed continually the beauties of having a pool of players but he had now found an eleven who fitted together seamlessly.

Chance played as great a role as anything else in Stein's selection that day. Stevie Chalmers only narrowly made the team at St Johnstone – he had needed treatment after setting up Charlie Gallagher's goal in the 5–1 victory over Clyde at Celtic Park three days earlier, during which Chalmers had skidded off the pitch and collided with a photographer, injuring his knee and ending up in the straw bales that ringed the pitch. Twenty tons had been laid on the field overnight in advance of the match on 11 January 1967 and had been used to cover the surface as a means of defying the freezing conditions.

Another individual who had comported himself energetically and with style against Clyde was Charlie Gallagher but he was omitted in Perth. It was to Stein's advantage that he would not explain himself, leaving players to figure out his team changes for themselves. It meant, productively, that the only responses a player could give would be to rebel against the manager's methods – a futile option with the steely Stein – or to try their best to please the manager in the hope of regaining favour.

As with many of Stein's players, Gallagher has mixed feelings about their manager as a man; acknowledging his genius in football matters but being less enamoured with his treatment of the human beings in his charge. 'He had massive hands,' Gallagher says, 'and when you were walking past him he would say, "How are you doin'?" and bang you around the ear. It would be sore as well. That would be his method of saying, "I'm bigger than you." He was a hard, hard man and nobody would argue with him.'

Stein could mistreat and abuse players to get a reaction. Once a player was entirely out of his plans, the individual in question could be blanked completely by Stein, made to train on their own, not even given a game with the reserves and excluded from attending matches at home or abroad with the Celtic party. These individuals could be players who had played vital roles in pivotal moments for Celtic under Stein but they would be cast aside the way a child might throw away a once-favourite toy. The hurt would remain with those players for years, decades, afterwards.

Facing Celtic at Muirton Park, Perth, on that concealed-red-letter day, was a team that was led in a manner that was almost as shambolic as Celtic was professional. Bobby Brown, the St Johnstone manager, was a considerably less-dynamic presence on the sidelines than Stein – when he was there, that is. The St Johnstone manager, when he found himself unable to handle the tension, might, as a match raged on in front of him, rise from where he was sitting, leave the stadium and spend quarter of an hour walking the streets surrounding the ground before returning to ask his trainer how the game was going and what was the score. In those less-scrutinised times, a manager could get away with doings such as those.

'That's when we were rubbish,' Benny Rooney, the St Johnstone centre-half on the day, recalls of the encounter with Celtic in January 1967. 'That was not long after I'd gone to Perth and we were a poor side, just out of the relegation zone. We were really well beaten by Celtic.

'The thing about that Celtic team, up front, was their pace. They had scorers and they had wee Jimmy Johnstone – you had to double up on him all the time. They were, all-round, a great side. The really important thing was how they gelled as a team. This was also the first time we had seen overlapping full-backs in Scotland, as they had. Their midfield players, Bobby Murdoch and Bertie Auld, were exceptionally good but Bertie Auld was a nasty wee bugger. You had to watch when you were tackling him – it was a case of watching who went into the tackle first . . . We used to have a few skirmishes together. Then, after the game, you would shake hands and blether away but he really was a handful both as a player and as a tackler.

'It was so difficult to defend against that Celtic team – Stein knew how to play players and they all knew exactly what they had to do. Stevie Chalmers was as quick as anybody. Willie Wallace was strong. Bobby Lennox and Jimmy Johnstone were hard to handle. You had to get in about them and when they didn't get their own way, they couldn't handle that, at times, and they weren't afraid to hand it out on the physical side as well. They could handle themselves – all of them. Wee Jimmy could retaliate. If Jimmy was having a hard time he would have a punch or a swipe. So there was that side of it. There was great spirit in their team.'

As with many of the great teams, contemporaries can sometimes be hasty in belittling them. Celtic's 4–0 win was their biggest away victory of the season up to that point but one St Johnstone player was not overly impressed; he was the first opponent to comment on this particular Celtic line-up, although he was wise enough to do so anonymously. He characterised Celtic as 'not the best team in the world' but a side that would simply wear down the opposition.

'That's a fair point,' Benny Rooney concedes, 'inasmuch as, as soon as the game started, they were at you all the time. You had to compete with that. They were an all-round team that knitted together at that time, through the system they played.'

Stein's team would pressurise relentlessly, moving on and off the ball with energy, and the opposition might hold out for an hour or so, only to be sucked under by an avalanche of goals. St Johnstone, in this case, had held Celtic at 0–0 until the 63rd minute. Once Celtic went ahead, though, the game would be up – literally so. This might convey the impression to some opponents that they had been unlucky or unfortunate but it was happening too often that season for it to be attributable in any real way to mere fortune. Bobby Brown, the St Johnstone manager, said, 'I thought my boys played well, possibly as well as they can play. Given a bit of luck we could have scored before Celtic did but once they went in front, no team could have stopped them. It was no disgrace to be beaten by a Celtic side playing as well as they did in the second half.'

Excellent saves from Ronnie Simpson had prevented Gordon Whitelaw and Alex MacDonald opening the scoring for the home side but once Jimmy Johnstone had scored the first goal, striking the ball from right to left across the goalkeeper, as he had done against Nantes, three further goals flowed like liquid gold, leaving players such as our anonymous St Johnstone man wondering how they could have lost so heavily from such a good position. Something similar had happened to Clyde in their 5–1 defeat the previous midweek and numerous other opponents over the season would go from being level or a goal down and in a seemingly sustainable position, only to end the match in ruins.

Tommy Gemmell had been in particularly buoyant mood as he held court for a clutch of pressmen on the day before that trip to face St Johnstone. He had been an object of interest to them because, against the Perth club, he would be notching his 100th consecutive appearance in a Celtic shirt. 'It's because I'm so young and healthy,' he said of his longevity at left-back. Gemmell, the most ebullient and extrovert of the Celtic players, was happy to be pictured posing in the car park in front of the stadium sitting on the elongated bonnet of his car, which lacked a personalised TG numberplate only because such a thing had yet to be invented. Owning a car was radically new for a footballer at Celtic – only half a decade earlier, few players had enjoyed private transport – but Gemmell was determined to take this new symbol of freedom to the extreme.

'Cars were a necessity,' Gemmell said, 'both as a means of

getting around and as a part of your image. It was great fun to drive up to the Park on matchday with all the supporters giving you the thumbs-up as you motored past them. Better than riding up to the ground on a bicycle, isn't it? We worked hard and played hard at Celtic Park under Jock Stein. It was always a hard shift in training under the manager so you earned your fun and that made me all the more determined to enjoy my time off as much as possible. Would I have been driving a smart car, a really fancy-looking deal, if I had still been an electrician at Ravenscraig? No – so I made sure I made the best of it.'

Inexplicably, Gemmell held up for the press photographers that January day a lucky pennant featuring nothing less than the club badge of Internazionale. The Italians were, as with Celtic, fellow quarter-finalists in the European Cup but Gemmell could not recall why he might have had such a thing in his possession or what his holding it on that mid-January day might have signified. The draw, after all, made in December, had paired Celtic with Vojvodina Novi Sad, not Inter, in the quarter-finals, and with the Milan side being paired with Real Madrid, the holders, their route to the final had been made more slippery than they would have liked.

Stein had taken thirteen players up to Perth, including Joe McBride. He was back in the squad after weeks of rumours that his career was over, and only a few weeks after Stein having said his season was over. After looking over the pitch, shortly before kick-off, and finding it to be on the heavy side, the manager opted to make one change from the match with Clyde the previous midweek. Gallagher, the left-sided midfielder, despite having excelled in the previous two games, made way for Bertie Auld – and the perfect starting eleven came together.

Three different four-goal triumphs inside a week had boosted Celtic. Dundee, the previous Saturday, had also been tanned by a four-goal margin but, unlike St Johnstone and Clyde, had been unable to hang on to parity for very long. They had been 4–0 down at half-time on a day when the professionalism on which Stein insisted had been displayed once again. Warm-ups in the 1960s consisted of the players taking the field five minutes before kick-off and stringing together, cursorily, a few token passes and shots on goal. Against Dundee, with the icy surface promising to be tricky, Stein's players had broken the mould by taking to the pitch twenty minutes before kick-off, to try out the pitch and to get their footwear right by testing three different types of boot, finally opting to use a short leather stud. Dundee, who opted for the traditional, aimless warm-up, subsequently spent the early stages of the match slipping and slithering around and half an hour into the game, Celtic were four goals ahead.

Stein had been jolted into taking a new direction with his team after a disappointing encounter with Dundee United at Tannadice on New Year's Eve that had seen Celtic tumble to their first league defeat since losing to Stirling Albion in February 1966. United, prior to meeting Celtic, had won only once at home in the league and had accumulated a mere 13 points but they were simultaneously anticipating a Fairs Cup tie with Juventus after having demolished Barcelona's chances in the tournament by defeating the Spanish club home and away in the previous round.

'That was quite a game at Tannadice,' Billy Hainey, the United forward, recalls. 'Celtic were such a good team and we had a fair team too at that time. We had a lot of good players and because of that, we played football similar to Celtic. When we were on song we were difficult to beat. Celtic had a formidable defence but I have to say that I never found them any more difficult than some of the other defences I faced. There weren't any big humps up the park from our team so that maybe contributed to the result. I'd have liked to have said it was because they upped the bonus – but they didn't!

'I travelled back to Glasgow on the Celtic team bus. I knew Joe McBride because I had played with him at Thistle and he said, "You can get a lift on our bus." The Celtic players were fine with me and when we got to Glasgow, I went part of the way onwards with Bobby Lennox and Jimmy Johnstone.'

If children are a reflection of their parents then football teams are a reflection of the league in which they perform and a defeat to a United side that had been struggling for domestic form emphasised the strength of the Scottish League. Stein, acknowledging that, had stressed the difficulty of facing Aberdeen, Dundee United and Rangers in quick succession during the festive period.

'If we can get through these games well,' Stein said, 'and are still four points ahead of Rangers, then I will consider we have faced and overcome the worst. I am not saying that we will have landed the league flag if we come through this period well, but it will certainly make things easier for the final run-in.' The match with Rangers at Ibrox on 2 January was postponed due to freezing conditions but stumbles at Pittodrie and Tannadice had meant that Celtic had failed to rise above the fray, as Stein had hoped. Instead, 1967 began with Aberdeen only two points behind Celtic at the top of the First Division. 'All of the games are important now,' Stein said.

Through learning from the defeat at Tannadice, Stein was propelled towards his team selection for the match with St Johnstone. John Hughes had finally been ready to return to action at Tannadice after being out through injury since late October. But his performance had been subdued and after similarly quiet games against Clyde and Dundee, he had been replaced by Bobby Lennox. Willie O'Neill, simultaneously, lost his place at left-back, conceding it to Tommy Gemmell, who was switched to make way for Jim Craig, and Craig never looked back after that.

Jim Craig was unusual for a footballer in that he lacked the seemingly essential working-class background that was common to his teammates. Not that he was a Lord Snooty exactly. As a youngster, he lived in the district of Mosspark on Glasgow's south side, a respectable area but not one of the city's rarefied, leafy suburbs. His father was a furniture-shop manager and Craig had begun studying dentistry at the University of Glasgow at the same time as embarking on a career with Celtic. It was while a student that he had received the offer of professional terms at Celtic Park and any doubt was dispelled for him when his father told him that while there were a number of people who were dentists, it was a rarer honour to play for Celtic Football Club.

Dentistry is one of the most demanding of university disciplines, requiring in-depth study allied to working on patients and for Craig that meant frequent attendance at the Dental Hospital in Glasgow to learn the practical side of the profession. Craig, who signed for Celtic in 1965, was temporarily defeated by the overlapping demands on his time of football and dentistry and when he decided to give his final university examinations his priority during the early part of the 1966–67 season, he dropped out of the first-team squad and trained on his own.

Ian Young, Tommy Gemmell and Willie O'Neill had all performed at full-back in his absence and Craig clearly lacked match fitness. He managed only two outings before Christmas 1966, after each of which he was immediately returned to the reserves, a source of some frustration for an individual who was totally confident in his abilities as a footballer. He began to feel serious disappointment at being left out, not least because he had played regularly in the previous season, albeit without ever becoming the automatic choice at right-back. So when Stein brought him in for the match with St Johnstone, Craig was aware of the necessity of seizing the opportunity to reclaim his place in the team. He had fallen down the pecking order in his absence and with Jock Stein it was impossible to predict how many more chances there might be to restore his position as a first-choice member of the team.

Craig was one of the less boisterous members of that Celtic squad. In a dressing room that held its quota of lively extroverts, he preferred to remain quiet, opting to speak only when he was sure he could be heard, as befitted an educated man. He could have been at a disadvantage because of that very education, not least because the ability to practise dentistry, a financially rewarding middle-class profession, removed him to some degree from the tight control of Jock Stein, who used the financial dependency of his players on football earnings as a means of motivating them and keeping them hungry for first-team action and its attendant bonuses. Stein was also most comfortable in a working-class milieu and could never understand how someone with a talent for football would wish to devote time to any other profession. Any doubts the manager might have held with regard to Craig would be dispelled by the player's ruthlessness in the tackle, his slick passing and his commitment to his sport. The advantage this one-time athlete held over those such as O'Neill and Young was an ability to glide, seemingly effortlessly, up the wing on the overlap, an attribute he shared with Gemmell, and one that Stein saw as essential to his overall plan for the team.

Beating the weather to play those matches against Clyde and Dundee had 'certainly improved our chances of winning the European Cup', stated Stein, ever wary of potential end-of-season fixture congestion. The 38,000 crowd that had been at Celtic Park for the match with Clyde had sung, insistently, that Celtic would be 'running round Lisbon with the Cup'. A representative of the Yugoslavian press had witnessed the match with Dundee and had expressed his admiration for the style in which

Celtic had dismantled their opponents' defence even on a mud-caked pitch, adding that Vojvodina, the Yugoslavian champions, would, by necessity, have to place great store in the talents of Ilija 'The Panther' Pantelić, their world-class goalkeeper. The matches with the Yugoslavian champions were still almost two months away, being scheduled for March 1967, but the tie was already having an electrifying, galvanising effect on Celtic.

CHAPTER 9

Master of Invention

A furious ambition and a rage for achievement possessed Jock Stein. This was a man who could see the time flashing by, who was terrified of being caught out through having failed to keep abreast of change. 'We cannot just stand still,' Stein said early in 1967, 'without trying to develop something new, something different. If we do, others will pass us.' So when a chillingly, mind-numbingly ordinary series of late-winter fixtures attempted to freeze his team's progress, Stein devised a means of putting fire under the players' feet.

By the last days of January the lacuna in this hectic season for Celtic had arrived at last. The fixture schedule suddenly relented noticeably as Celtic faced Airdrieonians and Ayr United, stragglers and strugglers respectively in the First Division, and received highly favourable Scottish Cup draws that placed them at home to Arbroath, of the Second Division, and Elgin City of the Highland League. Four victories would be duly secured in simplest fashion, with 19 goals sent crashing past opposing custodians with none conceded.

This segment of the season was the lightest and most undemanding Celtic would experience. It was all too quiet for the restless Stein, who was haunted by the prospect of complacency creeping up on his players to pickpocket them of their talents.

There was constant talk of league reconstruction for Scottish football – the eighteen-club top division allowed too much deadwood to float along with the more competitive clubs – but proposals to cut numbers in the top flight had been rejected by the league clubs in early 1966. Stein, faced with the repercussions of a non-streamlined competition, came up with a solution that would make his team more fully prepared for the fast-approaching tie with Vojvodina Novi Sad. He put into place a friendly match with Dinamo Zagreb, a club also from the Yugoslavian league, and one that was in the quarter-finals of the Fairs Cup.

One of Jock Stein's many attributes was that he was a great showman. A man who hated his players to smoke and drink, he was football's most flamboyant puritan and soon Stein had transformed, in the public imagination, the exhibition match with Dinamo Zagreb into something that promised much more than the usual half-paced, easy-going bounce game usually seen on such occasions. Stein's grandstanding would entice a crowd of almost 50,000 along to Celtic Park on that chilly, early-1967 evening thanks to his promise that they were going to see, as if by magic, something never previously witnessed in the game of football.

'Every tactical system in use is a copy or a modification of what someone else has tried,' Stein said in advance of the match. 'Why shouldn't we come up with our own, brand-new system? It could pay off and might be the basis for everyone else to try in the future. It is an original system – beyond that I am giving no clues. Every man will have a job to do concerned with attack. And everyone will be on the move. It is not a simple system. Each man will be numbered according to the job he has to do and the fans will be kept in the picture. We need a try-out in a full-scale game to see how it goes . . .'

Audaciously, Stein heralded this friendly as a match that would introduce a new, 'attacking' Celtic team – a bold promise, given that his side had been overwhelming opponents in exactly that fashion all season. It also helped, in enticing people out of their homes to see him unveil his 'experiment', that Zagreb would offer a contrast to his own team. Sitting second in the Yugoslavian league and jetting around Europe to play friendlies as a means of earning currency, credit and kudos, they had obtained success in contrary fashion to Stein's Celtic.

'Our success has been based on defensive play mainly,' Branko Zebec, the Zagreb manager, said, as he joined in the fun. 'Since Celtic are aiming to try something new in this match, then maybe we will try something new as well – although in our case it will be defensively. I welcome any idea that will brighten football and so we are happy to cooperate in an experiment but we will treat this game seriously and we will treat the result seriously.'

The grand experiment, unveiled by Stein with a conjuror's flourish, was to field the Celtic team in a 3-4-3 formation – pretty revolutionary given that everyone in British football had been playing 2-3-5 until relatively recently – with Davie Cattanach, the number 2, on the right side of a three-man defence that had Billy McNeill, number 3, in the centre and John Clark, number 4, on the left. Tommy Gemmell, wearing number 8 shorts, was fielded in midfield alongside Bertie Auld wearing number 7, and John Hughes, at number 5, on the right side of midfield, with Bobby Murdoch, number 6, inside him. Willie Wallace, number 9, Stevie Chalmers, 10, and Bobby Lennox, 11, were fielded up front. It was a radical formation for the late 1960s but during the second half, with the team struggling to adjust, Stein opted to revert to Celtic's more habitual 4-2-4.

'We were trying something new,' Stein said, defending his experiment. 'We did not claim that this was the be-all and end-all or that this would be our style of the future. We had to try it out in match conditions and I'm satisfied that it was not a wasted ninety minutes.'

Nor was it – even though, on the night, Celtic had looked tentative and testy in trying out the new formation. The three-man defence had been overrun on an evening when the futuristic 'wing-back' roles, in which Gemmell and Hughes had been deployed, made it an onerous evening for them, the latter having been especially cumbersome in the tracking-back, defensive aspect of his role. The back three were too often left exposed when opponents rattled past the midfielders; leaving big gaps in the defence. For the forwards, it had been equally tricky. Lennox, Chalmers and Wallace were expected to remain in the central areas so that Hughes and Gemmell would have space in which to come forward when necessary. This had left the highly mobile front trio cramping each other's style within the close confines of the penalty area.

'He was trying formations that no-one else thought about,' John Clark says. 'He thought, "I'll try it." He never played it much after that – it was maybe just a one-off thing. He believed in the system he had all the time.

'He was away ahead of his time there [in playing wing-backs]. It was a one-off game and he was experimenting. He was maybe seeing if he could find a way to improve certain positions on the park and to see if he could get more out of certain players by giving them different roles. The tried system was the best system that he had, you know, to the players that were available to him and it's amazing how he just got away with the players that he had – it wasn't the biggest pool of players and fortunately he never had a lot of long-term injuries. Oh yes, he was always thinking about the game, always thinking about formations.'

Stein had, in a non-competitive situation, learned much about the perils involved in gearing up a team for all-out attack. It would not stop him doing so on one significant day in the future but he would ensure that he got it exactly right on that occasion, when he would find a way for the forwards to be freed up, for the midfield to be supplemented in a quite different way; then he would employ his defence in an aggressive fashion that would bolster a team whose priority was to power forward at every opportunity. Stein was a quick and intuitive learner and while the fans consigned this seemingly unsuccessful evening to memory, it would be at the forefront of Stein's mind in the months to come. He was determined to discover the means by which he could attack an opposition side from any part of his team without hampering its own smooth functioning. In some ways, then, the match with Zagreb was as important as any of Celtic's European Cup ties in terms of what it told him about his team.

'Our defence is very strong, very well drilled,' Zebec, the Zagreb manager, said, 'yet Celtic still made chances. As I see it, Celtic's plan would mean much movement for the wing men and the full-backs and it has given me much to think about.'

The outcome was also positive in terms of Stein's commitment to updating regularly his team's attitude and approach to the game. His players had been given a mid-season refresher just at a time when they required perking up, in the middle of a series of humdrum fixtures.

'Naturally, the result is disappointing,' Stein said. 'We don't like to lose but surely there is something on the credit side? Surely any plan should be assessed on the chances made? And we made a great many. If the plan failed it was probably due to lack of practice. Anything new like this demands maybe months of work to perfect. We might have tried it out against weak opposition and made a big impact on football. Instead, we tried it out against a very good European side.'

It was also a final major opportunity to experiment as the season would soon engulf Celtic in three major tournaments each reaching a powerful crescendo. The European Cup was Stein's preoccupation but he did not expect the league championship and the Scottish Cup simply to fall gently into Celtic's clutches. On the evening after the Zagreb match, Rangers visited Clyde and won 5–1, a result that took the Ibrox club on to 36 points in the league, three behind Celtic.

A season that had been simmering gently was now rapidly coming to the boil. Tickets for the Vojvodina match on 8 March went on sale at Celtic Park from noon on Sunday 12 February 1967, were limited to two per supporter and were pricey at £1.10s for the centre of the stand and 6s for the terracing. Thousands of supporters still made the midday trek to Celtic Park as a means of securing their places for a night replete with promise. They stood from early in the morning in queues that snaked around the ground – the stand was sold out within three hours, the seats being part of an initial batch of 45,000 that swiftly melted away. Time had stood as still and slow for Celtic in the preceding weeks as it had for those dully queuing for those pieces of paper gold but now it would speed up to an almost immeasurable degree as a rush of colour flooded the lives of Stein and his players.

CHAPTER 10

The Mountain Lions

Around this time a French film crew was despatched to Glasgow to film the Celtic Park environment. The curious visitors scrutinised the dressing rooms, the vast and glaring floodlight pylons and the drama of matchday itself but they were equally intrigued by the slumland – no other word for it – that encroached threateningly on the stadium, filming it as lovingly and artistically as if it were a moonscape. The blackened tenement buildings grimly sat alongside vast gaps where others of their ilk had simply been unable to go on standing any longer – like one of the city's famous paralytic drunks – and had been razed to the ground, their macabre remains stacked where they had stood. For continentals, it must have been almost like looking upon the bombed-out ruins of Second World War Berlin only to find, amazingly, that these buildings were actually inhabited.

This was a city leading the way in post-industrial decay. The city council augmented it all magnificently by building their own new, modern, concrete ice-boxes while Glasgow's mouldering canals and tall tenements proved to be, simultaneously, pop-up playgrounds and living tombs for the young.

Non-swimmers proliferated in this era, so a tumble into a freez-ing, debris-filled canal could prove fatal, as could a child's fall from an opened tenement window on to the iron spikes that topped so many sets of railings below. One Glasgow resident of 1967 suggested that the housing problem in the city was so bad that it might have been better for the city to have been struck by the plague – that way, the authorities would have been forced to take the type of drastic action that they had opted not to do in relation to tackling the poverty and the run-down housing that infested the city.

The autumn of 1966 had seen Glasgow witness its first car bomb, when a vehicle owned by the 'gambling club manager' Arthur Thompson exploded when he started up its engine outside his home in Blackhill. Thompson was spared but his mother-in-law perished in the blast. On the outskirts of the city that autumn, a jilted 40-year-old man shot his 38-year-old former lover dead in a park and then turned the gun on himself in a dark parody of *Romeo and Juliet*.

Glasgow was not, then, a city without its troubles, so when the Celtic players arrived in Novi Sad to find it grey and gloomy, it meant that the home of Vojvodina Novi Sad, the Yugoslavian champions, really had made an impression on people whose daily place of work was a far cry from the multi-colourful world of the pop-cultured sixties.

Tommy Gemmell would characterise Novi Sad as a 'dump of a town', and Celtic's accommodation as being 'like a well-worn B&B' while Bobby Lennox saw it as 'not the nicest of places', where 'the weather was dull and depressing and the town was grey'. The poor impression that Novi Sad made on the Celts was odd, as Novi Sad was the cultural epicentre of Serbia, in eastern Yugoslavia, and at its heart a pretty city, the capital of the Vojvodina province described, in pre-communist times, as 'the Athens of Serbia'. Its wide boulevards, parks and squares survive, attractive as ever, although out of sight of the Celtic players, who always dreaded visits to Eastern Europe in the 1960s and who had perhaps been ready to have their worst fears realised after previous visits to such other masked Eastern European beauties as Zagreb, Bratislava and Budapest.

It may not have helped that Novi Sad was also emerging from its habitual freezing winter, which caused the football league to take an annual two-month break, post-Christmas, and Yugoslavia was subject to the privations visited upon Eastern Europe by the Soviet Union's imperialist domination. Things were changing, though. Yugoslavia, under Marshal Tito, was less stringently controlled, remotely from Moscow, than other Eastern bloc states, and in 1965 reform had begun that was taking the country down a more liberal route. Professionalism had been legalised in football and some of the country's multi-talented players were now seeping abroad. Clubs were allowed to deploy advertising hoardings and some teams even had sponsors' names on their shirts long before such a phenomenon had been allowed in certain parts of the capitalist West.

The Vojvodina Stadium would prove to be one corner of the city of Novi Sad that shone undeniably brightly for the local people. Two spanking-new, huge floodlight pylons – each placed in opposite corners of the ground – were to be unveiled for the match with Celtic and when Jock Stein visited the stadium with his players in advance of the game, with the manager ready and willing to kick up a stink if the lights were not at full strength, he was instead pleasantly surprised at the powerful illumination they provided.

'We have no complaints at all,' Stein declared, although he may have been rather more discomfited by the full-wattage greeting he received from Vujadin Boškov, the Vojvodina manager, when he told Stein at the official banquet on the Monday evening before the game, 'I know your reputation. I know you are good and your team is good – but I am better – and we will win 2–0.' It was almost as if Stein was confronting his mirror-image, but one with an extra dollop of virulent self-confidence. As Celtic were to discover, Boškov's words were far from being the empty boasts of a braggart – he had a strong basis for his bold prediction.

Boškov's provocation failed to rile Stein but, in advance of the match with Vojvodina, the Celtic manager was more wary, more cagey, than he had been before the encounters with FC Zurich and Nantes. 'We've got a hard tie,' Stein said. 'Remember, Partizan Belgrade reached the European Cup final last season and no-one had heard of them either. This team beat Partizan to the Yugoslavian league title.

'The trip to see Vojvodina in the play-off was important for me because I was able to see both teams [Vojvodina and Atlético Madrid] play their normal games. Normally, one team has exaggerated defensive tactics, the other exaggerated attacking tactics but here, in a play-off, that wasn't possible. They had to play their usual style and that helped me a lot. I know pretty well what they are capable of doing now.'

That encounter between Atlético and the team from Novi Sad had become turbulent and that aspect of the match with the Spaniards was clearly prominent in Stein's mind. 'If the Yugoslavs want to mix it,' Stein added, 'and they have a reputation in that line, let them get on with it. My orders will be to play football and to go on playing football. It isn't always easy. But our boys have shown in the past that they can restrain themselves and they can do it again. We must not allow this to become a physical battle on our side.'

The match would prove to be quite different to the battle that Stein appeared to have been anticipating, with Vojvodina perhaps surprising even Stein despite the Serbs having gone into the game minus Dobrivoj Trivić and Vasa Pušibrk, two vital attacking players, suspended after their indiscretions against Atlético, and by the loss of Takač, their most luminous star.

'Vojvodina was very weakened by the Silvester Takač transfer [to Rennes],' Vasa Pušibrk says, 'especially because, besides him, our second main striker Djordje Pavlić also couldn't play [having been transferred to MSV Duisburg of West Germany], so basically we had to face Celtic with two completely new players in the attacking part of our team.' Takač had scored two of the goals that had eliminated Atlético Madrid in the play-off at the tail end of the previous round and had been 'as good a player as I have ever seen', according to Stein, but Takač had gone off to France early in 1967, drawn west by the powerful magnet of money.

'It's true that I haven't played in the first match,' Pušibrk adds. 'I played only in rematch. From such a big time distance, it's hard to say how big a disadvantage that was for our team. All I can say is that, if we weren't suspended, both of us [he and Trivić] would also definitely have played against Celtic in Novi Sad, because, in that time, every team had a regular starting line-up. In that season, Ilija Pantelić and I had most appearances for the team.'

As with several of the clubs in that season's European Cup, Vojvodina were the product of years of careful construction, carried out away from the fierce glare of commercial pressures. A club in a quiet corner of Europe, and in one of the less well-advertised leagues, could at that time bring in young players and develop them over time without them being plucked away by a rapacious agent as soon as they displayed any sign of being a distinctive talent. Ajax Amsterdam had done this and so too had Celtic and Vojvodina.

'The major credit for Vojvodina's accomplishment in 1967 goes to general manager Vujadin Boškov and our team manager

Branko Stanković,' Vasa Pušibrk says. 'They were both excellent players and later they became famous managers. I especially need to praise Branko Stanković, because he allowed us to show everything that we learned about playing football, thanks to the amazing physical condition which we had because of him. We could easily play for 120 minutes and still keep enough strength to play even more.

'In Youth Academy of Vojvodina Football Club, everything was done systematically for years and most of the players who played in 1967 were raised in that academy. Some of them came from other clubs, but those were mainly clubs from province of Vojvodina [the northern part of Serbia], so we had a very good chemistry among us. In defence, we had experienced players, while in midfield and in front, all of us were very young.

'We were confident enough to believe that we could qualify for the semi-finals, because in round of 16 we had defeated Atlético Madrid, which was a very good team. Our confidence was extra boosted after we won the third match in Madrid, where the atmosphere was fantastic. Also, in those years, our stadium in Novi Sad was full on every match, and the first game against Celtic was historical for Vojvodina, because that was the first match on our stadium ever that was played under the floodlights. We played in front of lots of crowds, basically, everywhere where we played.

'Vujadin Boškov and Branko Stanković were very good men, and most of all, they were fair. Those players who were the best, they were the ones who got a chance to play. All of us who used to play football professionally know that quality is visible and notable. We had a very sharp competition in our team and at the beginning of the season, we had more than thirty players in our squad.'

Confidence was coursing equally freely through the mind of Radivoj Radosav, Pušibrk's fellow forward. 'After we dominantly won the Yugoslav championship the season before,' Radosav says, 'we were all convinced that we could do a lot in European Cup next season. Whatever Vujadin Boškov wanted, or whatever he promised and said that he would do, he did it.

'I think that one of the most important things was the fact that we already knew each other for years and played together even in youth squads of Vojvodina. In those years, every summer and every winter we spent on a tour. We went to Germany, France, once we even went to Mexico and the USA. Basically, we were moved to the first team all together and that's why we managed to become Yugoslav champions in 1966. The defensive part of our team had been built for years. In midfield and up front, only Takač was a player who had been with Vojvodina for long time, while all the others were basically fresh and new. Takač was a leader in our team, especially up front. For Vojvodina, Takač was just like [Jimmy] Johnstone was for Celtic.

'We believed in our style of play. If you compare us to English or German teams, I think that we had bigger quality than them, since in those years, Yugoslav football was known by its beauty, lightness, disdain . . . It was superior towards Western European clubs.

'At the time, there were no dozens of live matches on TV every day, so we didn't know much about Celtic squad. We knew only about Johnstone, who was very fast and had a good pass and good change of direction with ball in his feet. Even before the first match, Johnstone was the player who was announced as the biggest threat for our team. He played for Scotland's national team and he was short, but extremely fast, and with that he stood out from other players. Other Celtic players were pretty unknown to us.'

If Vojvodina had been made more flimsy by their suspensions, it proved impossible for the Celtic players to see the join at the Vojvodina Stadium on the first day of March 1967. The

Yugoslavian champions should, in theory, have been rusty, coming off the football hibernation enforced by their winter break – Stein had wanted the tie to be played in January but Vojvodina had delayed due to their winter shutdown. The deadline for the tie to be completed was 20 March so this quarter-final had been delayed as late as possible, allowing for a play-off on 15 March, but there were no signs of Vojvodina defrosting slowly after a scarcity of competitive action in the previous weeks. They proved, instead, to be quite exceptional: seamlessly tight as a team, ineffably comfortable in possession and a constant threat to the Celtic defence. Each player was highly comfortable on the ball, with even the defenders expert at creatively working their way out of tight corners.

Nor was there any sign of the type of over-aggressive approach that Stein had suggested might be possible. Instead, the Vojvodina players lived up to the reputation that Yugoslavs had earned as 'the Brazilians of Europe'. Boškov had asserted that, 'I did not win the championship with eleven men. I used many players and the four who come into the team are very experienced. We will beat Celtic home and away.' His team's polished performance stressed that the Vojvodina manager had every right to be proud of the squad that he had assembled.

'Celtic players seemed a little confused with the atmosphere on the stadium and with our approach to the game,' Vasa Pušibrk, a reluctant spectator that evening, says. 'We played very aggressively and with lots of energy, but not too rough of course. We managed to force upon [Celtic] our style of play and succeeded to win.'

For all Vojvodina's vivacity, the only goal arrived via a Celtic mistake and it came late on in the match but Boškov now changed his tune with Stein-like alacrity. 'This is the best possible result for us,' he said, 'because the team will be stronger for the Glasgow game.'

It was a triumph obtained, Radivoj Radosav explains, in testing circumstances for his team. 'I think that we played very well,' he says, 'regarding that our team was weakened for that match [through the suspended Trivić and Pušibrk, the injured Vladimir Savić and the transferred Takač and Pavlić].'

'We were attacking and trying to score as many goals as we could. We had some chances but, to be honest, those weren't some extremely good opportunities. The goal which was scored by [Milan] Stanić was more a product of luck than of some organised team play. However, we gave our best and managed to win 1–0. I believe that we did not score more than one goal because we were missing the players who usually scored for our team. In Novi Sad, Celtic didn't make any opportunities for goal and I believe that the final result was fair. I'm absolutely sure that if we had had Dobrivoj Trivić and Vasa Pušibrk in the team for the first match, we would win with a higher score. They would bring more quality and stability to our team.'

Watching from on high, Pušibrk was sanguine about the result for his side. 'We weren't disappointed at winning by one goal alone,' he says, 'because we still managed to win without conceding. While Vojvodina was not such a famous team, we had a character, strength and quality to face any team which we played against that season. Although I didn't play in the first match against Celtic in Novi Sad, even then I saw how good the Scottish team was. It was made of serious players, who were physically prepared excellently and had the potential and the quality to win the European Cup. But after that first match, when we won 1–0, we believed that, with our style of play, which relied on short passes, we could remain undefeated in Glasgow.'

Following a fraught match for Celtic, an impressed Stein played down the returns of the suspended Vojvodina players for the second leg. 'I doubt that Vojvodina will be stronger with those players than they were against us,' Stein said. 'In fact, the men they brought in were more powerful physically, better in defence, and that is what they will need for the second game. I think we have seen them as strong as they can be.

'We are quite happy with the result and I am sure we can win in Glasgow. Naturally, we don't like to lose any games but this was not a bad performance. Tommy Gemmell made the mistake that lost this one but these things happen. He has won games for us in the past so I'm not blaming him too much this time.' Gemmell, exuberant, irrepressible, admitted freely his mistake but was determined to use it positively.

'I made a bad mistake,' Gemmell said. 'I was short with a pass back. My pass was inaccurate. It fell between John Clark and Bobby Murdoch, their guy intercepted it and when it was moved on to Stanić he finished by placing the ball behind Ronnie Simpson. He knocked it away and we did well to keep the score down to 1–0 over the remainder of the match.'

Stein also, privately, expected that, under relentless pressure at Celtic Park, and verbally assaulted by a baying, swaying crowd, Vojvodina would fade physically. But he was to be disappointed in that assessment during the uproarious return, one week later. Celtic too would now be stricken by absences, being without Willie Wallace, ineligible for this round, and, of course, Joe McBride. Stein had tried to bring the player back in reserve matches after his breakdown at Pittodrie until, at the end of January, Stein had finally announced that McBride would take a complete fortnight's rest. Further attempts to restore him to fitness had failed, with rumours beating the air that his football career was entirely over, until he entered Killearn Hospital on the morning of 8 March, the date of Celtic's quarter-final with Vojvodina at Celtic Park, readying himself for an operation on a torn cartilage. His season was over.

It meant that Celtic would be relying on Stevie Chalmers as

their principal goalscorer, a situation acknowledged by Stein resting the 31-year-old on the previous Saturday, for the league match with St Mirren in Paisley, which the team managed to win 5–0 without the aid of the striker. Stein knew that he would require a specialist to slice Vojvodina open artfully. Chalmers found Stein not to be the 'most supportive of people' but Stein had the knack of going to a player individually in advance of a match and bolstering them by expressing how much confidence and trust he had in their innate ability. Stein now needed Chalmers like he had never needed a player before.

It all made for a powerful evening of drama. Tickets for the match had sold out rapidly although, quirkily, some seats in the wings of the Front Stand had been kept back, as they were exposed to the elements. Patrons were told that the £1 tickets for those areas would be sold on the night but only if the weather proved clement enough for those seats to be comfortable.

Three months' worth of pent-up anticipation was about to be spilled by the supporters that evening. They knew they had to hurl everything they had at the match in support of their team. The ground was full long before kick-off – to secure a prime spot, it was necessary to be early because tickets that gave access to the ground allowed fans to go anywhere on the terraces. The build-up had begun with the draw in December and had increased through the excited and passionate chatter in the queues for tickets that had stretched from the stadium down on to London Road and that had demanded hours of patience. The week since the narrow defeat in Yugoslavia, which had left the tie poised tantalisingly in the balance, had built the excitement to a crescendo and as the fans crammed into Celtic Park, the tension that sparked from one supporter to the next made for a near-frenzied atmosphere by the time the game began. This was one evening on which the supporters would be much more than onlookers. 'We have not come to play defensive football,' Boškov had said on visiting Celtic Park after arriving in Glasgow, where his players trained on the track after Stein had artfully told him the pitch was too heavy for a workout; in Novi Sad, Celtic had been similarly barred from training on the heavy pitch at the Vojvodina Stadium on the day before the match. 'We are here to beat Celtic again. It is a matter of prestige. I will play my best team and try to score goals.'

Stein was equally assertive when discussing his team's prospects. 'We all know in our hearts that the European Cup is what counts most,' he said, 'and I feel we have the players fit to wear the mantle of champions of Europe. I have told them so. Now it's up to them. I believe our boys and our style are good enough to win this match and the European Cup, with which nothing else compares.'

Those who were fortunate enough to have the hottest ticket in Scotland that month found that Vojvodina lived up to Boškov's words and were as relentlessly stylish and as physically resilient as they had been in Novi Sad. Their panache would not go unacknowledged by the enormous crowd pressed into Celtic Park on an evening on which Vasa Pušibrk and Dobrivoj Trivić were back in the side.

'When we ran onto the pitch before the match,' Pušibrk says, 'I had an impression that there are between 80,000 and 90,000 people on the stands, probably most of them boosted with a typical Scottish drink. They were waving and singing Scottish songs. The atmosphere was beautiful and playing in front of so many people was just an extra motive for us. I have never played in front of more spectators in my whole career.

'Personally, I remember the first half of that match when we played extremely well with our style of short passes and when Celtic players were pretty confused. They were unable to establish their way of playing, which was typical for British teams and completely different from ours.

'That first half is when I had a very good chance to score, since it was just me and the goalkeeper, but the ball went beside the goalpost. If I had managed to score then, who knows how the match would be finished? Of course, I remember it well. The goalkeeper ran towards me and I made a shot to his right side, but instead of the net, the ball [went past] the goalpost. That was definitely one of the most important chances I ever had in my career. However, even much better players than me can miss.

'The crowd was incredible. They supported their team very loudly and it was an example how the crowd should give their support. They didn't show any negative gestures towards us. On the contrary, when we came back to the pitch in half-time, some of them started applauding. I think that they liked the way we played. We were all very good technicians and able to keep the ball in our possession for a long time, just like Barcelona plays today. I would say that Celtic fans were impressed with us just like we were impressed with them.

'Celtic played very tough, with lots of energy and they weren't surrendering until the end. However, with every tackle, none of them ever showed any intention to hurt any of us. That was the way British teams used to play in those years and how, by my opinion, British teams still play today. I was impressed by [Jimmy] Johnstone, who played on the right wing. He was very fast and had an incredible technique, with an amazing change of direction when he had the ball. He is the one I liked most [from that Celtic team] as a player.'

The star attraction in the Vojvodina side was not a web-weaving forward but Ilija Pantelić, the goalkeeper, reputedly being watched by Internazionale and Real Madrid. 'If I must leave Vojvodina,' he said haughtily, 'I should like to move to Real.' He had been described by Stein, following the play-off with Atlético, as 'terrific' and he enhanced his reputation further at Celtic Park, exuding calm in the midst of the fray as Celtic battered against the defensive wall erected by the Serbs on the night. Over in Novi Sad, Lennox, at one point in the first leg, had slid in for a ball and lain grounded after failing to reach it. Pantelić had pulled the forward up by the hair and had hammed up the moment for the benefit of the crowd.

Stein, seeing his players perturbed by Vojvodina's style, decided to introduce some confusion of his own. As the second half began, John Hughes, fielded at outside-left, now lined up on the right alongside Johnstone. This gave Gemmell the space in which to ease forward and on 58 minutes he duly atoned for his first-leg error, sending over a fiery ball from the left and seeing Pantelić fail, for the first time on the night, to cut out the cross.

'Pantelić was lying sprawled out on the ground,' Stevie Chalmers says of seeing the ball reach him. 'I controlled it quickly, eased away from a defender, let it fall and clipped it over the line.' As the Celtic players engulfed Chalmers, Bobby Lennox ran to Pantelić to emphasise the goalkeeper's blunder; the only time in his career that the winger would gloat in the face of an opponent. It was a moment that signalled how the tension had become tangible but although it felt like a break-through for Celtic, the Vojvodina players remained composed and calm. A draw would give them a less hectic play-off in front of a modest, neutral crowd in Rotterdam.

'Physically, Celtic was an extremely strong team,' Pušibrk says. 'In defence, they had players who were very good in the air, especially comparing to us, who were naturally pretty short. It is them who eventually decided the match in Glasgow, since after a corner-kick from the right side, their player Billy McNeill managed to jump high enough and score a goal with his head.'

That corner had been taken by Charlie Gallagher, in the team after Bertie Auld had failed a late fitness test. The ball had sailed into the heart of the Vojvodina box, where hitherto McNeill had been unable to enjoy an unhampered attempt on goal.

'As the ball came across,' Chalmers says, 'I made a little run and just happened to get in Pantelić's way, as if by accident, when he came to meet the ball. That put the goalkeeper off his stride but I was keener to see how Billy might head the ball than how well Pantelić might be able to catch it.'

Stevan Nestički, the number 6 on the line, clawed at the air as he attempted to keep out McNeill's final-seconds header, while Pantelić stood stranded, close, but not close enough, to McNeill as the Celtic man, the Vojvodina goalkeeper and a balancing Stevie Chalmers looked to see if the ball was going to hit the target. It did. Only seconds remained of the game.

'Of course, we were very sad and depressed,' Vasa Pušibrk says. 'I remember that moment. Chalmers obstructed Pantelić with his back, enough to change the direction he was going. Our goalkeeper was basically about to catch the ball with his arms, but since he was afraid not to make a penalty over Chalmers, he took [a step] back and that is how we conceded a second goal. I knew that it was a foul right away and we protested to referee, but when Celtic scored a goal, the atmosphere became wild and everything was over.'

Shock engulfed Radivoj Radosav at the moment of McNeill's goal. 'We didn't even have the time to think about how we feel,' he said. 'When the ball went to the corner-kick, we thought that it was over and looked to the referee, but he said that there are four more seconds to play. After the corner-kick, a Celtic player scored with a header. There was a foul on our goalkeeper, but now we can only feel sad for that. Pulling and pushing in the box between the players used to happen much more often than it happens now, so it was basically normal. The crowd was really okay and they supported their team until the last moment.

I think that the second goal was actually a reward for them [the crowd]. However, I don't think that they had any impact on the referee [in convincing him to give the goal].'

It had been a tight squeeze for Celtic – a tumultuous but opportunistic victory that, Radivoj Radosav suggests, was aided by Vojvodina squandering some priceless scoring opportunities. 'The atmosphere at the stadium was much different from the ones in Yugoslavia,' Radosav says, 'since Celtic fans seemed much more disciplined than what we used to see here. Personally, I regret two incredible chances that we made in second half. Five minutes before the end, I made a very good pass to Vasa Pušibrk but with his shot he literally passed the ball to the goalkeeper. After that, I think that it was Vladimir Rakić who also had a chance, but he also didn't use it. Celtic was so lucky then, because if we scored, everything would be over.

'Honestly, Celtic was a tough team to play. They could run more than us and they were stronger. I think that was the only difference between us in their favour. Also, I need to accentuate that they were not too rough and they played very fair. We were trying to defeat them with our short passes and technique, while they were trying to win using their strength and physical power. They were playing with long balls in space and, basically, their style of play was relying on who will be faster. They were physically superior to us and that is how they managed to span the fact that we had better football technique.

'The finish of the second match in Glasgow brought a huge happiness for Celtic and a huge shock for Vojvodina. It was madness on the pitch and at the stadium, and after the final whistle, I can't remember exactly who, but somebody kicked the ball towards me. The referee never asked for it. I took it with me to the changing room and kept it for all these years, so today I have one very dear memory. It's a little scratched thanks to all the studs . . . but it's still good. At the time when it showed up, it was the best ball ever. It was very light and convenient for play, especially when the pitch was moist.'

The Celtic team had gone out to perform a lap of honour after the crowd had chanted for them to return, a rare event, but appropriate on an evening when the role of the supporters was acknowledged fully by Stein. 'How could anyone feel tired or uncertain of victory when these 75,000 were behind us?' he said. 'They willed the players to win. I thank them. It was almost as if they were on the park. At half-time, when it was 0–0, I told the players we would win. We proved to the world tonight that Scotland is still great at football.'

The aggressive assertiveness that Vujadin Boškov had employed on behalf of his team prior to both legs was now converted into gentlemanly grace as he acknowledged Celtic's forceful victory. 'Celtic fought like mountain lions,' he said. 'That McNeill goal was like being hit by an earthquake. I have no complaints. How can anyone have against such supermen?'

McNeill surreptitiously paid tribute to the role of Chalmers in providing him with the chance to score the equaliser. 'I knew Charlie was going to put over a long corner when I saw two defenders run out to cover Jimmy Johnstone at the flag,' he said. 'I'd been coming up for all the corners but hadn't got my head to any of them. The keeper was always there first to punch the ball away but he was a fraction late coming out this time and I knew somehow the ball was mine. Charlie doesn't float his corners. He hits them hard and if you connect the ball goes like a rocket.'

The dramatic element of luck, of chance, was not lost on Stein. 'I don't suggest that the game went the way I planned it,' he said. 'The first half was not a rewarding experience. We had aimed at making the Slavs do the maximum amount of work possible in the first half, in the belief that they would tire. They did look very weary towards the end and I think we had them on their knees but there were worrying times. In midfield, they were strong and their link men were quick to turn our attacks back on us. But there was never any question of us holding something back for the second half.

'At half-time it was obvious changes had to be made so I tried a shock move in a bid, at least, to confuse them with Hughes and Johnstone going through on the right together. It made the Slavs stop and think. And before they had worked it out Hughes was back on the left wing and running free. Charlie Gallagher moved up with the other forwards, Bobby Murdoch moved further forward into midfield and we were on our way. At half-time I told the players we would win. Maybe I had to convince myself as well and I admit a great weight was lifted when Chalmers got the equaliser. The winner came late but is there a better time to get one?'

The ground had shaken not only in Glasgow that night but across Europe and word of the white-hot crucible that Celtic Park had become had reached Helenio Herrera, the seemingly all-seeing, all-knowing manager of Internazionale of Milan. 'I would not relish a game in Glasgow,' he said. 'The Scottish crowds are frightening to the Latin temperament. Believe me, Celtic would be better having the advantage of one game against us on their own ground and take their chances of holding us in the San Siro. We can win the final wherever it is played but I don't want to meet Celtic in Glasgow. At home, before their own fantastic crowds, Scottish clubs play fast, clever football and have a determined spirit no foreign team could ever match.'

Vojvodina, to their own and Boškov's enormous credit, had almost done exactly that and it was hard on them to return home wondering about the variety of ways in which they might just have seized victory. 'We thought Vojvodina were the best side we played in the European Cup that year,' Tommy Gemmell said. 'They had class. Every one of their players looked comfortable on the ball, they held possession well and they showed

152

a lot of good teamwork. They gave us our hardest two matches in all my years in Europe with Celtic.'

That dramatic escape from a perilous play-off in Rotterdam was worthy of James Bond and Sean Connery duly honoured the team by turning up at Celtic Park on the following Saturday for the Scottish Cup quarter-final with Queen's Park, posing for a team picture with the players on the pitch beforehand. The reverberations from the Vojvodina match seemed still to be echoing around the ground as the crowd settled into their places but this seemingly innocuous tie against the great Glasgow amateur club would provide its own minor eruption.

Stein would be particularly nervous in advance of a match against a small club, especially in a cup tie. This would puzzle players who pondered why such an uncomplicated game would induce palpitations in such a strong man. It was because of the game being weighted, beforehand, so heavily in favour of the minor opponents. If Celtic won, they would receive next to no credit for doing only what was expected of them. If they drew, or lost, against game but limited opposition, well . . .

The proceedings, in a rollicking 5–3 Celtic victory, were most notable for Jimmy Johnstone receiving a booking two minutes from time for retaliating after a foul by Millar Hay, the Queen's Park player. Celtic, of their own accord, immediately suspended Johnstone for seven days, until 6pm on the following Saturday 18 March, ensuring he would miss the match with Dunfermline Athletic, at a stage in the season when the team had fallen fractionally behind Rangers at the top of the table. He would also, on Celtic's instruction, miss the Scottish League v English League match at Hampden Park on the Wednesday evening, involving Bobby Moore and assorted other World Cup winners.

Against Queen's Park, Millar Hay had hounded Jimmy Johnstone throughout until he brought Johnstone to the ground with a clumsy tackle. The winger snapped and motioned his head towards the rising Queen's Park player. Hay's head had veered in a backwards direction.

'Everyone at Parkhead knows where he stands – now or any time,' Stein said. Johnstone's actions had been unacceptable to the manager, who had acted swiftly to reveal to the player his displeasure. 'I have no grievance,' Johnstone said meekly. 'I know that when my suspension is up at six o'clock next Saturday, that is the end of the matter. All I want to do is get back in the team. Being suspended like this may actually help my game.'

It was a timely warning to Johnstone, following the euphoria of victory over Vojvodina, that, for all his talent, he was not set upon an elevated plinth, as far as Stein was concerned. The winger was a highly emotional player, and man. If he was omitted from a match, he would slump visibly in front of his teammates, unable to conceal the pain shooting through his brain.

It might seem counter-productive, superficially, to toy with Johnstone's emotions in this way but the reverse psychology of it was to spur the player on to avoid repeating the shattering blow of omission. Johnstone would be back and ready when he was most needed: the draw for the semi-finals, held in Vienna, had paired Celtic with Dukla Prague, the champions of Czechoslovakia, a side with a rugged record of competition in the European Cup, conquerors of Ajax in the quarter-finals and whose relentless progress in the tournament was just as impressive as the advance of Celtic.

'This one suits us fine,' Jock Stein said. 'It is not an easy one but none of them are at this stage.' His words would never be more true – Celtic were about to face another high-calibre test of skill, steel and style that would require every drop of talent and perseverance that was within their powers.

Jock Stein (right) in Bermuda in May 1966, with players and backroom staff at the start of their long post-season tour which would prove to play such an important part in drawing the squad together.

Pre-season training, and Bobby Lennox shoots past Bent Martin, with Stein keeping a close eye on everything.

Tony Dunne of Manchester United looks on as Jimmy Johnstone crosses the ball during their August 1966 friendly, which Celtic won by an emphatic 4–1 margin.

In the first minute of the League Cup quarter-final, Billy McNeill (second right) heads home against Dunfermline Athletic to set his side en route to a 6–3 victory, with Joe McBride watching the ball enter the net.

Billy McNeill, watched by Tommy Gemmell, heads clear at the Letzigrund during Celtic's 3–0 second-leg victory over FC Zurich in October 1966.

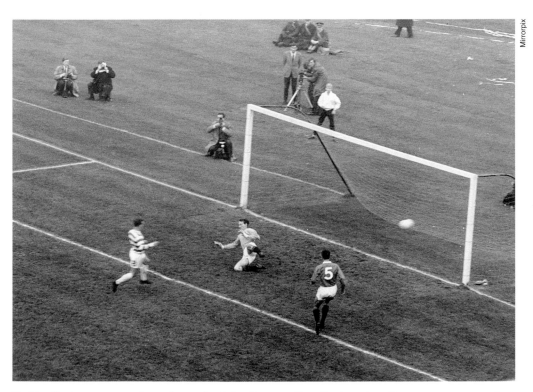

Bobby Lennox scores the only goal of the League Cup final against Rangers to secure the first major piece of silverware for the season on 29 October. There would be much more to follow.

Lennox strikes again to put the seal on a 6–2 aggregate victory over Nantes in the European Cup second round.

Jock Stein obliges young fans with autographs on the day after Celtic returned from Yugoslavia and a 1–0 defeat against the excellent Vojvodina Novi Sad in the first leg of their European Cup quarter-final. The result had left the tie very much in the balance, as shown by the tense expression on Stein's face.

(L-R) John Clark, Jimmy Johnstone, Tommy Gemmell, Jim Craig, Bobby Lennox, John Hughes, Billy McNeill and Bobby Murdoch celebrate after a last-minute goal from McNeill against Vojvodina had secured Celtic a European Cup semi-final spot.

Mr Bond, we've been expecting you … With Celtic's season building to a climax, even James Bond star Sean Connery was keen to get in on the action, taking to the field with the team prior to the Scottish Cup quarter-final with Queen's Park in March 1967.

Tommy Gemmell scores from the penalty spot to complete a 3–0 win over Hearts, the first time Celtic had won at Tynecastle since 1954–55.

Quick thinking from Jimmy Johnstone helps him score Celtic's first against Dukla Prague in the first leg of the European Cup semi-final.

Willie Wallace leaps for joy after scoring the first goal in the 1967 Scottish Cup final with Aberdeen, shortly before half-time. Bertie Auld (left), Tommy Gemmell (centre) and Billy McNeill rush to congratulate him while Stevie Chalmers ushers the ball into the net.

On a miserable, wet afternoon, in front of 78,000 fans, Celtic got the point they needed to complete the domestic treble with a 2–2 draw against Old Firm rivals Rangers. Here, the Celtic players celebrate and the Rangers players look suitably dejected after Jimmy Johnstone's astonishing second goal.

The Celtic squad train in the Estádio Nacional ahead of the European Cup final. Neilly Mochan (second right) takes them through a sprinting routine.

One of the key features of Celtic's 1967 European Cup final victory was Tommy Gemmell repeatedly advancing forward to provide extra thrust to the Celtic attack, a ploy that would ultimately result in him scoring the equalising goal.

Steve Chalmers scores the winner as Celtic complete their comeback against Inter.

Celtic fans inside Celtic Park on Friday 26 May 1967, waiting for the team to return from Lisbon with the European Cup trophy.

Bobby Murdoch, Bertie Auld and John Clark raise the trophy in front of thousands of fans at Celtic Park.

Jock Stein often looked anxious on the day after the final, as here, while being interviewed by a television reporter upon the team's triumphant return to Celtic Park. The burden of how to better his team's great victory was already weighing heavily upon him.

CHAPTER 11

Guile and Style

A grand old game of Cold War deception began raging quietly when Dukla Prague landed in Scotland for their European Cup semi-final with Celtic. Dukla were a team replete with Slavic guile; a side who would not overwhelm opponents but who were, instead, all about style and finesse, liable to finish off the opposition by killing them with self-confidence, lulling them into a belief that they were comfortably in charge before slipping in the poison.

Stanislav Štrunc, an angular individual, nominally a winger, but very different in style to Jimmy Johnstone, would lollop around looking uninterested or mildly discomfited at being on the field of play and would then despatch opponents spy-style, administering the killer blow professionally, efficiently and unexpectedly. Josef Masopust, already established as the greatest player in Dukla's history, was now a classical older player, unhurried, shorn of pace at 36 years of age but still able to propel the ball dexterously and dangerously; the ideal 'false number nine'. Dukla relied enormously on him, in his Indian summer as a footballer, and he had played a huge part in unpicking Ajax in Dukla's notable quarter-final-victory over the Dutch champions.

'The score will be 1–0 to Celtic,' Masopust said straight-facedly, inscrutable as a double agent duping a gullible stooge, at the team hotel, his distracting disguise a bushy hairstyle that could have passed for a guard's bearskin. 'Yes, the score will be 1–0 to Celtic both here and in Prague.'

An initial batch of 50,000 tickets had been put on sale for the first leg of the tie at Celtic Park from noon on Sunday 2 April, ten days before the match, with the ground and stand pegged at the same prices as for the quarter-final. Those tickets had melted away swiftly, into a multitude of eager mitts, with the remaining 25,000 soon to follow, as supporters bought heavily into the prospect of seeing another evening of grand theatre to match the one they had enjoyed so greatly with the visit of Vojvodina Novi Sad.

One concern for Stein and Celtic, amidst all the euphoria of qualifying for the semi-finals and the anticipation of enjoying further European Cup exhilaration, was that that climactic encounter with the Yugoslavs had created its own sweeping anticlimax. Little could live up to the evening when Celtic had diced dangerously but thrillingly with the prospect of elimination from the European Cup before concocting the most dramatic of climaxes just before the curtain fell. There had been a subsequent dip in form, the team looking uninspired occasionally, although also flaring, at times, into a carnival of colour. With players such as Jimmy Johnstone in the team, they could not remain subdued for too long but Jock Stein acknowledged that it had been a rather flat spell, one perhaps induced by the ordinariness of the tasks the team had faced.

'The danger for any team like Celtic going flat-out for trophies,' Jock Stein said, 'is not the tough games. It is in the less-important games that the standard drops. We still win but with less effort and, consequently, the edge is lost. We have had a run of games that, with due respect to the teams involved, did not require maximum effort . . . We lost the edge last season on a similar run and we didn't get it back. We were short of peak form at the most crucial part of the season, when we had the Scottish Cup final and two games against Liverpool.

'That is why I am so content at the moment,' Stein said as he awaited a Scottish Cup semi-final with Clyde in early April 1967. 'Our game did drop below the expected standard in effort but we have been able to raise it again recently against teams who traditionally make it hard for us – Dunfermline, Falkirk, Hearts and [Partick] Thistle. Our game has come back close to peak just at the right time. We are as ready for a hard run-in as we could ever hope to be.'

The looming encounter with Dukla and the semi with Clyde would require patience and flexibility on the part of Stein's team and they would meet his demands willingly. There was no question of a player insisting that he should be selected for one specialist position only and that he could not be expected to be able to play with competence elsewhere on the field of play. Bobby Murdoch had suffered an ankle injury against Heart of Midlothian in late March and Willie Wallace, the forward, was fielded in his place in central midfield for the next match, against Partick Thistle, and performed excellently – satiating Jimmy Johnstone's voracious appetite for the ball with a variety of superb passes.

Wallace happily remained in the heart of midfield for the tie with Clyde at Hampden Park, which looked a potentially tricky one. Clyde, after their early-season capitulations to Celtic, were having one of the best seasons in their history and were a talented team, with a strong and settled defence and a potent attack in the shape of Joe Gilroy and Harry Hood. They were making it an all-Glasgow top-three in the First Division and aiming for European qualification.

'At Shawfield, on the 31st of August, I had scored my first goal against Celtic that season,' Gilroy, the Clyde centre-forward, recalls. 'The ball came across and I sidefooted it quickly. It was an instinctive goal – there was not a lot of build-up involved, just a quick pass from Alex Bryce. I scored against all Scottish First Division and Second Division sides except Rangers. I struggled against Ronnie McKinnon who was big and strong and pretty quick, but I always felt I had a chance of getting a goal against Celtic. Billy McNeill was more gentlemanly, if you like, about the way he played. I found I could nip in for a header here and there. I never felt I couldn't score against Celtic; I always thought I had a chance. They were a terrific side, though. Everything they did turned to gold.

'Already, Celtic were a well-oiled machine, scoring goals galore, especially from Joe McBride. At Parkhead, on 11 January, I got my second goal against them that season. Strangely, I always seemed to play well against big Billy [McNeill]. I had gathered some interest – first from Celtic but they signed Willie Wallace from Hearts – then from Rangers but they signed Alex Ferguson from Dunfermline – and look what great careers they had!

'And so it was on to the next two games with Celtic – the Cup semi-final and replay and crowds of 56,000 in both games. Celtic were a great, skilful team but they could be hard as nails when needed. In Bobby Murdoch, big Billy, John Clark, wee Bertie [Auld] and Tommy Gemmell, they could mix it with the best. Harry Hood and I had struck up a great understanding and caused many teams problems that season. Big Jock [Stein] had a few words [with his players] to sort that out . . .

'At half-time in the semi-final, I had a huge swelling on my left calf thanks to a "tackle" and Harry had a very bad gash thanks to big Billy. Although neither of us was as effective in the second half, I nearly won the game. Late on, as the ball bounced at the edge of the box, I turned and hit it on the volley. As it headed for the top corner I jumped up, shouting "goal" then saw wee Ronnie Simpson flying through the air backwards to just tip it over the bar – chance gone! Ronnie was only about five feet nine inches tall but he could spring all over the place. [The game finished goalless.] Harry did not make the replay and, to be fair, I really was not 100 per cent and Celtic won 2–0.'

Goals from Bobby Lennox and Bertie Auld sent Celtic through to their third consecutive Scottish Cup final and, a week later, Murdoch was back to face Dukla, the Czechoslovakian champions, which released Wallace into the forward line after three weeks of operating at the heart of the team.

'Before a European tie, Jock would have gone to see the opposition, every time,' Jim Craig says. 'So the tactics board would go up on the Tuesday night at Seamill and he would discuss how he thought they would play. He would very often say – and it's a tribute to him that we believed it – "I don't think they'll play the way I saw them. I think they'll do this on the night and they'll want us to do this." The thing about that is that you've got to decide whether he was right or whether it was because we believed him that we forced them to play the way he wanted them to play. By us carrying out a counter-plan, did we force them into playing a certain way? We'll never know the answer to that but he was right far more often than he was wrong.'

There was a tendency for Celtic to start matches cautiously, even slowly, in Europe – Stein liked his team to play itself into matches with high-class and potentially treacherous opposition – and at home to Dukla Prague they certainly started slowly. The Czechs, with players soaked in World Cup and European Cup experience, attacked the home side from the start and won a corner in the opening 60 seconds. Dukla, assured and nimble, flitted across the Celtic Park turf as lightly as ghosts, all art and craft, and proved exceptionally good at holding on to the ball, defending assiduously and then hitting hard on the break.

'We had had a tough match against Ajax in the quarter-finals,' Vladimír Táborský, the Dukla Prague defender, says. 'Then Ajax was on the rise. Until then, Ajax was not so well-known team. They came up with a completely new style of play, then, with all players attacking and defending, figuratively speaking. It was a very interesting and difficult opponent but, then again, we got through. I think we did not play badly. Both matches were balanced. At the conclusion, the game came to us. Ajax took an own goal and another fell to us from a penalty. Their reaction to going behind made things look bad for us at times but finally we managed it.

'Although Dukla was known in Europe, the furthest we had got before was to the quarter-finals. That year, Dukla managed to go further. That year, our team was very good and mature. In the team intermingled older and more experienced players with young. It was the outset of Ivo Viktor [on the cusp of becoming one of world football's greatest goalkeepers]. We still had Josef Masopust. We also had a good coach; he was a good psychologist. And therefore he brought us so far.'

The testing tie with Ajax had seemed to be perfect preparation for Dukla confronting Celtic in the semi-finals but although the Czechs' confidence was duly buoyed upon making their trip to Glasgow, they were also slightly weighed down by fear of what they might have to weather in the East End of Glasgow. 'After beating Ajax,' Ivo Viktor says, 'we were fairly confident against Celtic, but we were afraid of the stormy atmosphere on their stadium. We had played both matches against the Dutch team at the maximum of our capabilities and I had the feeling Ajax underestimated us.

'At that time, a new Dukla team had begun to form under coach [Bohumil] Musil's lead. Only a few players from the old Dukla remained, with Josef Masopust among them. Celtic had become known for their vigorousness, loud supporters and also several very good players such as Johnstone, Chalmers, Wallace, McNeill and others. Then, during warm-up before the game, our experienced defender, Jiři Čadek, got injured and a novice [Ján] Zlocha had to get in. We had trouble with Celtic's vigour and speed and their simple but purposeful defence. Our fears of a very tough play and loud atmosphere came true. Celtic played very vigorously even for British standards, even insensitively or brutally sometimes.'

It was another momentous evening at Celtic Park. The vast crowd, swaying like an amorphous mass, saw Stevie Chalmers head a Jimmy Johnstone cross past Viktor in the early stages only for the effort to be mysteriously disallowed by Joaquim Fernandes Campos, the Portuguese referee. Chalmers had leapt with a defender to win the ball and send it on to Johnstone in the first place. It looked a fair challenge. Had rumours of Chalmers' actions in the final minute of the quarter-final crept through to the ears of Fernandes Campos? Or maybe Johnstone's alacrity in scurrying to the goal-line and cutting it back had caught out the referee and, puffing along well behind the play, he had been overtaken by disbelief at Johnstone's quickness in controlling and crossing the ball while also keeping it, just, in play.

That moment was soon subsumed by a memorable Celtic goal, in the 27th minute. Bertie Auld triumphed in a tussle in midfield and unhinged the Dukla defence with a natty pass through to Willie Wallace. When his shot was blocked, the ball went spinning into space in the vicinity of Jimmy Johnstone. The only problem for the winger was the massive, black-clad figure of Ivo Viktor rushing out from his goal-line to meet man and ball but Johnstone, beautifully brave, chested down the ball and, when it bounced up temptingly, leapt like a hare to volley it over the bulky Viktor and send Celtic into the lead.

'It was stormy but sporting,' Táborský says. 'The game was

fair. We counted on Celtic being strong and the crowd being big and loud, but the reality exceeded expectations. Spectators rushed the Celtic players forward. No ball for them was lost. They played simple. Dukla was the technical team that played for ground, and Celtic played simply forward and still wanted to keep their opponent under pressure. And we were under pressure.

'[We found out] that Scottish football is very tough, especially unpleasant for the attackers, who had to go into personal battles that were very hard. In a personal duel they were better than we were. It was hard to create a chance.'

One minute from half-time, Masopust was to be found once again at the centre of the action as several Dukla players helped to thread the ball carefully through the heart of the Celtic defence and when the ball finally made its way through to Štrunc, he hit the ball across Ronnie Simpson and inside the far post.

At half-time, Stein calmly informed his players, rattled by that equaliser, that they had been the superior of the two during the opening 45 minutes and told them that if they continued to play in a controlled fashion, their own momentum and the backing of the crowd would take them to victory. So it proved. Dukla, in the face of Celtic's forceful football, wilted and col-lapsed and were slightly fortunate to leave Glasgow with only a two-goal deficit.

'During our initial pressure,' Ivo Viktor says, 'we managed to create two chances. But practically the whole game we weren't able to get through Celtic's perfect defensive block [wall]. Celtic were one of the best teams we ever faced, a team with a very vigorous defensive game, speed, organisation and a fast counter-attack. We were under pressure for most of the game which was in, for us, an unusual environment. It was hard for us to create goal attempts. Even at 36 years, Josef Masopust was a personality and a conductor of the team. But he was also not fond of the British toughness of Celtic.'

With almost an hour played, Celtic went ahead again. A high, swirling ball, played by Tommy Gemmell from the vicinity of the halfway line, dropped out of the sky and into the Dukla penalty area, bounced once and sat up perfectly for Willie Wallace to whip it past Viktor from the corner of the six-yard box. Soon, Celtic had doubled their lead. Bertie Auld, crouched down as if to steady the ball before taking a free-kick, cunningly remained hunched over, deceiving the defensive wall, who had expected him to straighten up and move back to take the kick. Wallace was fully aware of Auld's ploy and it bought him a few precious seconds when Auld, still crouched over the ball like someone plagued by a painful back, nicked the ball to him, catching Dukla in slight disarray. The striker's low, 20-yard shot travelled past Viktor for the final goal of an absorbing match.

'The atmosphere was amazing,' Josef Vacenovský, the Dukla forward, says. 'They were known for their encouragement. I think it affected us – sometimes you succumb to it. Celtic was a typically British team, playing consistently on the body, hard, and Ajax was good at the technical side. That's why we played better against Ajax than against Celtic. In the game against Celtic we had always someone at our backs. We have not met with such style of game in that time in Czechoslovakia.'

The result was a good one for Celtic – a useful victory against a useful side. 'I got what I wanted from them all,' Stein said. 'Now the Czechs will have to come right out and attack us. We are all happy.' For all the manager's stated confidence, there had been worrying aspects to this game. The Celtic defence had faltered collectively in allowing Štrunc to score – Simpson's inaccurate throw-out had been intercepted by Masopust and McNeill, Murdoch and Jim Craig had all had attempts at stemming the surge forward from Dukla before Štrunc had cleverly sent his shot cutting diagonally across Simpson into the far corner of the Celtic net. It had been a terrible, sloppy goal to lose in such an important game. Dukla were a formidable force who were sure to be uncomfortably difficult to hold on their own patch, but Stein was insistent that his team would not be cowed by Dukla's potential potency at the Stadion Juliska.

'There will be no flat-out defensive game from Celtic here on Tuesday,' Stein said after flying into Prague on Sunday 23 April 1967, ready for the return two days later. 'I feel it would be foolish to hand control of the game to Dukla. Naturally, we will be cagey, very cagey but we intend to dictate the game, not just wait for what they have to throw at us.

'For us, this is the big one, the one we almost didn't dare to hope for. We want to be the first British team into the European Cup final and all our energies and thoughts will be directed towards pulling it off.'

On arrival in Prague that Sunday, the Celtic players were released into the city to enjoy its delights. Soon, a group of them, spearheaded by Billy McNeill, were joshing around on one of the city's trams, hanging on to the platform only by a pole, half in and half out of the vehicle and half in and half out of the European Cup.

CHAPTER 12

Czech-Mate

En route to Prague, Bobby Lennox had enjoyed a good laugh at Jimmy Johnstone's passport photograph. In revealing black-and-white, it made the winger resemble Harpo Marx, the comedian, whose light and voluminous curls lay piled up high on his head. Johnstone retorted, 'At least I don't have a mouth hanging so open that you could put a fishnet on top of it.' This was the winger's take on Bobby Lennox in his own photograph.

A Tuesday afternoon in the Stadion Juliska soon sobered up every one of the jolly ensemble who had joked and japed all the way across the continent. The ping of a ball hitting a stanchion was one of the most reassuring sounds in Bobby Lennox's world but in Prague in April 1967 it caused him palpitations. Lennox, one of world football's fastest and most dynamic wingers, oper-ated habitually in the vicinity of the opposing team's goal but, in Czechoslovakia, a determined Dukla Prague pushed Celtic back so deeply during the game that even the freer spirits in the team found themselves chained to defence. At one point Lennox, back with his teammates, saw a shot flash past him and, before he could turn around, heard it hit the goal-frame. Immediately he feared the ball had beaten Ronnie Simpson

165

but he instead found that the ping of ball on metal had been created by it hitting the outside of the stanchion after whistling past the post. Lennox and Celtic were able to enjoy a release of tension, for the moment, but this would feel like one of the longest afternoons of their lives.

'That was a nerve-racking game,' Tommy Gemmell said of the second leg against Dukla. John Clark, in turn, considers Dukla to have been of comparably high quality to Vojvodina and that while the Yugoslav side worked extremely well as a team unit, Dukla had several players who operated with considerable style as a means of opening up opponents.

Significantly, Lennox was the only change in the Celtic team from the first leg, coming in for John Hughes. Hughes believes that Stein had been 'dithering' between him and Lennox but Hughes had performed ordinarily in the first leg with Dukla. Every time Hughes got on the ball a huge murmur of excitement would rise from the crowd, which would give way immediately to an equally loud collective groan of disappointment whenever the player failed to meet the crowd's expectations. Lennox had also played well against England at Wembley on the Saturday in between the two midweek ties with Dukla despite a wild challenge from Jack Charlton in the opening minutes that had left Lennox with blood seeping from his knee.

Suddenly, the season was reaching its climax for Celtic. The excitement surrounding the club even eclipsed Scotland's victory over England, when the Scots had become the first nation to defeat the World Cup holders, who had been unbeaten in fifteen matches since early 1966. Celtic could, in the space of only a week, clinch the league title, lift the Scottish Cup and reach the European Cup final. They could also, equally, see all of those prizes slip out of reach. Prague would be the first of those dramatic tests and Jock Stein was now feeling the weight of expectation on his shoulders to an unprecedented degree.

The 3–2 win over England at Wembley had thrilled all of Scotland – and Alf Ramsey, the England manager, had congratulated the Scots after the match for their magnificent performance, describing them as 'a great team'. Although the five Celtic players involved were proud to have played their part in the national team's totemic win, the game had been a risky one for them with their club at such a crucial stage of the season: matches between Scotland and England were always bloody, bruising affairs. Lennox had discovered that he would be in the Scotland team while at Seamill preparing for the first leg with Dukla but states that, had he been given the choice, he would have opted to have participated in the first leg against the Czechs rather than at Wembley. Charlton's challenge had left Lennox with blood seeping through his suit at the reception after the match but the injury had not proved to be serious enough to keep him out of the return with Dukla. Tommy Gemmell, early on in the game against England, had suffered a bruised instep when Ray Wilson, the England full-back, went right over the top of the ball in a challenge; it stiffened up after the match and left Gemmell, he said, 'hirpling about', a worry for the player with all of those crucial games looming.

Ronnie Simpson and Willie Wallace had emerged unscathed but Stevie Chalmers had made a fruitless trip to Wembley. He had been first reserve – and in those days, when substitutes were not yet allowed in internationals, that meant he would take the place of any forward who pulled out of the named starting eleven. Yet when Jimmy Johnstone was held back by Jock Stein, supposedly because he was injured in the wake of the Dukla match, the Celtic manager used his powerful influence with Bobby Brown, now the Scotland manager, to send down Willie Wallace to England as Johnstone's replacement, leaving Chalmers out in the cold and suffering a disappointment that would remain with him for decades afterwards. It was manipulation by Stein but done for the greater good of Celtic – the manager had a special role in mind for Chalmers against Dukla and a tiring match against England would not have been the perfect preparation prior to his exertions in Czechoslovakia.

The win over the world champions would have helped boost the confidence of those involved, coming as it did ten days before the return with Dukla. Lennox believes his fine performance at Wembley, which included a goal, helped convince Stein that he deserved his place in the team that took the field in Prague. Stein also made a point of collaring Gemmell after the game and telling him that his two early tackles on Jimmy Greaves, the England striker, had rocked Greaves so badly that he had been mostly missing for the remainder of the match. The introduction of Lennox for Hughes made the Celtic team in Prague: Simpson, Craig, Gemmell, Murdoch, McNeill, Clark, Johnstone, Wallace, Chalmers, Auld and Lennox. It was only the third time that side had played together; an eleven who had previously been fielded exclusively for matches at St Johnstone and at home to Aberdeen. Bohumil Musil, the Dukla manager, was still without Čadek.

The 22,000 tickets for the Juliska had been in huge demand; not least because the stadium's capacity had been restricted to that number by one side being redeveloped and thus out of use for spectators. Celtic, based at the Intercontinental Hotel in central Prague, opted to walk the short distance to the ground but the game would be anything but a stroll.

'Three-one away was a bad result,' Ivo Viktor, the Dukla goalkeeper, says of the defeat that his team would have to try to adjust in Czechoslovakia. 'The defeat disappointed us but before the Prague game – the rematch – some chance was still there for us.' Vladimír Táborský, his teammate, was hopeful but wary of a Celtic team that had burrowed deep into the usually rock-hard Dukla defence. 'Every defeat is a disappointment,' he says, 'but if we won at home 2–0, we could play a third game on a neutral field. We had been in the game [at Celtic Park] but, on the other hand, we did not lose three goals to anybody. We always got along by losing just one goal.'

This was one match that seemed to spook the habitually super-confident Jock Stein. Unlike in Zurich, where Celtic had also arrived holding a two-goal lead, the Celtic manager had not ebulliently informed his players beforehand to dismiss any perceived threat from their opponents. This time, he acknowledged Dukla's quality by instructing Stevie Chalmers to play as a lone striker in a 4-5-1 formation, with Chalmers ordered to chase down every ball as Dukla attempted to play out from the back. Willie Wallace, goal-getter extraordinaire in the first leg, was now assigned to man-mark Josef Masopust. The inventive midfielder had been on Stein's mind before the return, the Celtic manager suggesting that he would not be surprised if the conductor of Dukla's tempo and mood were to be omitted because of his advanced footballing years. 'Our pace had them worried in Glasgow,' Stein said, 'and it particularly worried Masopust. I would expect them to attack directly from defence, cutting out the middle man if possible. We will be careful at the start and take it from there.'

With Chalmers isolated, the rest of the Celtic team were set up to blank the Czechs as the home side poured into attack as a means of watering down and then levelling Celtic's lead. Stein's team had tumbled at the semi-final stage in the previous season's European Cup-Winners' Cup, going down 2–0 in the second leg at Liverpool after going 1–0 ahead in Glasgow and that setback had haunted Stein ever since. He was determined to seal his team's goal, temporarily shelving Celtic's reputation for flowing, attacking football.

As the players prepared for the match, the official Celtic party, being given a tour of Prague by a guide, came across a statue of

Josef Stalin. The former Soviet leader was already a discredited figure and even in the Soviet Union itself, monoliths in his honour were being torn down. The guide explained wryly that in Czechoslovakia, a country with a long history of invasion and occasional subjugation, they did not feel quite ready to remove this image of Stalin. 'You never know when something might come back,' he explained with a half-laugh. Celtic knew that their Dukla Prague opponents might look as damaged, half-way through the tie, as Stalinism but that a comeback from the Czechs was quite a possibility.

For Táborský, the Dukla defender, it would prove to be one of the quietest afternoons of his career, one that began replete with promise. 'We had the support on our home field,' he says. 'The spectators came not only from Prague but also from the villages; as well as the supporters of other clubs. That was a big thing for us. It was a game where Celtic wanted to defend and we did not have much chance to score. But superiority yes; we did have that.'

Dukla's seizing of the initiative was visible from the open-ing moments of the match. 'I had a half-chance in the third minute,' Vacenovský, the Dukla forward, says. 'I did not score with it, unfortunately. They came to play a draw; a 0–0. They were two goals ahead so it was good for them. We played ugly football because it was important match for both teams. Maybe we were a bit nervous. We did not have enough confidence. The thing about us was that we did not have enough confidence in ourselves. For example, when we played with Real Madrid, we worshipped them, and overlooked the fact that we had also world-class players among us. The newspapers made them gods and we seemed so small.'

Viktor too was under-employed in the Dukla goal. 'We did not have any clear chances,' he says, 'only the two half-chances at the beginning for Josef Vacenovský and Stanislav Štrunc, but we did not get a goal and did not have any more chances. We played against a defensive block. We managed to create some pressure in the beginning, but for the whole match it was like conquering a fort. After a 0–0 half-time, it was obvious that the loss from Glasgow will be hard to catch up. Musil, our coach, was disappointed by our offensive game and by the single-sided defensive performance by the Scots that aimed to hold the advantage from their home game. I was still impressed by Chalmers' toughness and by McNeill directing the defence. It [Celtic] was one of the best European clubs we played against.'

Stein had told the players that a two-goal cushion from the first leg would see them into the final and when Stein said something with certainty and precision, clearly and easily understood, the players tended to believe him. The manager's words, backed up by his having been proven correct on so many previous occasions, helped bolster the belief of his players that they could play a game unnatural to them and obtain the required result.

The match proved a nervy, jumpy one for Celtic and Stein admitted that it had been a risky, unappealing strategy to set his players up with so few attacking ambitions. Bobby Lennox feels that if Dukla could have breached Celtic's defence with one goal, there might have been the prospect of an avalanche to follow. When the game ended goalless, it proved a considerable triumph for Stein, not least because he had never set his side up so defensively before. Any cracks in the edifice were brilliantly concealed as McNeill, at the heart of the back four, spurred his teammates on to the most notable goalless draw in Celtic's history.

'In the second match Celtic did not impress me,' Táborský says. 'It was a team that just defended. But in the first game there that you played on me, Johnstone had speed, hardness, good shot and a passion for the game. Then I remember Wallace and Chalmers. I think that relations between the Czechoslovak and Scottish players have been minimal, or we did not know anything about that team. We read about Celtic, the famous European team, but we did not know what to expect. They warned us that they will be tough, the Scots are harder than the English, and later it turned out that it was true. And the match was decided not because we were inexperienced internationally, but because we had no experience with the concept of Scottish football.'

Vacenovský is sanguine about the outcome. 'We did not score,' he says, 'and so when our coach said he was disappointed with how we had played, the comment was correct.'

That afternoon in Prague would be branded on the brains of the Celtic players long afterwards because it had been so unusual for them to play in the manner in which they did. 'To go and face Dukla and get a 0–0 draw was a great achievement,' Bobby Lennox says, 'but we didn't play particularly well. The boys were delighted after the game but we knew we had been rotten. Sometimes you've just got to get there – and we got there.'

Stein was only mildly apologetic, following the match in the Juliska. 'We played the only possible type of game for this situation,' the Celtic manager said afterwards. 'The boys did exactly as they were told and I am overwhelmed with joy. It is a great day for us. We had to plan our tactics not only to hold out but with a view to our commitments, notably the Scottish Cup final at the end of the week.'

Musil was downcast in the aftermath of a contest that deadened the senses of those watching. 'I was disappointed with my team,' he said, 'and neither Dukla nor Celtic played well. Celtic were so different with ten men in defence. I am very unhappy.'

Tickets for the European Cup final in Lisbon were quickly made available from the Scottish Football Association with the highest price being £2.7s.6d and the lowest 10s. The more expensive, funnily enough, sold most quickly but while the fans could look forward a month to the final, Stein had to ensure that the domestic season regained prominence in the players' minds. It helped that there was not too much hype around the sport. Commercialism in football barely existed – there were no souvenir stores with products yelling about the forthcoming grand occasion. All there was, really, was the next match – and the next match was such a big one that Stein had broken with tradition and flown Celtic home immediately after the game in Prague instead of allowing the players the usual chance to relax, stretch out and enjoy breakfast, camaraderie and a change of scenery in a foreign city.

'We had done something that had never been done by any British side before,' Tommy Gemmell said, 'and that was to reach the European Cup final. So, basically, the load was off our shoulders.'

Five hours after slipping into the European Cup final, Celtic were back in Glasgow and preparing for an eight-day week that would bring their domestic season either to a crisp, shuddering climax or to mournful, damning defeat. Stein swiftly took the team to Seamill the day after they returned from Prague for two days of golf and relaxation. 'The aim is to keep everyone ticking over,' Stein said, 'so we are not doing a great deal.' With no serious injuries having been sustained in Prague, Stein opted to choose for the Cup final the same side that had steered the club into the European Cup final.

Amidst all the jubilation over Celtic's reaching club football's most elevated plateau, a meeting with Aberdeen at Hampden Park four days later, in the Scottish Cup final, looked relatively mundane; as much as that was possible at a national stadium that had a crowd of more than 126,000 crammed into every cranny and teetering on their toes to follow each scrap of action. It promised to be a trap for Celtic – any cutting out of concentration or intrusion of complacency in the wake of the elimination of Dukla might prove deadly in the face of a fine Aberdeen side who were expected to test Celtic in the same stringent fashion as the punchy, pawky Pittodrie side had done in becoming the only side to draw both of their league matches with Celtic over the season. Aberdeen and Hibernian had drawn around 80,000 to their quarter-final ties at Easter Road and Pittodrie and another 30,000 had seen Aberdeen's semi-final with Dundee United at Dens Park. The Pittodrie side could claim that their route to the final had been more testing and invigorating than Celtic's and they had also enjoyed ten days of pure preparation for the final.

It proved to be even more anticlimactic an afternoon than the most curmudgeonly of supporters might have expected. The footballer's cliché after a poor performance is to suggest that the team simply 'didn't turn up on the day' and in Aberdeen's case that afternoon, that was not only figuratively but almost literally true.

'I was still at college, in my senior year at Jordanhill [College of Physical Education, in Glasgow],' Bobby Clark, the Aberdeen goalkeeper, says as he recalls the day of the final. 'So, as I was from Glasgow, I got a "blue train" from my home in Shettleston to Queen Street and a blue train out to Hampden for twenty to two. The rest of the team had prepared for the final at Gleneagles so I went to the dressing room on my own – to find that the Aberdeen team was not there. When it got to two o'clock I put my head out of the dressing room door to check that there was a game on … The rest of the players didn't turn up until two-thirty because Eddie Turnbull [the Aberdeen manager] had taken ill. [From memory] I feel it was his liver – it was certainly something fairly serious to stop him being at the final.

'The players all came rushing in – threw out all the stuff – and the team was out there before we knew where we were. So we rushed on to the field and I don't think we started playing until we were two goals down. Coming off, we knew we had never played Celtic. I felt a lot of it came from Eddie not being there. Davie Shaw, our trainer, was there to take over from Eddie but this was in the days before assistant managers. Not taking anything away from Davie but Eddie Turnbull was a terrific coach. Eddie was a tracksuit manager – and it was because of him that I had gone to Aberdeen. Eddie always had all the footballs out for every exercise whereas previously at Queen's Park, where I had first worked with him, it had been running all the time. Everybody always looked to Eddie for inspiration and tactics. When he wasn't there for the final it was a huge blow.

'That Celtic team – nowadays we talk about high pressure but they would pressurise teams. They were very good at pressing, not giving you a minute, but I felt we had a good defence. We had some special players, such as Jens Petersen, a really smart player, a Danish international who had represented Scandinavia against the Rest of the World, and Frannie Munro, who would go on to have a fantastic career with Wolves.' Jimmy Smith, a young player admired by Jock Stein, and audaciously nicknamed 'Jinky', would soon go over the border to Newcastle United for a substantial fee and to some acclaim as a cult hero. 'Davie Johnston was fast, two-footed, could hit the ball,' Clark adds. 'Then we had older pros such as Ally Shewan and wee Jimmy Wilson. Harry Melrose was the old head in the side.'

That assembly of talent fairly floundered on the day – 'lost and rudderless' as Clark puts it – without their manager, and prised apart by a Celtic side that, although unchanged from the one that had drawn with Dukla in Prague, had been 'freshened up' by Jock Stein switching Stevie Chalmers from the centre of attack to the right wing and playing Jimmy Johnstone at inside-right. It was a switch designed to cause chaos in the Aberdeen defence and would have been difficult enough for them to cope with even if Turnbull had been present. Stein intimated that Aberdeen had been over-confident prior to the final through having obtained their two draws with Celtic in the league. It seems significant too that, for such a major match, Stein opted not to change his side but merely to readjust his favoured starting eleven. It was as if he now knew the very team that would serve him best whatever the tactical requirements.

Prowling the left side of defence for Aberdeen that day was Shewan, a 'no-frills' defender, a type of player that thrived in the 1960s but who would flounder if their direct opponent – in this case Jimmy Johnstone – were to go for a wander, leaving them with no one with whom to get up close and personal. It left Shewan disorientated, temporarily at least, and sowed some confusion in the Aberdeen side when Stevie Chalmers was switched to the right wing and Shewan was uncertain whether to mark him or to follow Johnstone. Stein had perceived that the winger might exploit space by being shifted further inside to hound Harry Melrose, 31 years old, and Jens Petersen.

'I remember Jimmy Johnstone playing through the middle,' Bobby Clark says. 'That might have been to protect Jimmy from Ally! If we had had Eddie Turnbull with us, he would have noticed that [Johnstone at inside-right] and would have known how to fix it but we had nobody there of that calibre. For most of us, this was our first [Scottish] Cup final and that was a match where we didn't do very much in the first half. We didn't start playing until 2–0 down and, funnily enough, that was when we were playing into the wind. I remember coming off and saying to myself, "I hope I get another shot at this."'

Four days later, Celtic had the opportunity to land the domestic treble for the first time in their history. They required only a point from a rearranged, Wednesday-night fixture with Dundee

United to win the league title and now it was Stein who seemed perhaps too confident that victory was firmly within the grasp of his side.

'This is it,' Stein said. 'The boys know what they have to do. Get out and win. There will be a parade of honour if we win but I must warn our support that any attempt to encroach on the park [during such parade] will mean the team being withdrawn at once. I am sure that will not be necessary on a night like this.'

It was not but, then, neither was the planned 'parade'. Celtic suffered an unexpected 3–2 defeat on an evening when Charlie Gallagher replaced Bertie Auld and John Hughes took over from Stevie Chalmers. It gave Dundee United the exalted status of being not only the sole Scottish side to have beaten Celtic that season but to have done so twice. Glasgow's 'team with no stars' had been undone by their Dundonian equivalents.

Billy Hainey, scorer of a 35-yarder against Barcelona earlier in the season, got United's first, shortly after half-time, to claw back Tommy Gemmell's first half penalty-kick. Dennis Gillespie again scored against Celtic to make it 2–2 after Willie Wallace had put Celtic ahead once more. Twenty-year-old Jackie Graham, a boy from Drumchapel, and described by Jerry Kerr, his manager, as the best inside-forward prospect in Scottish football, grabbed the winner in 71 minutes.

'I remember at one stage at Parkhead they brought the [championship] trophy out,' Sandy Davie, Dundee United's genial goalkeeper, recalls, 'but we scored late on in the game. They came down the tunnel with it, ready to present it, and they carried it back up the tunnel. I felt sorry for them, the people at the club.

'Our reaction to winning that game was just one of shock, I think. We were ecstatic. We'd beaten them and stopped everything although I can remember a couple of close calls late on in the match. I've got a photograph of a shot that nicked the outside of the post. It meant, didn't it, that Celtic had to get something from their game against Rangers and it seemed more appropriate for them to try to win it there.'

As Davie correctly recalls, it left Celtic seeking their title-clinching point at Ibrox in a rearranged fixture three days later. Stein, in the interim, became very irritated when nine Celtic players were selected in Scotland's squad of sixteen for the international friendly with the Soviet Union, to be played on 10 May, just over a fortnight prior to the European Cup final on 25 May. The arrangement of the friendly international forced the postponement of Celtic's final league game, with Kilmarnock, to 15 May, ten days before the European Cup final.

'These two factors have completely upset the arrangements of my club in their attempt to win the league championship and the European Cup,' Stein said. 'I had hoped Celtic would be free around that time so that we could get away for European Cup preparation and, let's face it, no club, and that includes Celtic, has nine players of real international quality in their team.' The Celts named were: Ronnie Simpson, Tommy Gemmell, John Clark, Bobby Murdoch, Billy McNeill, Willie Wallace, Jimmy Johnstone, Bobby Lennox and Stevie Chalmers. Sift out the imposter internationals from that lot, if you can.

The pursuit of the point to take the title now took Celtic to Ibrox Park. The match with Rangers had been postponed from 3 January due to freezing weather that had made the pitch unplayable but it was in little better condition, on 6 May 1967, when Rangers needed to win, in their final fixture, just to remain in contention before Celtic rounded off their programme against Kilmarnock. The sodden pitch caused serious pre-match concern for Celtic, whose players were aware that the surface would soon cut up and that that would be a greater disadvantage to Celtic given that they were the superior footballing team. They would still attempt to play the game in the most pleasing fashion possible.

It had proved to be one of the oddest seasons in the Ibrox club's history. They would be facing Bayern Munich in the European Cup-Winners' Cup final on 31 May but had also garnered their most notorious result ever, when defeated by tiny Berwick Rangers in the Scottish Cup, in January. Rangers, in December, had appointed Bobby Seith as coach in an attempt to catch up with Celtic but with Scot Symon still the manager, they continued to flag.

No-one at all had expected Berwick to defeat Rangers. Matt Busby, the Manchester United manager, the previous day, had commented on how such shocks simply did not seem to happen in the Scottish Cup because the superior fitness of the full-time clubs always told. Much had been made before the game of Seith, Rangers' new tracksuited coach, a scarecrow-imitation of Jock Stein, putting the team through a furious training session and musing on how, 'The mental attitude is probably more important to us than the physical.'.

Jock Wallace, the Berwick player-manager, had responded bluntly with, 'This will be the shock of the year.' So it proved, Berwick winning 1–0 and Scot Symon, the Rangers manager, stating that he was 'shocked and distressed at the lack of urgency shown by players we should have been able to rely on – there were men in the Rangers jerseys today who should not wear them again.' The result had, of course, generated much deep and genuine joy among the Celtic support but it had also concentrated minds at Ibrox and the team had picked up from that point to go on to compete closely with Celtic for the title.

Special guests abounded in the main stand. Sean Connery, fresh from filming *You Only Live Twice*, and Helenio Herrera, Internazionale's Argentinian manager, were looking on as rain pelted down incessantly to give them a great big Glasgow welcome. The pitch was a mere superficial obstacle for Celtic, who overcame a slowish start and settled down to seal the point that Rangers had been seeking to steal. A magnificent goal from Jimmy Johnstone put Celtic 2–1 ahead with only a quarter of an hour or so remaining before a late goal from Roger Hynd pegged the result at a 2–2 draw. The point was secured, and Celtic were champions.

'They were a good side,' Jim Craig says of that Rangers team, 'and the reason we did well against them was because Gemmell, McNeill and myself took care of our immediate opponents. Willie Johnston was the best outside-left I ever faced. Wee Willie just put the head down and came right at you. He was terrific, at least as quick as me, and, of course, he got a start because he was facing the way he was going!

'Rangers were an excellent side but we were the better all-round team. We were quicker. Every morning at the end of training, we played a match – bibs against the non-bibs – and it was always two-touch football; sometimes even one-touch. It was a matter of pride that you remained with the same side over the season. It meant that we played really, really quick, passing football and I think that we were just quicker at playing the game than them. I think we were quicker and faster than them and probably better runners in terms of stamina. There were never any problems between Celtic and Rangers players even though it was a tough, physical battle. One thing is that as the game drew on, I would be standing beside my immediate opponent and hear them gasping for breath. That gives you quite a boost when you hear that; it makes you feel great, knowing that you are on top physically.'

Herrera had not planned, initially, to attend the match at Ibrox, having expected it to be a fixture-filling formality – he, along with so many others, had expected Celtic to tie up the title by defeating Dundee United. When that did not happen, even the Argentinian could not resist the magnetic lure of an all-or-nothing Glasgow derby. He flew in from Italy by a private jet that had been provided by him by Giovanni Borghi, the industrialist, and he would leave three minutes from the end to hurry back to northern Italy for his team's vital league match against Juventus in Turin on the Sunday.

It was only because the private-plane arrangement made it so easy for Herrera that he had graced Glasgow that afternoon. It had seemed too dauntingly awkward to make his way to Scotland through various necessary stop-offs across Europe and he had generously offered, before leaving Italy, to allow Stein to share the jet on its return journey so that the Celtic boss could cast an eye over Internazionale in competitive action. 'If it is safe enough for Herrera, that will be fine for me,' Stein said in response to the offer. Then Herrera, just as swiftly, withdrew his invitation, stating, ungenerously, that there was not enough room on the plane for Stein, who was, the slight, dapper Herrera suggested, 'a big man'. This ugly piece of Machiavellian manoeuvring did not deter Stein. Determined to see his opponents, he duly left Glasgow at 7.35pm in the evening after the Rangers match, and, via Rome, found his way to Turin in time for the following day's vital title match.

'When Rangers scored,' Herrera said after his visit to Ibrox, 'Celtic threw ten men into attack, moved upfield and Johnstone equalised. This was very impressive. Too impressive for me to sleep peacefully. The defence is good and I worry a little that it will be difficult to score against them. In attack, Celtic looked very difficult to check because the players have no fixed positions. They move freely and you can never be sure where they are. It is the sort of movement that could have lost me the final in five minutes if I had not had a chance to study it in Glasgow. Still, I think that, individually, my Inter players have more class.'

Jock Stein was more circumspect in assessing Inter after their 1–0 defeat at Juventus, averring that, 'I may have seen Inter at the wrong time, so it is best not to read too much into this game. If Herrera had seen us losing to Dundee United last week, he would have had a very different impression of us, wouldn't he?

'After the goal was scored against them, I saw them at the point of desperation, with everyone up. When they came out like that, it looked as if they might have left a few doors open.' Stein came away from Turin impressed by how Inter had comported themselves in a 1–0 defeat, in which they had played it tight before going behind to a 70th-minute goal.

There remained a diamond–hard aura of confidence around Herrera a week before the final. 'If Celtic come to Lisbon for the European Cup final wearing kilts,' he joked, 'then there can be only one result. We will leave them in their underpants.' Matters were less comical for him in relation to football itself. His team's attempt at retaining their Serie A title was beginning to falter as it reached its concluding stages and four days before the European Cup final, Inter drew with Fiorentina at the San Siro to bring Juventus almost abreast of them. 'We must be better in Lisbon,' Giacinto Facchetti, Inter's rangy left-back, asserted.

Inter were booed roundly by their own supporters as they left the field, following their flawed performance against Fiorentina; a less than fulsome send-off to Lisbon that contrasted with Stein being carried shoulder-high by his players as they performed a lap of honour following their 2–0 victory over Kilmarnock in their last public appearance before the final. 'We cannot play like that again,' Herrera said sadly after the Fiorentina game, his side's fifth successive match without victory. Compounding his anxieties, Jair, his Brazilian winger, was removed from the action with a pulled muscle. Jair had faded since his vivacious performance had inspired Inter's 1964 European Cup win over

Real Madrid and had been unlikely to figure in the starting line-up in Lisbon; nevertheless, his absence decreased Herrera's options. Armando Picchi, cornerstone of *catenaccio*, ended the Fiorentina match with a strained back, requiring treatment. Celtic players, meanwhile, were relaxing at home that weekend after a week of nicely paced workouts at Seamill and the outing against Kilmarnock, who had been happy to save themselves for their Fairs Cup semi-final with Leeds United.

The timing of the rescheduled match with Kilmarnock, on Monday 15 May, could hardly have been better. With the game all but a dead rubber for both teams, Celtic enjoyed a competitive workout without worrying about collecting serious injuries through the players over-straining themselves. They then had nine days to prepare for Internazionale, dissipating tiredness, knocks and niggles, with Stein expertly ensuring that they would be mentally and physically relaxed for this, the greatest challenge of their lives. They spent the rest of the week at Seamill, training lightly, recuperating, playing golf and board games, watching recordings of notable football matches.

'Jock was great at keeping the focus on the game but relaxed as well,' Jim Craig says. 'Hard sessions would suddenly be interspersed with a bit of fun. You'd maybe be doing shooting practice and then it would stop and you would have a game of rounders. Then you would go back into something serious again.'

Stein told the players his team on the morning of Monday 22 May, three days in advance of the European Cup final, but did not release it to the public until the following day, just as Celtic departed for Lisbon. It was the same team that had drawn in Prague, drawn at Ibrox to clinch the league title and defeated Aberdeen in the Scottish Cup final.

The only player who had featured in the first leg against Dukla Prague and who missed out against Inter was John

Hughes, the storming outside-left, who had played, instead of Bobby Lennox, against Dukla at Celtic Park but who had subsequently been replaced by Lennox.

'It was a dry, windy night, the park was bumpy,' John Hughes says of the game with Dukla, 'and the wee full-back I was playing against was lightning-quick. I had a nightmare. I just didn't play well at all. And that was it. He dropped me and I knew that I wouldn't be playing in the Final. And that was down to me. It's my biggest regret.

'He played Bobby Lennox in the return with Dukla and in the final. As it happened, in between I played in a league game [against Dundee United]. I got a kick on my ankle and it got poisoned. I went to the European Cup final but spent almost the entire time in Lisbon in my bed because the journey by air had aggravated the injury.' There is no guarantee that Hughes would have played in Lisbon even if he had been fit. Indeed, the team that Stein sent out for the final looked perfectly balanced, almost incapable of being improved; Stein knew that in Lennox, on the left wing, he had a player whom he could trust entirely to fulfil his instructions.

'When we got to Estoril,' Billy McNeill said of the team's base on the Portuguese Riviera, 'the hotel [Palacio] was absolutely magnificent. It was perfect, with a beautiful swimming pool and gardens. It was extreme luxury. But the big fellow gave you half an hour or so in the pool and then said, "Right, get out of the sun because it will tire you." Whether the sun would have tired us or not is another matter but I think what he was doing was reminding you that you were here to do a job of work.'

Stein's instructions were based very much on precedent. Three years earlier, Manchester United, having defeated Sporting 4–1 in the first leg of a European Cup-Winners' Cup quarter-final tie, had lazed in the Lisbon sun prior to the return and had been hammered 5–0 in the Alvalade. Stein, tipped off about this by

Matt Busby, was determined not to repeat such an error. 'My players will get a very small ration of sun indeed,' he said.

'He wouldn't allow us out in the sun until five o'clock at night,' John Clark says. 'He felt the sun would drain your strength away. You had to stay in the reception area, the hall or in the shade [just outside the hotel building itself]. We trained at half-five [on the day of arrival] because that was the time of the game.'

There was always a sense of things happening, and happening fast, around Celtic, with Stein in charge. As if their arrival for the final was not enough, representatives of Real Madrid were ready that Tuesday to request that Celtic perform in Alfredo Di Stéfano's testimonial – the club's most illustrious player had retired one year earlier and Real officials tied up the deal in Lisbon, committing Celtic to visit the Bernabéu thirteen days after the European Cup final. It endorsed Celtic as the hot date in Europe; not Inter.

'Don't make any predictions, just keep quiet, don't say anything at all,' Stein had told his players as they were besieged by the press on arrival in Lisbon, exerting full managerial control once more. For all his anxiety over the players making a slip in speaking to newspaper reporters, there was also a keen sense that the pressure was now off, to a large extent. Celtic had made history in becoming the first British club to reach the European Cup final and *La Grande Inter*, stuttering league form notwithstanding, were widely expected to swat the Scots aside.

It was, though, a tetchy Herrera who arrived in Lisbon, now shorn of Luis Suárez, his playmaker, who had picked up an injury against Fiorentina. The bus that would take them to their hotel was late, making for an irritating start to their stay. As a means of cheering himself up and lifting his team, he decided to take his players to watch the pasty-faced Scots training on the Wednesday morning at the Estádio Nacional, in blistering sunshine. It was an occasion that involved much hilarity on the part of the Inter players.

'We could see the Italians laughing away at us,' Stevie Chalmers recalls. 'They were sitting on the wall of the stadium and they weren't hiding their laughter either – it was loud enough for us to hear. Honestly, Inter Milan must have thought that we had no chance of winning the match.'

For Sandro Mazzola, Inter's star scorer, Herrera's insistence on Inter watching Celtic train was a miscalculation. 'I remember that at that time, The Magician wanted us to follow closely the training, at close quarters, of our opponents,' Mazzola says. 'That was a most serious error. The Scottish players turned up in the middle of dozens of supporters, all well sustained by pints of beer. More than that, their coach limited them to fitness exercises without the ball. Then, at the end, they organised a little match against the journalists. We were looking on and quite staggered by this and it got us laughing uproariously. At that point, that time, this was so unusual.'

John Clark himself finds hugely amusing the idea that Stein would have reprised the training session that he had undertaken in Nantes with journalists. 'No,' he says refuting Mazzola's idea that press people would have been roped in to assist as Celtic honed their preparations for the final. 'That might have been Sean [Fallon] and Bob Rooney and Neilly [Mochan] joining in the session on the park. That other thing . . . the idea that they were reporters . . . John Mackenzie, Hugh Taylor . . . they couldn't walk!

'The Italians watched us and big Jock said to us to make sure we did everything sharp and we did everything intensely. They were watching us and our training had to be A1, sharp. He said, "Let them know how sharp you are." I remember we had to put on a show. "They're watching – let them know you can do things properly." The Italians thought, [in a condescending fashion], "Scottish guys . . . " Well, they paid the penalty for it.'

If Celtic had looked in any way eccentric to Mazzola, he ought to have seen them later that evening. A match was being transmitted on television – England v Spain – but it was unavailable at the Palacio. So the Celtic players, less than twenty-four hours before the European Cup final, descended on a golfing complex run by a man called Brodie Lennox, an exiled Scotsman, to watch the international. Darkness was obscuring the way as they sought to return to the Palacio and so Neilly Mochan, the trainer, opted to take a shortcut that led to the players stumbling in the dark down a rocky outcrop after Mochan had seen the hotel's distinctive six-floor, creamy, cruise-ship-at-anchor outline in the distance.

'That was the famous walk,' John Clark says, 'when we came to a brick wall, with barbed wire, that we had to climb over to get back to the hotel.' A twisted ankle or a serious gash would have denied any one of those players a glimpse of making history but when they got back to their hotel, late in the evening, they were all, thankfully, still physically intact.

'I have no ambitions for myself,' Stein said as the match neared. 'I am completely impersonal about the glories of winning the European Cup. The praise is for Celtic. Win or lose we have created a fine image of Scotland and Celtic. I have worked around the clock for my club because I believe they are one of the greatest in the world and deserve nothing but the highest honours.'

An intense man, Stein was consumed entirely with football in every waking hour and slept for only a few hours a night, staying up and chatting over pots of tea with whatever company might be around. Fine for him but not for his young athletes.

'We'd maybe have a wee half a sleeping pill to make sure

we got a good sleep,' Bobby Lennox says. 'That would make us quite sharp. And sleeping was preferable to listening to Johnstone singing. We'd maybe lie and have a blether about what could happen and what could not happen, you know. I always slept quite well but I would be nervous before a game – until it kicked off and then it would just be a game of football.'

A year and a day after cantering to a nonchalant win over the cobbled-together collage of a football team that was the Hamilton Primos, Celtic were going in against the world's richest club, cut from the finest cloth money could buy. Their day and their hour had come.

CHAPTER 13

Artistry and Arrogance

'This is going to be a great final of great class between two great teams,' Helenio Herrera, the manager of Internazionale of Milan, said in advance of the European Cup final of 1967, 'and this is going to be Inter's year again.' As with all the iconoclastic managers, Herrera's character was reflected in the approach of his players and there was an artistic arrogance about the footballers of Inter as they strode out for the final, prepared to paint Celtic into a corner. They looked self-contained and self-satisfied and sleek and smooth – as if, with a few languid strokes, their superior art on the ball would brush away Celtic's presumptuous tilt at wresting the European Cup from the grasp of southern Europe. Only the great clubs of Italy, Portugal and Spain had, until then, won the trophy.

Inter displayed an assurance that all would go well for them on the day. European Cup finals, after all, had become their natural milieu. They were in their third final in four years, in the comforting surroundings of a great southern European city and the prickly heat was something considerably more familiar to them than it was to their fair-skinned opponents. The clean green and white of the hooped strips worn by the Celtic players enhanced that pale complexion in contrast to the smoulderingly suave, black-and-blue-striped outfits worn by the Italians, as if to emphasise at once, when seen in direct comparison for the first time, the apparent lack of sophistication of the Scots with the languid, easy self-confidence of the Inter men.

'I remember looking at the Italians,' Billy McNeill said, 'and looking at us in the tunnel and thinking that they must believe that they are playing a Scottish pub team. They had their stunning blue-and-black shirts, they were tanned and handsome-looking.' It was noticeable, though, that while Celtic strode out like a team, every player in line behind Billy McNeill, their Inter equivalents straggled out as anarchically as the traffic in central Milan. That was possibly nothing more than a subtle cultural difference but it did reveal the unity and purposefulness among the Celtic players.

Herrera had watched Celtic's semi-final first leg with Dukla on television and commented, 'I was greatly impressed by Celtic's speed, rhythm and staying power. Their flowing football, non-stop attacks and very fair play made it a most enjoyable game. I was particularly impressed by [Jimmy] Johnstone's brilliant wing play and [Bobby] Murdoch's dangerous foraging. Celtic looked a team of considerable all-round strength and they should be very worthy finalists. Celtic are the toughest, fittest, most professional team I could have run into this year in the European Cup but we are now in the final and getting back to our best at the right time. Apart from [Renato] Cappellini, my team has played together for four years. They can go through all the moves with their eyes shut.'

The day of the game had passed uneventfully for the Celtic players. They had been paired in their rooms, tactically: Ronnie Simpson and John Fallon, the goalkeepers; Tommy Gemmell and Jim Craig, the full-backs; Billy McNeill and John Clark, the central-defensive players; Bobby Lennox and Jimmy Johnstone, the wingers; Bertie Auld and Willie Wallace, a midfielder and a striker with whom he might link; Bobby Murdoch and Stevie Chalmers, likewise. There were back-up squad players in Lisbon but Stein had settled on his team long in advance of their arrival in Portugal and so the rooming arrangements were calculated on the basis of which men were playing. John Fallon would be the sole substitute. The players had been allowed to sleep late, a favourite indulgence of Stein's, and then have a light breakfast in bed – tea and toast and marmalade. That had been followed by a light workout beside the swimming pool, in the beautifully manicured gardens of the Hotel Palacio after the churchgoers among them had attended Mass to mark the Feast of the Ascension. A light lunch at one o'clock had been followed by a rest period, in bed, during the early afternoon before another gentle limbering-up session, a collective cup of tea and then departure for the Estádio Nacional at 4.10pm, singing and laughing and chatting all the way on the coach that took them to the ground. These were no headphone-wearing isolationists, stuck in their own little bubbles.

'It was a Holiday of Obligation,' Jimmy Gordon, the film-maker assigned to Celtic that year, recalls, 'and I remember Jock Stein saying to Desmond White [the Celtic secretary], "Those priests should give us half their gate – they've never had crowds like this in their lives ..." because planes were leaving Glasgow at one and two o'clock in the morning and flying out. It was a great occasion.' It is not recorded whether White, an accountant to the tip of his head and a man with a voracious appetite for cash, actually approached the said clergy with Stein's light-hearted suggestion.

Even when a snag tore at Celtic's well-worked arrangements, it worked in their favour. It was that kind of a day. A police escort had failed to turn up at the Hotel Palacio, leaving the Celtic coach trapped in a traffic jam. A passing police motor-cyclist was eventually flagged down and he led the delayed squad to the stadium, which they reached with only thirty-five minutes remaining before kick-off, thanks to the terrible traffic on the west side of Lisbon. Inter had already been there for forty-five minutes when Celtic arrived but the time lapse worked in the Scots' favour. They had only a few minutes available to check the pitch and get changed before taking the field. There was no time to be overawed or engulfed by nerves.

'The Inter fans were numerous,' Tarcisio Burgnich, the Inter right-back, says of a crowd for the final that contained thousands of Celtic supporters, 'the Scottish fans too – but they were not so much like the English, not as forceful as the English, who really made you feel something during that era. The Scots actually resembled the Italian supporters in terms of their passion. The atmosphere was beautiful; not at all oppressive.'

Lisbon's Estádio Nacional has to be the most unusual setting for any European Cup final. Most such venues are on inner-city sites – when Inter won their first European Cup they did so in Vienna, at the vast, bowl-like, Prater Stadium, with a backdrop of several large banks of advertising, tiers of the stuff stacked up glaringly on the Austrian terraces. The Estádio Nacional was hoarding-free and it sat isolated in woodland like a fairy dell, six miles west of the centre of Lisbon. It was designed as much to be an athletics venue as it was a football stadium. A long-jump sandpit stretched along the main-stand side while a running track ran around the pitch area, which accommodated at both ends space for field events. One side of the stadium actually had no permanent terracing or stand at all. A modest, temporary construction was instead erected to house a few hundred spec-tators and the press. The other three sides of the ground were altogether more grand, with 120 rows of marbled bench seating rising to a rostrum in the main stand where the brand-new model of the European Cup sat gleaming, its two elongated grips awaiting the hands of the winning captain.

The 1967 finalists were competing for a brand-new trophy. The original European Cup had been retained by Real Madrid once they had won the competition for a sixth time, with the defeat of Partizan Belgrade in 1966. Hans and Jorg Stadelmann, father-and-son jewellers based in Berne, Switzerland, had been commissioned by Hans Bangerter, the general secretary of UEFA, to design a new trophy; the original European Cup had been designed along the lines of a Greek urn.

'We put the design together like a jigsaw puzzle,' Jorg Stadelmann said of the new cup, which took the Swiss 340 hours to create and which is 62cm high, weighing 7.5kg. 'It was a "bastardised" design, yet I like it, and I think everybody in football likes it as well.' The very bastardisation of his design would make it the enduring symbol of the premier European club competition: its long, smooth, convex body and slim, elongated handles meant it looked unlike the traditionally more squat football trophies. Celtic and Inter would be the first to see who could take this unusual prize home with them.

It was common currency during that era to suggest that Internazionale were a defensive side but that is too simplistic a description of a footballing institution that had, with considerable élan, become the dominant name in club football. Certainly Herrera was keen to keep the goals scored against his side to a minimum – and in doing so he was fulfilling to a large extent the requirements of the crowd at the San Siro. Italians have a great love of seeing a team that is efficient at eliminating mistakes in defence – a team such as Stein's Celtic would not have been to their taste because they would notice too many seemingly unnecessary risks being taken. Instead, Italians, paradoxically colourful but conservative, prefer to see technical players manipulate the ball expertly, keep it, hold possession.

There was also a multi-dimensional attacking threat from this Inter team. If Inter were so defensive, how had they defeated, for example, Real Madrid, the holders, 3–0 on aggregate in the quarter-finals? Italian sides were supposed to gain a 1–0 advantage and then sit on it. Inter's victory over Real suggested they could defend efficiently and ally that with some prodigious attacking.

Inter's semi-final had been trickier than Celtic's, the Italian side discovering, as Celtic had done, how much talent one of the less-renowned Eastern European clubs could contain. CSKA Sofia had pressed them hard to draw 1–1 in both legs and had been due to play off in neutral Graz, Austria. Instead, jittery Inter offered Sofia a considerable cash inducement to switch the venue to the Stadio Communale in Bologna, northern Italy, still supposedly neutral but close and convenient enough to Milan to pack the ground with followers of Inter. As an inducement, Inter offered to provide Sofia with, reportedly, two-thirds of the takings from a crowd of 45,000. The Bulgarians took the bait – and threw away a potential place in the final; that went to Inter thanks to a Renato Cappellini header, the only goal of a play-off that Inter dominated with great assurance.

'If we keep them busy, the result might be interesting,' Stein had said after his sole viewing of Inter performing 'live', a 1–0 defeat to Juventus in a league match between the top two in Serie A. Having seen Inter lose a 70th-minute goal after attempting to chisel out a draw, Stein wondered how the Italian side would react against a team that scored the first goal considerably earlier than that, to force the Italians into a more expansive game.

'There was a confident feeling among us,' John Clark says, 'and we knew we had the ability but we never thought, "We're going to win." Nothing like that ever came into your head.

In your own mind, you're wanting to do your best because it's the biggest game in Europe – or the world – a European Cup final. So everybody's looking in. I don't think we ever gave it a thought that we could get beaten. We felt confident all the time that we were a good team and this was a stage on which we could prove we were a good team.

'We knew we were playing the cream; the top team in the world at the time. They were the team that nobody could beat and they had a style of play that nobody could break down.'

At the heart of Inter's success was the aplomb with which they could transform a defensive situation into an attacking one. Sandro Mazzola, possessor of an economics degree and a fine footballing heritage, was the spearhead of the Inter attack and epitomised Herrera's desire for efficient calculation. Graceful, quick, light of movement and rapid of thought, Mazzola was wonderfully elusive and had the potential to sweep from deep into the dark heart of the opposition defence. For the final in Lisbon, he would be flanked by Cappellini and Angelo Domenghini, swift and streamlined forwards who had the ability to dart dangerously into positions poisonous to the opposition. Inter would not attack with any great abandon: Mazzola, who had reportedly been laid up in bed a week before the final with a high temperature, was their top goalscorer, with 22 goals from 42 games.

The recollections of Jimmy Johnstone were at variance with the measured assessment of John Clark in relation to how the Celtic players felt in advance of the final. 'For the Cup final, we thought, "Here we go,"' Johnstone recalled. 'You know? "Inter Milan – we are going to get a doing!" Oh aye, Inter Milan, we had watched them. They had been world champions twice. At that time, they were the best defensive side in the world. They would score one goal, even at home, and think, "That's enough. That'll do us." Even in European football, they would do that because they felt that in the second leg the other team had no chance of scoring.'

All of Inter's attacking efforts relied on the coiled spring of *catenaccio*, epitomised by Giacinto Facchetti, a left-back who had been converted from the position of striker. The idea was that attacking teams would be drawn on to the rocks of Inter's defence by the Italian team retreating calmly; Facchetti, springy and long-legged, would then emerge suddenly with the ball to sting the over-committed opposition by streaking up the left flank to turn defence into attack. All of the defenders were free to range forward as and when they saw fit – when they did, Armando Picchi, the sweeper, was expected to fill their position in their absence, locking the defence like a bolt. Celtic, with their thirst for attacking football, were ideal opponents for Inter.

Inter's dangerous trident of attackers was of less concern to Stein than his own players maximising their attributes. 'Jock's team talk in Lisbon was, "You've made history. You've got to the final. Go out and play to your capabilities,' recalls Bertie Auld. 'He never mentioned any individual or how they would play.'

A myth has arisen that the Internazionale players were somehow unsettled and shaken by their Celtic opponents belting out riotously 'The Celtic Song' ('Hail, Hail, the Celts are here!') in the players' tunnel in the minutes prior to kick-off. This seems fanciful even if it is true that the echoing underground passage, similar to a very narrow underpass, which leads to the pitch from the courtyard beside the Estádio Nacional's dressing room, was atmospheric and claustrophobic. A short delay had seen the two sets of players standing side by side therein for some moments. Auld had initiated the singing, which may have helped assuage any Celtic nerves and emphasised their togetherness. 'For us,' Tommy Gemmell said, 'it released the tension because we were getting a bit uptight; we just wanted to get out there on the park and get on with it.'

Johnstone, too, relished those pre-match moments. 'When we were talking among ourselves,' Jimmy Johnstone said, 'we were saying, "Oh, we're going to get a doing here. Ach, we'll go out and give it a go anyway. At the end of the day ..." You know? Anyway, wee Bertie, the wee Glesca, Maryhill boy ... we were standing near them [Inter, in the players' tunnel prior to the final], you could feel them breathing, smell the Ambre Solaire off them, you know, and wee Bertie says, "Wee man, look at this big yin!" The Italian says, "What ees this?" Then Bertie says to the Italian, "You tell your maw you're going to be late. Your eyes will be burling." The Italians were saying, "*Loco, loco!*" That's all we heard.'

Inter, on emerging from this initiation into Celtic ways, still looked composed, calm, untroubled by the occasion. As with Celtic, all of the Inter players were from the nation they represented and, given the greater size of Italy, this team could, as with Celtic, also claim to be something of a fairly local selection. They did not hail from within a 30-mile radius of the club's stadium, as the Celts did, but they did have common ethnicity in that they were all from northern Italy. Sandro Mazzola was the equivalent of Bobby Lennox in terms of birthplace, being the furthest flung of the Inter players. While Lennox had been born 30 miles from Glasgow and brought up right on the Ayrshire Coast, on Quay Street, Saltcoats, Mazzola had first seen the light of day in Turin, where his father Valentino had been a star with Torino, around 220 miles from Milan. That, though, had been an accident of birth for Sandro as his father was a Milanese and only the wanderings of a professional footballer had taken him west.

None of the Inter players, surprisingly, had been born in Milan itself – the most local among them was Facchetti, who was from Treviglio, 19 miles away. Most were from small towns, apart from Mazzola and Mario Corso, who hailed from Verona, 100 miles or so from Milan.

Both sides, as they emerged into the sunlight of the Estádio Nacional for the 5.30pm kick-off, were wearing strips untarnished by sponsors' logos, colours that would go unchanged from season to season to show that this was a football club first and foremost rather than a profit-driven commercial organisation; colours that would be worn home and away unless there was a clear clash with the strips of their opponents.

The Inter players may have looked like catwalk models but this was to be no fashion show. Bill Shankly had, in spring 1965, when Liverpool faced Inter, described European Cup games as 'little wars that have to be fought'. Stein had sent his players out prepared to perform in style but 'he never forgot it was a battle', as Jim Craig puts it. A green-and-white mascot, resembling a Zulu mask, which had been handed to Ronnie Simpson before the Scottish Cup final, was prominent among the Celtic players as they lined up smilingly for the final. John Fallon, the Celtic reserve goalkeeper, carried out a Celtic teddy bear.

It would have seemed ludicrous at that stage in the 1960s to state that attacking football performed at its best would always get the better of its more defensive counterpart. Yet that would have been as true then as in any other era. An attacking team is always the one with the initiative. An attacking player has the advantage over a defender of knowing exactly what he is going to do and that gives him a few seconds of an advantage; vital in a game such as football. A defender is always reacting and if the attacker is sharp and stinging and precise and quick in their execution, they will prevail. If Celtic were to get the better of Inter through attacking them, they would have to be as sharp as knives.

CHAPTER 14

A Matchless Mercurial Maverick

There was a lot to observe in the body language of the Celtic team as they took the field to face Internazionale of Milan in the European Cup final on 25 May 1967. Billy McNeill, the captain, whose father had soldiered in Africa, strode out at the head of the team, with full military bearing, head erect, chest out, club pennant in hand to symbolise his role as leader; the perfect figurehead. Bobby Murdoch, a magnificent playmaker but a self-effacing man, took up the rear, as unassuming and invisible as it was possible to be on such a day. Bertie Auld, his partner in midfield but contrastingly extrovert, was the only man in the Celtic team to be holding a football, symbolising his role as ball-player extraordinaire.

The players formed an orderly, northern-European line, striding out in single file behind McNeill, except for one, Jimmy Johnstone, unwavering in his role as the maverick in that Celtic side. He loved, he explained, seeing other people taking on defenders and beating them, just as he loved seeing film of himself doing the same thing, which had won him fame around the world. He did so through being unvaryingly unpredictable – on and off the field of play.

While his teammates strode resolutely and purposefully out on to the pitch at the Estádio Nacional, eyes on the centre-circle, where they would line up alongside Inter, Johnstone approached the game in his own style. With his red hair frizzed up, he was unmistakeable anyway but now, dodging out of line, he gesticulated at the Italians wildly, repeatedly, not in confrontational fashion but in an attempt to obtain the attention of Giacinto Facchetti, the totemic, overlapping left-back in the Internazionale team. Facchetti, understandably concentrating on the task ahead, saw Johnstone but looked away quickly, perhaps anticipating a degree of gamesmanship from a notable opponent. That did not deter the Scot. He continued to signal to the Italians – using his hands to indicate someone tall – until Tarcisio Burgnich, Facchetti's fellow full-back, noticed Johnstone and realised that he was attempting to get the attention of Facchetti.

Eventually, as the cavalcade of players from both sides converged on the centre-circle, there was a flurry of activity among the Italians as they strove to understand Johnstone's wildly extravagant arm and hand gestures, and, just as the teams lined up, it was conveyed to Facchetti that the purpose of the Celtic player's histrionics was to obtain a guarantee from Facchetti that it would be with Johnstone that he would swap shirts at the conclusion of the match. Having finally got his message across, Johnstone gave the Italian the thumbs-up.

It would have made more sense for Johnstone to have had this exchange in the players' tunnel, as the Scots and Italians hovered nose to nose, awaiting the start of the match, rather than doing so only once a melee of dozens of photographers and match officials and a great swathe of the pitch was separating the two sides, but it was always in Johnstone's character to do things in the most unconventional fashion. If Jock Stein gathered his players around him at training to get a point across, Johnstone would be at the rear of the circle, playing keepie-uppy with the ball as the manager spoke.

'He wasn't being cheeky,' Stevie Chalmers says, 'it was just his desire to be on the ball all the time. No-one else would have been able to get away with that – anyone else who tried it would have stood a good chance of being drummed out of the club.'

Johnstone's approach to life and the game of football may have owed much to the freedom he was given as a boy, roving the wilds around his native Viewpark. He was free to roam all over Lanarkshire during the school holidays with no restrictions placed upon him. Jimmy could simply disappear as often as he liked. After such a childhood, it was hard for Johnstone to embrace any form of discipline and lapses in behaviour would be a regular occurrence. Teammates who collected him from his home in Lanarkshire would often have to wait – Johnstone would have been asleep in bed on their arrival but would give the thumbs up at the window before rapidly breakfasting, dressing and performing his ablutions while they waited in the car. Few would hold a grudge against him – his fun-loving nature made him popular throughout the club.

It was, suitably, Johnstone who was to the fore for Celtic once the match kicked off on that late afternoon. A mere 14 seconds of the match had passed when he streaked up the right wing and whizzed almost to the Inter goal-line before sending a 'square' pass across goal. Armando Picchi, the sweeper, the cornerstone of Helenio Herrera's *catenaccio*, collected it with ease and spread it left to Mario Corso. Only a further 30 seconds had passed before the ball had been fed to Johnstone once again – and even this early it looked clear that Jock Stein had set Celtic up, at this stage, for the almost one-dimensional purpose of ensuring that Johnstone got on the ball as often as possible. Every time a Celtic player received possession, he looked right, down that wing, in search of the diminutive redhead.

'I saw myself as an entertainer,' Johnstone said, 'as someone on a stage and the fans loved it. My job on the day was to get on the ball from the opening minute if I could and I was to twist and turn at the Italian defence. That was what the manager had told me to do. That was what he wanted from me. I was specifically to take on and try to beat as many of the Italians as possible, with no restrictions on it. He said that I was to keep doing it even if it meant I lost the ball.' Helenio Herrera had witnessed the man he called 'The Little Flea' exert a powerful influence on the 2–2 draw with Rangers three weeks earlier and would have warned his players of him in advance. Through propelling the ball repeatedly in Johnstone's direction, Stein was showing them that, for all Herrera's advice, there was nothing Inter could do about him.

When Auld's pass, in those opening minutes, looped through the air to Johnstone, lying slightly infield, he twisted right, away from Tarcisio Burgnich, and then left, to elude the Italian right-back's flailing attempt at a recovery challenge. Facchetti hovered behind them, like a dancer on his toes, wisely keeping his distance from the fray by leaving the hard work to Burgnich, who now found himself wrong-footed a third time, as Johnstone veered back on his tracks and again made for the outside. Burgnich was so disorientated by this latest change of direction that he almost lost his balance and had to steady himself by using his left arm to make contact with the ground and prevent himself taking a tumble – it was all too humiliating for such a distinguished Italy international. Johnstone then turned back infield once more and showed the dizzied Burgnich the ball again before laying it off to Auld, much to the Italian's temporary relief.

It was impossible not to be captivated by Johnstone's incessant invention, movement, trickery. Stein's focus on getting the ball to Johnstone smashed into oblivion the idea of the sides beginning the match with the equivalent of gentle, introductory formalities – Celtic were aiming straight for Inter's heart in deadly fashion.

'I always loved seeing someone going up to another player,' Johnstone said, 'skinning them, nutmegging them, going by them, coming back again, doing it again. That's what sport's all about – entertaining people. That's what people want – they want that all the time. It was all about that – it wasn't about trying to decry anyone or bring anybody down.'

Soon Johnstone was once again streaking towards the Inter penalty area. This time he was purposeful and business-like and, confronted by Picchi, he cut inside to evade the sweeper, just inside the Inter box, danced round Angelo Domenghini's flailing challenge, and, menaced once more by the persistent Picchi, let fly with a low shot with what he called his 'bad foot', the left, a shot that Giuliano Sarti, the Inter goalkeeper, managed to hold at the second attempt. Picchi, whose body had been contorted grotesquely through attempting to charge down Johnstone's shot, scampered back clumsily, off-balance, from his prone position to provide cover for the goalkeeper, looking panicked, flustered, for the first time in the match.

All of that crafted magnetism from Johnstone had been packed into the opening five minutes – at one stage he had had five of the legendarily tight markers of Inter forming a wide circle around him but with none of them willing to take the responsibility of tackling this little football fury – and before the clock had ticked towards its sixth minute he would top all of those earlier efforts with an unexpected flourish. Bobby Lennox, switching momentarily to Johnstone's usual beat, darted down the right wing and crossed for the diminutive Johnstone to send a header angling in the direction of Sarti's top right-hand corner. The goalkeeper arched backwards and got his fingertips to the ball to propel it up from underneath his crossbar and over for a corner-kick before rocking back on his heels in temporary relief.

'I used to go out after training at Celtic Park,' Johnstone said, 'and just run with the ball, twisting and turning, sprinting with it, keeping it up, using my head. I'd carry out five, six seven different exercises. The whole thing about the game is mastering the ball. Everybody talks about "one-touch" but to me that is a lot of rubbish. All the tactics in the world mean nothing – if a manager tells the players to go here, there and everywhere – if you cannot do anything with the ball when it comes to you. To me, it's about control and to get that you have to work with the ball all the time. When you get that, it doesn't matter what way the ball is coming to you. I stand by that – because I did it. I proved it.

'When I was a boy, I had no distractions. I feel sorry for modern kids, with all their distractions and if their parents can take them places. They become lazy. I went out in the hail, rain, snow and played with a ball all the time.

'I always worked at my game. For example, when I was starting out, as a teenager, I could get past a player but within ten yards, he would get back to me. So my father gave me a pair of his miner's boots and I used to play in them for half an hour every night and do 50-yard, 100-yard sprints in them. It strengthened me – so I could get away from players. After five, six, seven weeks, I really felt the benefit of that. I also did press-ups to strengthen my upper body. And where we had played Cowboys and Indians as children, I found a metal bar and used that [as a weight] to build up my strength too. I worked all this out for myself. Nobody ever taught me anything in my life. I did all that from an early age. No coach ever came up to me and said, "Here, I'll show you this."

'One thing I always did, when I was working with the ball on my own, was to put myself in a match situation and not do anything at half-pace. I always imagined there was somebody chasing me and I was trying to shake them off and somebody in front of me and I was trying to go by them. You knew when you had done it well but if you didn't, you would go back and do it again and again until you got the right feeling.'

Now, Tarcisio Burgnich was respected throughout Europe as a hardman with finesse, a player of physique and dedication, a hitman in shorts who was ready to rub out anyone through assiduous man-marking. Where had he been at the point when the little Scot had climbed up for his header? The match was only minutes old, the players were fresh and so Burgnich ought to have been buzzing with concentration. Yet the winger had been allowed to hover, entirely alone, on the penalty spot, of all places, then given a 'free' header as well. Burgnich had been yards away, looking distracted, as Johnstone had climbed to head and Gianfranco Bedin, looking askance, spread his arms wide as if to ask his teammate just what was going on. It was an early indication that the Italians' well-laid plans were going awry.

As if to stress that there would be no let-up, Johnstone, following Sarti's save from his header, went across to take the corner himself and played it short, to Auld, but when the winger received the return ball, it was Johnstone whose stray pass conceded possession. Inter capitalised by breaking sharply to secure the penalty-kick from which Sandro Mazzola gave them the lead.

It is one of the stranger aspects of the final that, from then on, Johnstone all but disappeared from sight, as far as someone with such an eye-catching style and appearance possibly could. He certainly kept working away for the team, dragging Burgnich all over the place, but rarely was Johnstone seen again on the ball and causing the kind of havoc in the Inter defence that he had done in the early stages.

His admirers had to satisfy themselves with thin rations of his genius for the remainder of the game. It would be unfair to say he failed to get another touch, but he had lost that early incisiveness and threat. The persistent attentions of Burgnich, who followed Johnstone everywhere on the field of play, appeared finally to be paying off and there was some evidence too that the heat took its toll. Johnstone's attempts to go past Italian defenders began to look tired, unenergetic.

It is tempting to suggest that this tussle between Tarcisio 'the Rock' Burgnich and Jinky Johnstone was uneven – to portray Jimmy Johnstone as an artiste of a footballer, thus delicate and fragile and likely to be fragmented by crashing tackles. That would be to underestimate him. Anyone fortunate enough to meet him would be struck by his chunkiness, his resilient physical strength. Small and compact he may have been but Johnstone was powerfully muscular – blunt physicality held no fears for him.

'Jimmy was a hard wee guy,' John Clark says. 'He was solid, with a strong body on him. He'd come back at you – he wouldn't let you away with anything.' His advanced professionalism could also be easily overlooked – as a young player at Celtic, his pre-match preparation involved stretching, immersing himself in a cold and then a hot bath – 'so that you were tingling' – followed by a massage.

'I didn't have a particularly good game in the Cup final,' Johnstone admitted self-effacingly, 'simply because it was a hard, tense game. It was down to man-to-man marking too, which was difficult to play against. We forwards did our bit but the people who really excelled there were the midfield and the full-backs. They had a field day but we had to be up there in the packed areas, trying to take men here, there and everywhere to create this space. Doing what I wanted to do – running at them – that was cut to a minimum. I had my moments in the game – the header, a couple of dribbles and this and that – but it's all about it being a team game.'

CHAPTER 15

A Grand Overture

The opening ten-minute passage of the final had done nothing to disabuse the Italians of the idea that the outcome of this match was pre-ordained in favour of their pedigree, poise and class. Certainly Celtic were fiery and energetic in the early stages: the Scots' tackling had been sharp and purposeful. But Inter would have expected that from a determined provincial outfit in any cup tie; and to those who favoured the Italians, facing Celtic was much the same scenario.

Yet there were signs, even then, that Celtic were attempting something unusual. Jim Craig, the right-back, had appeared at the furthest extremity of the right wing to curl over a cross that was, ultimately, too long, while Bobby Lennox, the outside-left, had popped up on the same right wing to cross for a tiny winger, Johnstone, occupying the position of centre-forward, to head for goal. Nor was there anything forced about it, as if players were squeezing uncomfortably into ill-fitting disguises. It all looked supremely natural and smooth and effortless.

Still, the better efforts on goal were from the Italians in those early stages: a flashing header from Sandro Mazzola after less than three minutes for which no blame might have been truly attached to Ronnie Simpson, the Celtic goalkeeper, if it had beaten him low to his left, rather than him scooping the ball away. Mazzola had used the pace on the cutback from Cappellini to meet the ball squarely with his forehead and send it pelting downwards, fast and hard – the perfect header, which Simpson had shuffled away, almost clumsily, with his left hand. It was encouraging to Inter that they had cut open the Celtic defence at only the second attempt and that doing so had proved so simple. When the ball had met Mazzola's intelligent brow, the player's assertive header had symbolised how Italian willpower was intended to dominate the Scots – and Simpson's scruffy response had appeared to confirm how Inter were up against football's equivalent of country cousins. Herrera had pinpointed Simpson as a figure who was a possible weak link in the Celtic side but this early test of his powers had seen the goalkeeper shape up strongly.

'It was just early in the game, wasn't it?' John Clark says of that incident. 'He [Stein] said, "Just watch because they'll try and catch you on the break." That was maybe one instance where what he was trying to tell you would happen, actually did happen. After that, they were closed down. We never saw that again because everybody then did their job properly. We did the things that we were good at.'

Then there was the raking move out of defence – classic Inter – when, after Johnstone's corner was intercepted, they had whisked the ball upfield with brisk and unfussy efficiency. Mazzola took the ball from Mauro Bicicli and went wheeling along freely in midfield, before sending a smooth pass down the right channel for Cappellini. Jim Craig got too close to the Italian as the winger took the ball and, in a simultaneous movement, whipped it away from the Celtic full-back to head directly into the penalty area. Craig collided with the Italian and made no protest at the decision of Kurt Tschenscher, the referee, to award a penalty-kick; a clear suggestion, in the moment, that the defender knew there was substance to the German's award.

The Celtic player cut a resigned figure, alone with his gloomy thoughts, near the goal-line, as a series of his teammates took it in turns to do combat verbally with Tschenscher in protest at the referee's decision. Stevie Chalmers, in particular, protested long and hard, before Billy McNeill intervened to push him roughly away. Cappellini, in the interim, was being hauled gently to his feet by the Inter trainer and doctor, as if he had collided with a juggernaut rather than tripped over Craig's boot. Gemmell, after confronting Tschenscher, gave the linesman a long, hard stare but throughout Craig remained mute, ambling slowly from the goal-line on the left of Simpson's goal across to the edge of the 18-yard box on the other side of goal, where he looked as sheepish as this university-educated, supremely self-confident individual might ever do.

Simpson, hand on the shoulder of the outraged Clark, settled for a mere quiet word with the referee before barking at his teammates to give up on their futile quarrel with the official. Perhaps this was the confidence of the goalkeeper who was sure he could pass the test of saving the penalty. If so, Simpson's hope was misplaced. Mazzola limbered up, running on the spot, then sprang forward gently over the turf, angling his body so that it appeared he was going to sweep the ball low, with his right foot, into the right-hand corner of Simpson's goal. 'I'm not sure he made clean contact with the ball,' Billy McNeill would say of Mazzola's penalty but, even if not entirely intended, Mazzola brushed the ball into the other side of goal, leaving Simpson only to collect the ball from the back of the net. There had been only 6 minutes 20 seconds on the clock when Tschenscher had made the award and almost a minute of protest had passed before Mazzola could take the penalty. The Italian had been put off briefly by Simpson moving around on the spot prior to the kick being taken – Mazzola had never seen that done before – but still looked utterly unruffled in sending the ball past the goalkeeper. Seven and a quarter minutes had been played and Inter looked in charge.

'The team that scores the first goal,' Stein had said before the match, 'will win the Cup.' It looked a dizzying blow for Celtic.

At that point, Celtic's urgency could be mistaken for haste; their rapidity at moving the ball forward for unfocused enthusiasm. 'These men from the north,' Herrera had said prior to the final, 'run as if they want to be the first men on the moon.' It was a comment that contained a hint of contempt together with a degree of apprehension. The Italians, in contrast, were unhurried and, even at this early stage in the game, indulging in the frippery of the occasional backheel, carried off successfully. It looked for all the world as though Celtic's energy would fade, not least in the broiling sun, and that class would out. Inter must surely have thought so.

The only drawback in having cavalier full-backs, such as Jim Craig, is that cavaliers tend to treat the more mundane tasks in life with a haughty disdain. It was never, though, a habit of Jock Stein to accommodate luxury players. He expected Craig to produce, on a consistent basis, the flair and dynamism of an unpredictable, attacking wide player in combination with the steady, solid, sensible approach of a real roundhead of a defender.

Craig would later argue that the actions of his that resulted in the award of a penalty had been an example of sensible defending: seeing Internazionale counter-attacking swiftly and efficiently, Craig had been equal to the Italians' quick-thinking, and had switched to the left side of the defence to cover for Tommy Gemmell, grounded after crashing into a tackle on the edge of the Inter penalty area. Craig alertly spotted

Cappellini's intention of making a run from the centre of the attack to the right to take advantage of Gemmell's absence and Craig, with alacrity, pursued the Inter striker along the edge of the Celtic 18-yard box, like a heat-seeking missile. The full-back's intention was to guard against a pass from Mazzola, who was hovering on the ball, waiting to wound Celtic by sending Cappellini free to carve open their exposed flank.

Craig matched the svelte Cappellini for speed but as the Italian went to take Mazzola's pass with the outside of his right boot, he moved towards his teammate and away from Craig, drawing the diligent Craig with him. When Cappellini then veered immediately back towards Craig, almost in the same motion, the Celtic man was in trouble. Perhaps surprised by the Italian's sudden reversion to his original pathway, Craig was caught too close to him and when Cappellini pushed the ball into the penalty area, Craig had the option of clipping the forward's heels or pulling out of a challenge and allowing Cappellini to run freely in the direction of goal. It looked like a well-practised dodge by Cappellini straight from Serie A. Craig, caught in the midst of a micro-second crisis, tapped the Italian, who rolled over . . . and over . . . again . . . and again . . . and again . . . and once again. Kurt Tschenscher, the referee, pointed to the penalty spot.

'What did you do that for?' Stein asked Craig after the game. The full-back would insist that he had merely angled his body to ensure that Cappellini would bump into him if the Italian attempted to get the ball on to his preferred left foot. 'He collided with me,' Craig says. 'I didn't tackle him or anything like that. I just angled my run so that the two of us would bump into each other. Very few referees would have given a penalty for that so early on in a European Cup final.'

While Cappellini writhed on the ground, Craig, with his back to Tschenscher, gathered the ball and was on the goal-line

to the left of Simpson's posts when he was arrested by the referee's whistling for the penalty. Craig listlessly kicked the ball back
in the direction of the penalty spot and then strolled, seemingly
uninterestedly, away from the revolving scrum of protesting
Scots and clamouring Italians, making no comment to anyone
and glancing at the scene like a passer-by noting a futile street
dispute that has nothing to do with him. Craig then took up
position on the edge of the 'D' in anticipation of the penalty
being taken. Bent over, with his palms resting on his thighs, he
appeared resigned to Celtic's fate, duly executed by Mazzola.
'Yes, it was a penalty,' Tommy Gemmell stated.

'It was definitely a penalty,' Billy McNeill concurred. 'We
would have wanted a penalty for that but them scoring meant
that we had no option but to push forward and we had players,
like wee Jimmy [Johnstone], who could destroy anybody.' Not
to mention the potency of Craig himself, as a supplement to
the attack.

The late, speedy and dynamic run was one of Craig's special-
ities as a Celt and his arrival in the team for the final had been in
that mould. Injury had consigned him to the sidelines for much
of the first half of 1966 and he had missed the tour of North
America that summer owing to his commitments as a student of
dentistry. Willie O'Neill, at left-back, had been a revelation on
the tour and had remained in that position throughout Celtic's
autumn fixtures, with Tommy Gemmell flying along at right-
back, in place of Ian Young. Craig, with his final examinations
looming and under pressure to pass, had been provided with
a fully paid sabbatical by Stein, on the kindly advice of Jean
Stein, the manager's wife, but, following the defeat to Dundee
United on New Year's Eve 1966, he had been carefully inserted
back into the side, with O'Neill jettisoned ruthlessly by Stein.
During his time off, Craig had gone on extensive runs around
Bellahouston Park and Pollokshields and this, he believes, built

up the type of stamina that enabled him to make run after run in the European Cup final.

It had been hard on O'Neill, who, after seven years with Celtic, had finally been enjoying the chance to establish himself in the first team. Proprietor of a grocery shop in Govan, O'Neill had contributed steadily to the victories over Nantes and Zurich, in Craig's absence, yet Stein might always have had in mind the return of Craig once his studies were complete and he had qualified in dentistry. His athleticism and pace were exactly what were required of a Stein full-back.

'Jock always had this idea that he wanted his full-backs to come forward,' Craig says. 'I'd always overlapped – I'd always got a row at school for doing so, even when I was playing at centre-half. It was something I continued to do when I went to Celtic Park. Full-backs traditionally didn't get the ball very much so if you got it, you weren't going to give it away to anyone.'

Craig, in Lisbon, time and again went roving down the right and Helenio Herrera, with a close-up view of Craig immediately in front of his bench, just behind the touchline on Celtic's right flank, must have felt immediately apprehensive at this privileged sight of the force his opponents were unleashing. Stein's use of Craig as a flying full-back was similar to the type of *catenaccio* for which Inter were famous but now upgraded and enhanced with a fresh dimension of athleticism.

With a player such as Craig who has highly developed athletic abilities, it is often tempting to damn them with the faint praise of being a running machine but Craig was an elegant passer of a football. It was he who had sent a pristine 40-yard pass confidently into space for Bobby Lennox to collect and then use to deliver the cross from which Johnstone's early header forced Sarti into an agile save.

There was little sign of Craig suffering unease or a whittling away of his confidence in the aftermath of his conceding the penalty. With his lithe, elegant, long-distance-runner's frame, the distinctive Celt was soon picking up the ball on the right and driving again at Inter, setting up Celtic's first scoring chance after the goal. He threaded the ball diagonally through to Bobby Murdoch and the midfielder's 20-yard, left-footed shot cleared Sarti's bar. This was a match in which Craig did very little wrong – except for the concession of the penalty – and he would eventually have the opportunity to make up for that.

'Jock never forgot that it was a battle,' Craig says. 'He never forgot that it was a contest as well as a game of football. He would go into a lot of pre-match detail about the opposition but just before going out he would say to you, "By the way, I don't think this guy's too brave so let's see with your first tackle how brave he is." You must always use everything.' Craig's Inter opponents would agree that in Lisbon the player carried out those instructions to the letter.

CHAPTER 16

Keeping Calm

'What time on Saturday, boss ... if selected?' Ronnie Simpson would ask Jock Stein. It was a simple, accurate reflection of the Celtic goalkeeper's outlook. Simpson blended consistency and dedication with the experienced professional's wariness of a game in which complacency was any player's greatest and most ever-present rival.

Simpson's worn face testified to the vagaries of a career that had already spanned more than two decades by the time of the 1967 European Cup final. With his lined and creviced visage, he could have been taken for a jockey or a sailor; someone who has spent life facing into the wind. Now, in Lisbon, at the age of 37, he was seeking to add further to the two FA-Cup winner's medals he had collected at Newcastle United in the 1950s. 'All I want from the game is another couple of years,' Simpson said in 1967, adding wittily, 'and if life really does begin at 40, I could then start my career all over again.'

The declaration from Jock Stein before the 1967 European Cup final that meeting Internazionale would be no more difficult than confronting Rangers was a cheeky one. The manager's intention was to reduce the scale of the task to a large but manageable one; but Simpson might have gone further and compared it to facing Ayr United or Stirling Albion and in doing so he would have been entirely respectful of the Italians because when he walked out in the Lisbon heat that afternoon, clutching his peaked cap, he was preparing for a stint on the turf that would be no more taxing physically than facing one of Scotland's more modest clubs.

Many of a Celtic goalkeeper's matches in the Scottish league and cup competitions were of a nature similar to that which Simpson would face that day. The testing thing was to ensure that concentration levels were maintained at the highest level throughout the 90 minutes so that on the sporadic occasions when the opposition did manage to break through and threaten the Celtic goal, they would be facing an imposing final barrier.

Simpson had made vital saves time after time over the season, often in matches in which he was troubled only once or twice. Yet if he had failed to remain focused, Celtic could have lost a goal – and lost a game.

Bony and light of frame, with a rather long, lugubrious face that fitted well his dry humour, and popular with his team-mates, Simpson was quiet, in the main, off the field but would talk his defence volubly through every game. Jimmy Simpson, Ronnie's father, had won league championship medals as a centre-half with Rangers before the Second World War and that heritage, plus Ronnie's vast experience, accumulated over two decades, made him, behind the unflustered John Clark, one of the points of extreme calm in a team that was sprinkled with vibrant, excitable extroverts.

Ronnie seemed to have done everything before his late-career stint at Celtic. He had even spent a spell on loan from Queen's Park to Rangers as a teenager but the Ibrox club had decided he was not what they required. His amateur status at Queen's Park allowed him to perform in the Great Britain team at the 1948 Olympic Games, in London, before he progressed to Newcastle United and then back up the east coast to Hibernian, where he had been jettisoned by Jock Stein. Not only could Simpson recall being dumped by the Hibs boss but he knew that Stein also had a deep distrust of goalkeepers, bordering on hatred.

'He hammered the goalkeepers in training,' John Clark says. 'He really punished them. For some reason he wanted the goalkeepers to get more work than normal.' Stein, to whom control was everything, felt that he could set his team up to perfection but that the one aspect of a football team for which he was entirely unable to legislate was the doings of the man between the sticks, who could fritter away all the good work that had been done by those in front of him. Still, such was Stein's admiration of Simpson that the manager described his goalkeeper being 'as great off the field as he is on it'. It was high acclaim for a man who stood only 5ft10in tall and who was dwarfed when walking out on to a football field; alongside people such as Tommy Gemmell, Jim Craig and Billy McNeill, Simpson looked seriously small – a 'wee guy'.

It was understandable, then, that despite establishing himself as Stein's near-immovable number one, Simpson would state, only a few weeks before the 1967 European Cup final, that he remained uncertain of his place in the team. 'I still don't consider myself a regular at Parkhead,' he said. 'A first-team pool is operated at Celtic Park and I just play from game to game. I could be out at any time.' This despite his not having missed, at that point, a league match for fifteen months. 'At times, I've thought I couldn't go on much longer,' he said, 'but I can honestly say that I may have another year or two left in the game. I am as fit – if not fitter – than I have ever been and I am enjoying the game more than ever.'

So, having expressed his confidence in a goalkeeper whom he

felt he could finally trust, what thoughts must have been coursing through the mind of Jock Stein when Simpson put his own inimitable stamp upon the European Cup final with a moment of goalkeeping eccentricity that would have had the manager gasping for oxygen if executed at lowly Forfar or Brechin, never mind in the grand setting of the Estádio Nacional, Lisbon?

It was a moment that Stein must have dreaded. The first half was almost up and Celtic were pushing for an equaliser, when they were caught out by a moment of basic football from the usually elegant Giacinto Facchetti, of all people, simply hoofing the ball from the edge of his own area high into the air, for it to drop, like a bouncing bomb, midway inside the Celtic half. With Angelo Domenghini haring forward in pursuit of the ball, Simpson advanced to meet it, trapped it under the sole of his boot, concentrating visibly, as if trying in slow motion a new and slightly tricky dance move, drew the ball back behind him cutely and backheeled it out to Celtic's left flank, where John Clark collected the ball and got another Celtic attacking move underway.

'I was annoyed that because we only had two cameramen we didn't get every instance in the game,' says film-maker Jimmy Gordon. 'Ours was the only colour film [of the 1967 European Cup final] in the world but we didn't get the bit for when Ronnie Simpson backheeled the ball. Jock actually was annoyed at that. I said, "I'm sorry we didn't get that." Jock said [with one of his growls], "Just as well – he should never have done that."'

It looked reckless and it looked risky but it fitted perfectly with the endlessly creative, intuitive, instinctive approach displayed all afternoon by Celtic. More practically, with Domenghini expecting Simpson to belt the ball away, the goalkeeper avoided, through his backheel, the Italian charging the ball down just as Simpson was about to strike it. It was reminiscent of the flick of a bullfighter's cape that sent Domenghini careering blindly forward: continuing on his driving run, he was visibly bamboozled at finding no ball at his feet or anywhere in his vicinity as he continued to run into space. Once the Italian had put the brakes on and was ambling sheepishly back, Simpson eased gently, carefree, across Domenghini's path, back to the sanctuary of his penalty area.

'It was clever, wasn't it?' John Clark says of Simpson's piece of improvisation. 'That was him being so calm. That was typical Ronnie. He was good, great. You don't know how you do things at times and, just instinctively, he's done it. Can you picture it if he had made a mess of it, though? He'd have been the forgotten man by now, wouldn't he? He'd have been in the books all right – the bad books. No, I knew what he was doing because I was shouting that I was coming to the side of him. So he knew I was there because I was giving him a shout.'

Clark avers that if Simpson's clearance had been intercepted by Domenghini and the Italians had gone into half-time 2–0 ahead, Celtic would have found it almost impossible to get back into the match. That moment, for all Simpson's sangfroid, emphasised how dangerously Celtic lived in pursuit of the equaliser. It made them marvellous and admirable but had they lost a goal on the break they might also have appeared foolhardy rather than brave.

'When Inter got the early goal,' Billy McNeill says, 'I think they underestimated the skill and the quality we had in the side. I don't think Inter expected the amount of creativity that was in the side.' Even from their prototype sweeper-keeper.

One of the many wonderful things about Celtic on the day was the way in which they refused to sit back and live off the interest accrued from such moments. They continued to press Inter relentlessly. A corner from Johnstone reached the head of Stevie Chalmers but the forward sent his header wide. At the resultant goal-kick, Tschenscher showed some worrying eccentricity. This was a referee who had stood back and allowed Pelé to be roughed up during Brazil v Bulgaria at the 1966 World Cup, an episode at variance with the referee's own view of his talents as an arbitrator.

'I had a clear and firm grasp of the rules and the ability to assert myself,' Tschenscher said. 'A referee has to be a person who commands respect. When the players heard that I would referee their game, they said: "Watch out, boys, take care!" I'm surprised how much today's referees are willing to take from the players. You must keep the players in check. Nobody could give me an earful.'

Here, after Sarti had played the goal-kick to Picchi, who was outside the penalty area, Tschenscher raced back to stop play and to tell Sarti to take the goal-kick again – it was a stricture against timewasting that had been ... a piece of timewasting par excellence! The Italians had done nothing to contravene the rules and it was therefore incorrect of Tschenscher to stop play and order a retake. Nor did it prevent the Italians using goal-kicks to melt away some moments – Picchi really put considerable artistry into every pass back to Sarti – crouching over the ball and clipping it with studied precision back to his goalkeeper. The passing of the ball back and forward between Sarti and Picchi from almost every goal-kick awarded to Inter became almost like a formal folk dance.

In other aspects, Inter looked less than efficient in terms of making time their own: curving one free-kick up the wing and out of play; giving the ball away directly to Celtic players. Yet, crucially, Inter had not conceded a goal – and to the Italians that was everything.

It was notable that Simpson's first notion, every time he seized the ball, was, almost in the same movement, to send it whirring away as swiftly as possible, often to Jim Craig at right-back, to get Celtic moving again. From goalkeeper to goalscorers, Celtic were designed to take every opportunity to get on the attack. It was how they had played throughout the season – apart from in Prague – and the presence of *La Grande Inter* on the same field of play was not going to stop them now.

It had been a busy season for Simpson, one in which he had won his first cap for Scotland, and against England, no less. He had been named in the Scotland team just two days before the first leg with Dukla Prague.

'I had put the thought of international caps behind me long ago,' he said. 'I was with Britain's Olympic team in 1948, so long ago I don't remember a great deal about the experience. I do remember the tremendous excitement of two [FA] Cup finals and nerves that disappear with the first touch of the ball. Newcastle, my team, won both finals in which I played – 1–0 against Arsenal and 2–1 against Manchester City. If there were highlights for me in the course of the games, I don't remember them. These games often seem like a blur afterwards.' Capping his cap, three weeks before the European Cup final, Simpson had been named Scottish Football Writers' Player of the Year, a rare accolade for a keeper.

On the grandest of all of his footballing occasions, Simpson cut an isolated figure, such was Celtic's domination of possession. Simpson was not only custodian of his goal but of his own and several teammates' 'falsers', which he had placed carefully inside his net. Dental care, at that time, was not all that it might have been and even these fit, healthy, young men rarely had all their own teeth. Simpson could reflect upon looking at his false teeth how he was not only highly fortunate to be in Lisbon but to be alive at all. He had played with them in place while representing Newcastle United and in one match a forward had charged him to the ground, leaving Simpson struggling for his life, due to his false teeth being lodged in his trachea. It required a quick-thinking trainer to identify the problem with alacrity and remove them before the goalkeeper choked to death.

There was no such alarm in Lisbon but the sultry heat must have been at least as great a problem for Simpson as for his teammates. The danger of wilting was sharply illustrated shortly before half-time when, on the Inter left, Bicicli played a free-kick short to Mazzola and the forward stood with his foot on the ball, almost static, seemingly with little clear intent, before darting towards the penalty area and clipping a low, right-footed shot in the direction of Simpson's goal, one that went weaving through four Celtic bodies and that might have taken an unkind deflection. Instead, it flew straight and true towards the right side of Simpson's goal and he crouched down, drawing its sting, quick to gather it up at the second attempt as Cappellini and Domenghini closed in, seeking to snap up any spilt crumb. It had been a long stretch since Mazzola's penalty – the last attempt on goal by an Inter player.

It was a key moment for Celtic, just as important as Simpson's decisive backheel. More than a few European Cup finals have been lost by the superior and more attractive side and if Celtic were not to go the same way, it would require serious concentration from numbers one to eleven.

CHAPTER 17

The Brush

Jock Stein had had his players together for the best part of ten days in advance of the European Cup final – a period during which onlookers might have expected him to be imparting deep and serious detail as to what exactly he would have been expecting from each of them on the day. John Clark confirms the opposite, with an amused smile at the thought of the Celtic players taking the field laden down with tactical baggage.

'"Just play the game how you see it." That's all I was told,' Clark says. 'When you think of the names you played against, that didn't bother you – you played against Pelé, Eusébio, Mazzola and all them, Jimmy Greaves, all of these guys . . . It didn't bother me . . .

'It was more or less up to me how to work it out on the pitch [as to where to position himself and whom to mark]. The only time he [Stein] would maybe change you a wee bit [in terms of providing specific instructions], maybe, would be if he wanted you to come out and mark a player, deeper . . . a midfield player. He would tell you to push out a wee bit. If the other player [the midfield player] was maybe a bit lazy going back the way [returning into midfield after joining an attack] he [Stein] would

223

maybe tell you to shut him down a wee bit but, other than that . . . he would tell you to work out your own way of doing things. It wasn't a case of "You stand right at the back [fixed in a certain position]." Nothing like that. Maybe Mazzola . . . would be lazy going back the way but he was clever on the ball so he [Stein] would maybe say, "Push out on him a wee bit [mark him tightly] to make sure that the space is not there."

'Also, if big Billy [McNeill] was nearer him at the time, you'd say, "Well, you take him and we'll look after this area here." It just came instinctively. It wasn't a case that he drummed into you, "Do this and do that." He gave you the licence and the knowledge to play where you thought it was of more benefit. It meant you weren't a bag of nerves, saying, "I'd better watch him." You just played the game as you saw it.'

One player whom Clark and his teammates did not have to worry about was Luis Suárez, ruled out of the final through a thigh injury sustained against Fiorentina four days earlier. The Spanish midfielder, crucial in dismantling Real Madrid's defences in the quarter-final, was Inter's prized possession, for whom they had broken the world transfer record six years previously. He had however been in rather patchy form over the preceding year, so much so that he had been in danger of being usurped as the main item on display at the San Siro – Pelé in 1966 had been offered US\$1 million to join Inter, bankrolled by Angelo Moratti, the club's oil-magnate owner, and the Brazilian star's club Santos had been offered the same sum to release him (£358,423 at the exchange rates of the day). Pelé had turned down his Italian suitors, saying that he did not need the money and did not fancy European winters.

'The truth is,' Tarcisio Burgnich insists, 'that Luis Suárez was injured for the match. He was truly the man who could make a difference to our game, our extra weapon. He launched our counter-attacks, he held the ball, he added colour to our game. We opened the scoring, that's true, but without him it was very difficult to leave our own half. And their right winger, Johnstone, he went on so many extraordinary dribbles . . . We felt besieged.'

It is not only a team's more colourful stars, though, who make the difference in any match and John Clark's understated performance in Lisbon emphasised that point. If Jimmy Johnstone was the blaring trumpet in the Celtic orchestra, John Clark was its rumbling cello. Johnstone's histrionic, high-maintenance, capricious presence was counterbalanced by the type of steady and unobtrusive contributions made by Clark, the team's soothing balm, an individual willing to submerge his identity for the benefit of smoothing his side's progress through each match. One of the greatest players the game has seen was happy to bear testimony to this.

'You maybe do not always notice him,' Pelé said of Clark, 'but he is covering quietly for other players and always there to stop a man.' Those words were uttered after the friendly between Scotland and Brazil in June 1966, when the two players had been in direct opposition and when Clark, on his debut, had had his usual quiet but effective game. Notably, Pelé, the man he had been marking, had had a quiet game too.

The quality of leadership displayed by Billy McNeill was vital to Celtic but it was Clark who was the beating heart of the defence. His job was to tidy up around him with his deft, unfussy brush-and-pan feet. 'Play to your strengths and disguise your weaknesses,' was always one of Stein's great mottos. Clark epitomised that aphorism.

'He hated people trying to play above themselves,' Clark says of Stein. 'He would say, "If you've not got that kind of ability, that's not your style, it never will be and you'll never achieve that. Do what you're good at and you'll be able to play and you'll be looked upon as a player."'

John Clark played the perfect game in Lisbon. He proved a steady, calming presence at the tiller, wonderfully composed on the ball, ineffably quick to read the play and one of the most fierily motivated Celtic players on the day, desperate to do everything in his power to earn victory. That was revealed glaringly when Clark proved to be the first to complain to Kurt Tschenscher, the referee, about the penalty award made against Jim Craig. Clark, softly spoken off the field of play, shouted and gesticulated in the referee's face before being hauled away by Bobby Murdoch. He then shouted in the direction of the linesman before returning to snap at the referee and this time it took Simpson to emerge from his goal to restrain his sweeper. Hands on hips, a figure of fury, Clark awaited the penalty and, with Mazzola easing into position to take it, Armando Picchi ambled over in Clark's direction as if to communicate to him that, for all his protests, understandable as they may have been, it had indeed been a penalty. Picchi employed body language to signify relaxed authority in intimating that it was futile to resist the idea of defeat to *La Grande Inter* now that the Italians were in front.

'I don't know if I was more motivated for that one than in most games,' Clark says of the European Cup final. 'You wanted to "get there" [to win]. People say, "You played right in behind people" [in the Celtic defence],' Clark says. 'I didn't play in behind. I tried to anticipate the passes and played where I could make sure I could be in the areas [of attacking threat] all the time.'

If there were any concerns that Clark might lose his concentration in the face of the perceived injustice of the penalty – he proved to be an agitating presence around the referee once again after Mazzola had stroked the ball into the net – they were dispelled by the manner in which he swiftly picked up his performance.

Celtic looked rather ragged in the immediate aftermath of the goal and when a misdirected McNeill pass went straight to Mazzola inside Celtic's half, Clark retrieved the situation by entering fiercely into a tackle on Mazzola that stopped the Italian dashing in the direction of the Celtic goal.

'When you see defenders winning tackles,' Jimmy Johnstone said, 'you get a bit of confidence and you say, "It's our day." I think it's the same for defenders when they see you in front of them going by players and skinning them – they're getting a boost, they're getting a buzz.'

Such was the singularity of the occasion that Clark, defender par excellence, could even be seen going for goal. A clever pass from Bertie Auld was played into his path during the first 45 minutes and, finding himself in space inside the Inter half, Clark collected the ball and edged forward cautiously as befitted a man who rarely ventured out of his own territory, to a point where he was 25 yards out from goal and could try, of all things, having a shot on target; this in a European Cup final from a man who had scored a mere two competitive goals in his eight years as a first-team player. The shot proved to be a less than smooth action but it forced a block from Picchi, using his left heel, and it had a telling effect. The Inter man was still regaining his bearings as Auld scooped up the rebound and, using Picchi's temporary disorientation, went veering round the Inter captain and then Mauro Bicicli for a left-footed shot that flashed off the face of the bar. After an uncertain spell, Celtic had clearly re-established a foothold in the game and Clark had played a vital part in providing the platform for that.

'Good players?' Clark adds wryly as he thinks back to the day and Inter's stellar performers. 'Their guys were all top-bracket. [Giacinto] Facchetti, the left-back, [Tarcisio] Burgnich, [Armando] Picchi, [Giuliano Sarti], the goalkeeper, [Mario] Corso; they were a fair old team. . . . [Angelo] Domenghini had a bit of pace all right. He was up against big Tommy [Gemmell]. That's what I'm saying. We knew what to do. He [Domenghini] would maybe get a bit lazy and let Tommy go forward and that's how they catch you on the break [by catching the full-back out of position as at the opening goal]. So you'd maybe come across and mark that area; not mark him, mark the area, so that if the ball is going to get played in, you were round about the area, where their danger was going to be. You knew where to be – you understood each other. You knew what you were doing. I think it was just that your brain was working all the time seeing situations – "Get there! Get there!"'

There is barely a Celtic move in which John Clark, the brainiest of footballers, was uninvolved. He could be seen administering a small shove, when and where necessary, as doled out to Domenghini in the vicinity of the halfway line, or gathering a long, aimless ball from Picchi, almost at the corner flag on Celtic's left flank, then unfussily turning the play over by bringing the ball out of defence with alacrity, feeding Jim Craig, taking the return, feeding Bobby Murdoch and starting another attack. This is uncontestable evidence of a footballer, in the truest sense of the word, at work. Such interventions took place almost unnoticed, as the fans looked to the glittering whirl of Celtic's attackers for more eye-catching entertainment. And so it went on for the duration of the match: Clark as both defensive and attacking fulcrum of the Celtic team. 'The Brush', a most appropriate nickname for this most tidy and neat of players, was operating with magnetic bristles, fully aware that a single slip would allow the Italians to punish Celtic.

There was no flaw in this diamond at the heart of everything Celtic did. When, shortly before half-time, Clark's clearing header was picked up by Sandro Mazzola, the Italian saw the opportunity presented and surged in the direction of the Celtic goal. Clark stood tall against the maestro, mobile yet immovable, forcing the Italian to hesitate over what to do, with Clark standing off him expertly – just far enough to make it impossible for Mazzola to commit the defender but close enough to present the forward with a sizeable obstacle. Mazzola dallied, like an uncertain gambler, trying to decide whether to go right or left. When he chose his right he veered straight into Clark's tackle-trap, the sweeper squeezing the ball away and defusing yet another potentially dangerous moment.

There was no more fervent disciple of Jock Stein than Clark, who saw the manager as 'a kind of father figure'. Stein, Clark suggested, 'made us more tactically aware. It was no longer just about going out on to the field and playing. He asked you to think about how you play and how you play your position and explained it all to you on a tactics board. He asked you to try to think for yourself and you found you developed your game and your concentration got better.'

That high level of concentration was evident throughout proceedings in Lisbon and Clark's crispness contrasted dramatically with the lassitude displayed by Armando Picchi, his opposite number. The Inter sweeper was determined to hang on to the ball, slow things down as far as possible whenever the ball came within his sphere and do little to get the play rolling forward for Inter.

'Big Jock would maybe be looking for the likes of our full-backs,' Clark says, 'when they did go forward, to go forward with a purpose and that they didn't get caught out too much. When they did go forward, you'd be thinking, "I'll just go across a wee bit and maybe a wee bit more that way, so that the space is shut down." We had two full-backs that didn't want to come back the way, they just wanted to bomb forward. More or less you were just kind of looking after things, you know.'

CHAPTER 18

A Question of Balance

It was midway through the first half that the 1967 European Cup final began to settle into a groove. Celtic had the ball; Inter the concealed threat. Tommy Gemmell shot into the side netting and a Bertie Auld shot zipped over the Inter crossbar to be palmed down by a besuited man behind the goal, who let it bounce and then, with fine accuracy, on the volley, directed it straight back to Giuliano Sarti, who caught it on his foot and then let it bounce away from him so that he could respond with a serious glare in the man's direction, a visual warning to all behind the goal that he did not wish to have the ball returned to him swiftly. In such moments as that and in their delaying of the taking of goal-kicks, Inter were already showing a desire to slow the game down and waste time and to sit and brood on their one-goal lead.

Both sides, at that point, could still be relatively happy with how the game was going. For Celtic, Bobby Murdoch and Auld were beginning to have a greater influence on the play, having taken over from Johnstone as the main prompters of Celtic's attacks. Gemmell was enjoying a growing attacking involvement on the left flank, but Celtic's efforts on goal, such as that shot into the side-netting from Gemmell, the one that cleared the bar from Auld and one that went chirruping high and wide from Johnstone, had still left Sarti and his defence largely untroubled.

'We were getting through the Italian defence but our final pass was just that wee bit out,' Stein said. 'The task had been hard enough but to come back from the penalty was a true test of the team's calibre.' It was a characteristic of Italian football to allow the opposing team to have the ball until the final third, when the tackling would become tight and tough, and so Inter still looked sleek and confident. Neither side was on top – Inter were slowing the game down, as was their wont, while Celtic were still performing at pace, as was theirs. Inter must have thought, more than ever, that the Scots would surely tire, that the heat would inevitably have its effect.

In forcing attacks, and using full-backs in advanced positions, Celtic were also leaving gaps at the back that might still be exploited by Inter's pacy attacking trio, but on 34 minutes Celtic almost levelled. It resulted from a move that was pure, distilled essence of Celtic on the day: Simpson, as clearly instructed, gathered a loose ball on the edge of his own penalty area and swiftly recycled possession by hurling the ball out to Jim Craig on the right, whose exchange of passes with Murdoch led to the midfielder's cross into the heart of the Inter penalty area, where Domenghini, back in defence, headed the ball towards the edge of the penalty area. It fell for Gemmell, hovering 15 yards from goal, to catch the ball perfectly for a volley that found a clear route to goal between Domenghini and Willie Wallace but which made Sarti stretch flexibly to his left and turn the ball round his post in considerable style. 'I still don't know how he got to it,' Gemmell said.

'We were told before the game,' Bobby Lennox says, 'that Inter had one weakness and that that was the goalie but in the game, their goalie was great.'

High in the main stand, Jimmy Gordon, Celtic's appointed film-maker, was enjoying this encounter in Lisbon's fairy dell, convinced that the match was going to reach a propitious conclusion. 'Well, I thought there would be a fairy-story ending,' he said. 'I remember once interviewing Billy McNeill, earlier on that year, over at his house, and I remember saying to Billy, "There's something about Celtic – there's a fairy-tale quality." When you look back at things like the Coronation Cup, they won that – not on form – and they had a habit of pulling things out of the hat.

'My feeling was that there was something magical about Celtic on the big occasions – that they would win things that they weren't expected to win. It was, for me, blind hope rather than any rational belief in superior ability. You had the feeling that sheer willpower was going to get them through. The actual final, to go a goal down and then come back at Inter the way they did . . . I was with the Celtic party – Bob Kelly, Des White, that brigade – about four or five seats below where the Cup would be presented. The game was tense, a blur.

'We had started off doing this half-hour film on the club's origins and then they started doing quite well in the European Cup and they said would you like to come to Czechoslavakia for the Dukla Prague game? I then said, "I think we should try to cover the final."

'Normally, you would need about six people working on one camera, let alone the number of people you would have nowadays. Well, we had one cameraman and his brother, as an assistant. The night before the game, I said, "Mr Kelly, we don't have any passes for the camera crew." So he approached Hans Bangerter [general secretary of UEFA] and explained that this was a film for Celtic consumption and Celtic supporters and he wrote out the two passes in the name of Cinema Celtic and that's what I called the company that did the film.'

On the field, Celtic also continued to improvise and to rewrite the script, re-emerging after the half-time break with renewed spirit after their brief encounter with Jock Stein, who was always precise, succinct and to the point with his instructions.

'At half-time we were despondent,' Billy McNeill said, 'because we thought the penalty they'd won was a wee bit dubious, to say the least, but big Jock was not willing to entertain the idea of us dwelling on that decision. He wasn't a person to be negative. It had been sickening to us to lose the penalty. At half-time we were all having a go at the referee, giving him pelters. It took Jock time to calm us.

'He told us that we had been the ones on top in the game, that we were running it, and that it had only been [Giuliano] Sarti that had stopped us getting the goal that we had deserved on the basis of our play and performance. Most importantly of all, he insisted that we would get the breakthrough that our play deserved in the second half as long as we kept playing the same way.' Stein had told his players much the same during the interval in the match with Vojvodina, when it had been something of a confidence trick to coax out of them a new and improved performance in the second half. It had worked and in Lisbon, when Celtic resumed the match, as against the Yugoslavian champions, they swiftly swung into unrelenting attack.

McNeill was not having his best game ever in a green-and-white shirt. Not that it was his worst, simply that it was not really his type of game – that was more the encounter with Rangers, say, in mid-September 1966, when the Ibrox side hopefully – or hopelessly – hit cross after cross into the penalty box for the magnificent McNeill to head clear time and time again. Internazionale were different. This was a team that relied largely on guile and craft, cute cutbacks, backheels and penetrating passes performed with the telling precision of a master surgeon. The Celtic captain looked slightly uncertain, nervous almost, as he attempted to settle into the flow of the game.

It would still have been utterly unimaginable for Celtic to have won the European Cup final without McNeill. A top-level football club is like a well-run nation, with a collective consciousness that imperceptibly acts as a guide through the most testing of moments and Celtic had desperate need of McNeill, on that day in Lisbon, to provide his inimitable leadership, endless enthusiasm and sense of purpose.

Rock-like hardness as the cornerstone of the Celtic defence had made Billy McNeill an indispensable figure in Jock Stein's team. His role as Stein's eyes and ears and the manager's direct link to the players was reflected in the extra salary he was paid surreptitiously by Stein for his duties as captain. It is indisputable that he was worth his money – his almost stately bearing commanded respect among teammates and opponents alike. As a young Celtic player, he had been nicknamed Cesar by his teammates, after the suave actor Cesar Romero, but the name had mutated slightly into Caesar, the conquering Roman emperor, as McNeill grew into his leadership role at Celtic. There was an almost indefinable quality about McNeill, a complicated mixture of humanity and aggression, commitment and restless energy, natural enthusiasm and a formidable intelligence that lifted and encouraged those around him in an inspirational rather than a dictatorial fashion. He had the indefinable quality of exuding leadership, was utterly loyal to Stein and regularly reinforced the manager's own authority.

'His ideal is to have eleven good footballers who will blend into a hard-hitting unit,' McNeill said of Stein in the autumn of 1966, 'but with a sufficiently sound technique to allow for individual expression. I think it is the extent to which Jock Stein cares about us and for us which makes us so determined to do well for him and the club. The boss won't invite us all to sit down and then tell us what we'll do. We will, in fact, all get the opportunity to say what we feel, to disagree with one another if we want to and to ask his advice. Under Jock Stein's leadership, nothing is impossible.' Prescient stuff.

Billy McNeill was much more than the stern, watchful man on the bridge of the ship. His thoughts on football and on life in general, allied to his intuition and respect for people, made him a compelling presence. He was an enthusiast, high on life, a hard competitor in football who would nevertheless express his delight at seeing the Christmas trees lighting up house windows during the festive season. At parties in the house of Mike Jackson, his great friend, opposite the Queen's Park, McNeill would leap, in fun, at the great globular paper lampshade in the hall to re-create his heading feats on the field of play.

A simple ambition for her son's working life had driven McNeill's mother. She simply wanted him, she said, to be in a job where he wore a collar and tie. It was a desire to see her son progress into professional life that led to his working, as a teenager, in office management for an insurance broker in Charing Cross, Glasgow, the busy business adjunct to the West End of the city. McNeill had been presented with a real dilemma as to whether to remain there and go full time or opt for signing as a professional with Celtic. Having done the latter, he would bring the same commitment to training as he did to a match, launching into powerful, physical aerial challenges that would see him clatter into teammates who did not expect such a juddering replication of reality in a practice setting. By 1967, McNeill and John Clark had played together in Celtic's central defence for almost a decade and had a near-seamless understanding with one another.

McNeill would later comment that he could easily have sauntered through the European Cup final while reverting to his office gear of collar, tie and suit. It was a match that McNeill described as 'the easiest of the season' but John Clark, in contrast to McNeill, maintains that the encounter with the Milanese side was extremely testing. That was perhaps because this was a game that drew more on Clark's complementary talents of interception and positioning; the intelligence agent alongside the commanding officer.

CHAPTER 19

Taking the Initiative

En route to the dressing room at half-time, the Celtic players had angrily informed the Inter men that it had not been a penalty and Bertie Auld continued a conversation with the referee with the second half about to start. The midfielder, though, had now become calmer, less agitated, as he chatted steadily away. That mirrored a resolve within the Celtic players to approach the task of dismantling Inter patiently. Stein had soothed the bristling backs of his underdogs and convinced them to channel their energy constructively as a means of righting the perceived wrong that had been done to them.

'We were playing too much into the ruck of the Inter defence,' Stein said. 'I told them to keep the crosses back a few yards from the wall [of Inter defenders].' The manager had been 'reasonably happy' with the team's performance in the first half.

Consistently Celtic had started slowly in European Cup matches that season, sometimes losing goals. This was a slow-burning team but one that, once revved up, would hurtle along rapidly, almost unstoppably. That was true but the excellence of their football that season meant that they had only ever been behind in ten matches. Even then, they had always recovered a goal quickly. They had never been behind in any game for as long as they were in the match with Inter and the longer that went on, the more it would play on their minds.

Inter were also renowned experts at holding on to a single-goal lead – it was their preferred situation in a match, although Herrera had told his players that they would need to score more than once against this Celtic side. Giuliano Sarti, Armando Picchi and Mauro Bicicli had all been timewasting noticeably before half-time and this was where the battle between the managers began to be won and lost, with Inter sitting deep and Celtic told by Stein to keep attacking.

'Inter were a tremendous side,' Tommy Gemmell said, 'they just oozed class, but they played like we tried to play in the second match against Dukla and there wasn't a side in the world that could afford to give us as much of the ball as they did without being beaten. We had nine potential goalscorers and they gave us the ball.'

Within seconds of the restart, with Celtic pressing hard, referee Tschenscher's ongoing lack of serious control was further evident when he blew his whistle for a Celtic free-kick to be taken. Five of the nine-man Inter wall were already rushing towards the ball at that point and Gianfanco Bedin was so far advanced that he could block Auld's shot, after Wallace had played the kick short to him, and the ball flew away to Billy McNeill on the left side of the Inter box. The Celtic captain neatly clipped it back to Tommy Gemmell on the edge of the penalty area, and his coolly played shot caught the foot of Armando Picchi and began travelling goalwards only for Sarti to stretch backwards and gather the ball on the line. When Stevie Chalmers appealed for a goal, the normally unflustered Facchetti, along with Sarti, yelled and gesticulated furiously in the face of the Celtic man. Inter were becoming rattled as the contest became, increasingly, an epic one to see whether Celtic could score or Inter hold out.

'In the final,' Bobby Lennox says, 'the shots all came from Tommy Gemmell, Bobby Murdoch and Bertie Auld. Playing against the Italians, big Jock said, "You make sure you keep moving guys and moving defenders." The boys further back got lots of shots on goal because the Italians were playing [in those parts of the field] where we were moving them. The thing is, a lot of teams would not have midfield players or defenders who could come and do that [shoot accurately on goal]. Our players could come and do that.'

When Lennox did get on the ball he did not waste his moments in the sun. When, in the first half, a Bobby Murdoch curved pass dropped to the ground fractionally outside the Inter penalty area, Lennox brushed it with his shins into the path of Willie Wallace, whose 20-yard shot forced Sarti into a fine, leaping save.

'He [Stein] always wanted me just to keep running across defenders,' Lennox says, 'running behind defenders, just keep working them, off the ball. Jock always felt that football was not all about the man on the ball. You need movement and move- ment creates room and that's how footballers play.'

Lennox was a fine reflection of the discipline that Stein had instilled in his team. A dedicated professional, Lennox was the perfect player for any manager to handle in that he barely required guidance, only a prompt or two to follow instructions. Not that this goalscoring winger was an automaton; this was a player whose initiative enabled him to perform both as a winger of singeing pace while also an unerring and regular goalscorer; two players in one.

'I think you feel underdogs playing Inter Milan in the European Cup final,' Lennox says, 'but in our camp, I think the boys all knew, "We've got a lot of good players here." I felt we could have gone anywhere and got a result. We'd beaten a lot of good clubs.' But could they beat the most formidable club of all?

The game became ever more fierce. John Clark hurled the ball in the direction of the grounded Sandro Mazzola after the referee had given a foul for a challenge on the player by Bobby Murdoch. Petty infringements began to litter the game – not what Celtic wanted but precious to Inter. A handball here, a trip there from the Italians slowed the action as time ticked away but the Inter players were viscerally aware that what Herrera would call 'Celtic's force' was quite different to anything they had ever met before.

'We had the strong impression,' Sandro Mazzola says, 'especially during the second half, that the match was being played solely in one half – ours. They played with a variation on the classic Anglo-Saxon 4-4-2 because their two wingers – Johnstone on the right and Lennox on the left – played really like wide attackers. As a result, [Tarcisio] Burgnich and [Giacinto] Facchetti were plagued by their speed. Giacinto, who represented at that time our attacking left-back, was unable to make a single attacking move into the opposing half. Celtic had the ball all the time.'

That friendly match between Celtic and Zagreb three months previously, played on a cold winter's night in Glasgow, was now having an influence on the European Cup final as Celtic turned up the heat on Inter even further in sweltering Lisbon. Against Zagreb, Stein had sought the means to use the flanks and midfield in a more dynamic fashion but the experiment had failed on the night because the forwards had been static inside the penalty area, making that area overcrowded and cramping the team's style. Stein had learned from that and now, against Inter, the forwards had been instructed by the manager to go roving here, there and everywhere, freeing up plenty of space for the full-backs and midfield players to come forward and enjoy uncluttered space in which to shoot.

A telling incident occurred on the hour. Murdoch flopped a lame, left-footed 25-yard shot well wide of Sarti's left-hand post, the ball moving slowly enough for one of the photographers – an innocuous-looking figure with a paper hat on his head and two cameras slung around his neck – to tap the ball, left-footed, back to Sarti in the Inter goal. As in the first half, the Italian erupted in anger at this seeming good deed, a mini Vesuvius, battering the ball away with his right boot and rounding on his antagonist with fury for returning the ball so swiftly.

The match was aflame with tension. Stein felt that 'some desperation was creeping into our play at this stage and a goal was badly needed'. Tommy Gemmell, in the vicinity of the halfway line, went to tackle Gianfranco Bedin but missed the ball and then swung his left boot at the Italian, sending him to the ground. Bedin writhed and Gemmell roamed away in the immortal style of footballers who know they have committed a bad foul, determinedly not looking left or right until almost back into position, before venturing a quick glance round to see Tschenscher, the referee, scribbling in his book; it appeared to be a booking for the left-back. Bedin was attended to by a couple of Inter's backroom people while McNeill snapped at the referee in long-suppressed anger and Gemmell made the return journey to the scene of the crime to display some concern for his stricken opponent, patting him repeatedly on the back.

Tschenscher, when he had finished writing, held up his fingers in the direction of Gemmell as if to say he had noted his name yet the following day, on running into Tschenscher at the airport, Gemmell would be told by the West German that, no, he had not booked the Scot. That begs the question as to what was being written down at that point. UEFA confirm that there were no bookings in the final.

Bedin was down for a good minute before getting to his feet, tentatively moving around stiffly as if to shake off the pain. When the free-kick was taken and the ball arrived at his feet, he was suddenly gamine as a young deer once again.

Patience and persistence were as elemental to that Celtic team as their attacking flair and it finally told. With slightly more than an hour of the match having passed, Willie Wallace moved to take a throw-in on Celtic's left wing, near the corner flag, Aristide Guarneri, the Inter centre-back, followed him over.

Wallace had the intention of throwing the ball directly into the penalty area to provoke further panic in the Inter defence but the hulking Guarneri stood directly in front of him like a silently threatening and confrontational bouncer; the Italian blotted out the forward's view of the penalty area and prevented him following his intended course of action. Tschenscher did nothing. Wallace was forced to throw the ball back to Gemmell who spread it wide to Jim Craig, who then moved the ball on to Murdoch.

Nine of the Inter team were now back in their own penalty area and it was Angelo Domenghini, an attacking player, who dispossessed Murdoch on the corner of the box only for the ball to bounce away to Jimmy Johnstone, scuttling backwards. He passed it back to John Clark, close to the halfway line, and he bisected two Inter men in giving it back to Murdoch to feed Craig on the right. The full-back gathered the ball and ushered it into the Inter box until he was around 14 yards from goal and confronted by a hastily assembled defensive phalanx of seven Inter players plus Sarti, all scrutinising Craig's feet and body for a hint of what he might be about to do. Gemmell, meanwhile, had come powering forward all the way from the back.

Stein, at half-time, had advised his players to consider cutting the ball back to the edge of the penalty area because Inter were crowding the heart of the box – and this was a case in point. And so, Jim Craig, being a thinking player, and also clever enough to remember his manager's words, did exactly that. Craig coolly disguised his intentions until the time was right and then released the perfect reverse pass into the path of Tommy Gemmell, who came hurtling on to the ball to catch it perfectly with his instep and send it fizzing over Sarti's right shoulder and into the corner of the Inter net. The Italian goal-keeper made a valiant attempt to get to it and almost did so but, this time, even he could not keep the ball out.

Craig leapt in the air joyously at the sight of the ball hitting the net, arms swinging, relief at his redemption expressed in his rotating body. This was a man who considered himself not a passionate individual, who would stand back and keep his own counsel in the dressing room when those such as Auld and Gemmell were letting fly with their fast patter; a reserved, intel-lectual figure. Not at that moment – and no wonder because Craig's timing of his pass was almost as important as Gemmell's crisp and accurate striking of the ball.

'Three times I shouted to Jim to square it to me,' Gemmell said, 'and he held it and held it and held it . . . until he gave me a great pass, cutting it back to me while I was at full tilt. I hit it with my instep, as hard as I could, and when I did I was confi-dent that it was on target. It was a tremendous feeling to score because as soon as the ball hit the net I knew we were going to beat them. There was a clear difference between Inter's attitude to losing a goal and the attitude we had shown after Mazzola's penalty had gone in. It was strange – you would expect to see a bit of spirit from a team fighting for its life in a European Cup final.'

Sarti rolled over on the ground and stretched out both arms in an indication that two Celtic men were offside and, technically, he was perhaps correct – two Celts had been on the edge of the six-yard box as Gemmell hit the ball with the Italians pushed in front of them – but neither had been interfering with play. Sarti might also have questioned Picchi, supposedly the symbol of defensive reliability, advancing towards Gemmell but then stopping and turning his back in anticipation of the full-back's shot. Had he continued, more bravely, Picchi was in line to block the Celt's effort. At half-time, Gemmell had enjoyed a quick shower, peeled off his sweat-soaked strip, put on fresh kit and replaced his leather-studded boots with rubber-studded ones. There had been a commensurate freshness and energy about the shot that cruised past the previously indomitable Sarti.

The performance of Tommy Gemmell in the 1967 European Cup final epitomised Celtic on the day. He may have been categorised as a defender but there was nothing in the left-back's nature to take a safety-first, defensive approach to life and he carried the same approach on to the field for a game of football.

Gemmell had been nerveless in advance of the match with Internazionale and it showed in his subsequent performance.

'I think Inter were happy to be facing us in the final,' Gemmell said. 'Facing a team from the Scottish League, they would have gone into the game thinking that they were going to control it.' Few did more than Tommy Gemmell to disabuse the Italian side of that idea.

It is an oddity of that game, then, that Gemmell proved to be the final Celtic player to get a touch of the ball at the start of the game. Four minutes had elapsed before Gemmell got his first touch and, even then, he employed it only to execute the most basic of passes. Once he had wriggled his way into the game, though, Gemmell exerted an influence that made the overlapping forays of Giacinto Facchetti, the Internazionale left-back, look like the ham-fisted efforts of a well-intentioned amateur. As Facchetti and his fellow Italians faded, Gemmell simply got better and better.

'I could have had a hat-trick,' the ebullient Gemmell said.

Time and time again, Gemmell forged down each wing, occasionally being toppled but more often powering irresistibly past watery, weak challenges and endlessly seeking to convert Celtic's possession into the hard currency of a goal.

'It was a perfect example of what we'd spoken about at half-time,' Stein said of Gemmell's equaliser, 'the ball getting cut back, away from the defence with the oncoming defender getting a clear look at the goal and Tommy Gemmell certainly made a good job of it.'

It was typical of Stein to be so calm, controlled and cool in his judgement of a moment so sublime and stylish that, with a full-back streaking up the pitch to score a forward's goal, it contained within it everything that he had conjured into imagination as manager of Celtic.

CHAPTER 20

Facing the Chop

'If you look at the game up until Tommy scores,' Bobby Lennox says, 'we've played well and made good chances. It was just a matter of one of those chances going in. See, once that went in, I think the boys thought that was the game won.'

Celtic continued to pursue goals. Craig, again zipping down the right wing, fed Murdoch and his shot screeched over Sarti's crossbar. A Murdoch shot, left-footed, caught perfectly on the volley, went bending beautifully towards the same corner of the net that Gemmell had troubled but Sarti proved to be its equal, revolving across his area to flip the ball up and over the bar. All of this had happened within two minutes of Gemmell scoring.

'At this stage of the game,' Stein said, 'even if we achieved nothing other than keeping the Inter Milan team working hard, we were bound to come out on top even if it went to extra-time. This thought didn't make us afraid at all. It would only be to the Italian team's advantage to slow the game down as they were hopelessly unfit compared to our players. It would be dangerous now to let them off the hook.'

There was no possibility of Celtic relaxing now that they were on level terms and after his save from Murdoch, Giuliano

Sarti lay flat-out on the ground, exhausted by his lengthy after-noon's work – and by the knowledge that it was still far from over. When he got to his feet, Wallace sportingly applauded him but there was no respite for Sarti. Within seconds he was sprawling on the turf again after saving a low, left-footed shot from Gemmell.

'It took us a long time to break Inter down and that is a testimony to how good they were,' Billy McNeill says. 'They also carried a lot of luck.' That view is confirmed by Tarcisio Burgnich, the Inter right-back. 'I remember that, at a certain point, Picchi turned towards our goalkeeper and said, "Giuliano, we had a chance but the chance has gone. Sooner or later, they are going to score the winning goal." I had never imagined that I would hear those words, never imagined that my captain would tell our goalkeeper to abandon hope; to throw in the towel. But that showed how badly we had been destroyed by that point. And that our agony was only being prolonged.'

Inter were now a passive presence on the field. Facchetti did win a free-kick on the left wing but when Mario Corso took it, he lazily drifted the ball into the heart of the Celtic penalty area, far too close to Simpson, who leapt to clutch it under no pressure at all. Much more dynamically, Tommy Gemmell, unconventionally, even for this game, collected the ball in the left-back position, and went galloping forward all the way from back to front. The Inter players melted away from him although Corso made a fluttering, cursory attempt at a tackle on the half-way line, the equivalent of an indolent traffic policeman waving a finger at a speeding motorist. The Italians allowed the Scot to advance to 30 yards from goal, where he pinged a left-footed shot over the bar. Picchi knocked the goal-kick long, only to see Gemmell collect it and come hurtling back at the Inter defence. The Romans must have experienced something similar when confronted by the Picts.

'They were competitive,' John Clark says, 'and among themselves you could see them getting on to each other and the boy
that moaned a lot was a boy called [Gianfranco] Bedin. He was
kind of yapping, the boy in midfield. There was no way they
could get out of their area. We just kept coming at them and
coming at them but you had to be alert in case they did catch
you once or twice.'

A freakish goal almost came Celtic's way as the match
careered towards its conclusion. Gemmell, on the left wing,
scooped out a high, left-footed cross that veered over the heads,
collectively, of Sarti, Facchetti and Lennox and on to the crossbar, from where it rebounded to the feet of Bedin. Inter now
looked half-hearted, discouraged, while Celtic were driving
forward incessantly, but threat still lurked in the flashing feet of
the Inter attackers.

Nothing, though, could discourage Celtic. Bertie Auld, as
confident and impudent as ever, teased Mauro Bicicli by revolving his left foot over the ball, repeatedly, on the run before
cleverly bringing his right foot over the ball and clipping it,
almost in reverse, to Murdoch on the left side of the penalty
area. He, in turn, had Armando Picchi dangling, as if on the
end of a string, before pelting a left-footed shot at Sarti that
the goalkeeper parried desperately. This pounding of Sarti's
goal was now becoming routine. Within ten seconds of that
Murdoch shot, Gemmell had fed the hungry midfielder for a
second shot from the same angle and again Sarti clawed the ball
away manfully. 'Never in my long career have I been hit with
such a barrage of shots from every angle,' Sarti said.

Johnstone drove at the Italian defence and lost possession to
Picchi. As the Inter captain eased away with the ball, he jerked his
left elbow, nastily, into the Scot's face leaving Johnstone clutching it in pain. It was the Italians who were really hurting now,
though, their pride wounded, but they could find no respite.

So when a low ball from the left, delivered by Tommy Gemmell, stole into Inter's six-yard box it prompted serious alarm, like a fox in a chicken coop, among the Italians. Aristide Guarneri attempted to shuffle the ball back to Sarti but Wallace intercepted, got in between them and nudged the ball goalwards. Sarti, in desperation, stretched out on the turf, appeared to try to clutch the ball from the vicinity of the forward's feet and when that proved impossible, he grabbed Wallace's right leg with both hands – a clear infringement for a penalty. Tschenscher did nothing and the ball was hooked away by Bedin. Sarti draped a consoling arm across Wallace's shoulders and then spread his arms wide theatrically as if in silent admission that he had got off the hook with that one.

'I thought the referee was bad in the European Cup final,' Bobby Lennox says. 'That was a stonewall penalty.'

Ten minutes remained for Celtic to crack Inter's defence but Sarti, ignoring Armando Picchi's suggestion to him that defeat was inevitable, remained steadfast, unwaveringly defiant in the face of all that Celtic might wish to throw at him.

Central to all this pressure on Inter was Bobby 'Chopper' Murdoch, whose influence rarely waned despite a severe early collision with Mario Corso, on the edge of the Inter penalty area. As both players stretched for the ball, Corso's foot came down heavily on Murdoch's right boot, leaving the Celtic midfielder in agonising pain for the remainder of the match. His foot would become so swollen that he feared that if he took the boot off at any point, to attempt some pain relief, he would be unable to put it back on. With only a substitute goalkeeper allowed, that could have been a deadly blow for Celtic. There was no complaint from the hardy Murdoch. That would have been inappropriate – after all, in his determination to make a mark on the final, he had himself had a couple of chops before that at the ankles of Mauro Bicicli and Mario Corso.

'Our team, with Auld and Murdoch and people like that,' Bobby Lennox says, 'always tried to play through teams rather than simply hold on to the ball. That excites you more. People get more excited when the ball is in the box. We faced teams whose players tried to get the ball off us so it made sense to take the game to them and play it in their half. We were fortunate to have players who were built to be like that.'

Murdoch could look heavy, ungainly, off the field but he would be transformed by the presence of a football. 'Jimmy [Johnstone] was the most spectacular of the Celtic players,' Jimmy Gordon, Celtic's film-maker that year, says, 'but people like Murdoch ... I remember in the film doing some slow-motion stuff because the sheer balletic grace of somebody like Murdoch suddenly just swerving, was brilliant. There were a lot of great football brains in that team. You felt total confidence in them.'

Of all the Celtic players in Lisbon, Bobby Murdoch seemed to have the most space and time when taking possession of the ball. Partly this was because he was operating largely from just within his own half but partly because he had such masterful control of the ball, looked so relaxed when on it, that it was transmitted clearly to opponents that it would be futile to try to encroach on Murdoch's footballing space. In doing so, they might also face the chop.

CHAPTER 21

The Final Flourish

It is too easy to fit a narrative to a football match after the game has gone. A winning goal for Celtic was never inevitable. As Celtic chased the winner, they received warning that Inter too might strike the decisive blow. When the languid Mario Corso – 'he plays in the shade of the San Siro' as the Inter fans' slogan went – took a free-kick, wide on the right, midway inside Celtic's half, he drifted the ball expertly into the Celtic penalty area where Angelo Domenghini extended his long right leg into the air as he stretched to the full, opening out his body like a giant pair of scissors in trying to get to the ball. The ball was a mere inch away from his toe. It needed only the slightest touch to divert it past Ronnie Simpson but it eluded him and Inter, boats against the current, were soon attempting to repel a tide of Celtic attacks once again. None of Celtic's previous heavy pressure would have counted for much against the hard fact of an Inter goal – and victory – at that stage.

'To go and win a game,' Bobby Lennox says, 'you've got to be prepared to lose it. If you send people forward, you're going to be short at the back.' Almost as a reaction to the Dukla match, Stein had committed Celtic to blanket attack in the final – at numerous points, there were only two Celtic defenders in their own half.

With five minutes remaining, a tired-looking Renato Cappellini was played offside close to the centre-circle. Billy McNeill took the free-kick, placing the ball on the edge of the circle and making a simple pass to Murdoch, midway inside the Inter half. The Italians looked frazzled now and the midfielder was unhampered as he sent the ball out to Gemmell advancing up the left wing. He was confronted by Aristide Guarneri and then Mario Corso at the corner of the 18-yard box. Their idea, clearly, was to block the direct route to goal but Gemmell, as with Craig before him, followed Stein's simple instruction to think about cutting the ball back. Gemmell held the ball steadily, performed what he described as his 'Ali shuffle' in honour of the boxing great, and then slotted the ball in reverse to Murdoch, on his toes just outside the box and ready to let fly with his left foot. It cut through a cavity in the Inter defence and looked to be going wide until Stevie Chalmers nipped in behind the Inter defence, stuck out his right boot and deflected the ball gently past a stranded Giuliano Sarti.

'When the ball left Bobby's foot,' Chalmers says, 'I had a feeling that it was not going to be on target. I was on the blind side [of Gianfranco Bedin] as the ball came across and he never twigged that I was moving round him. He was not paying attention to me. I stayed just far enough away from him to stop him making a block but I think he was ball-watching anyway. I hit it first time, with the instep of my right boot and it went to the left of Giuliano Sarti. The ball was in the net before I knew it.'

After Chalmers' goal, Armando Picchi, the Inter captain, crumbled to his knees, a sign of a thoroughly defeated man.

'We'd do that at least three days a week in training,' Bobby Lennox says of the drill that saw Murdoch sweep the ball low across the face of goal for Chalmers to edge it past the goalkeeper. 'It was great for the forwards – Stevie, myself, Wispy [Willie Wallace], Joe [McBride] before he got injured, big Yogi [John Hughes]. The boys would play it to Big Jock [Stein] and he would send them away and they would smash it across. Wee Neilly [Mochan, the trainer] would be on the other side and we would be in the middle smashing it in. It's not as if the ball came across goal and Stevie was lucky to be there. We also cut balls back every day at training [as at the opening goal]. And it worked. It just shows you – practice makes perfect.'

Greed and selfishness are seen as positive qualities when it comes to strikers in the game of football but Stevie Chalmers proved that a goalscorer can be both a rounded person and an effective player. There were few greater testimonies to that than his performance in the 1967 European Cup final, when he sacrificed the prospect of personal glory in favour of the all-round requirements of the team – and ended up scoring the most important goal in the history of Celtic Football Club.

Chalmers had been instructed to rove around but to stay out of the penalty area during the final in Lisbon – his task, as with Willie Wallace and Bobby Lennox, had been to provide a distraction that would move the Inter forwards around and create space for his teammates.

Throughout the afternoon of 25 May in Lisbon, Stevie Chalmers obeyed scrupulously the instructions of Jock Stein. His role, he had been instructed, was to act as a decoy: to stray away from the penalty area and take his markers into wide areas that would leave space for the midfielders and the full-backs, when they came powering through, to use their momentum to shoot for goal. Yet just as Celtic's first goal came from Tommy Gemmell using his initiative to subvert one of Stein's rules – that only one full-back could attack at a time – so too did Chalmers' winning strike.

When Chalmers put the ball in the net, he had had enough roving around the pitch everywhere from the full-back position to the wing and finally, in frustration, reverted to the position of striker where he most naturally belonged, nipping round Gianfranco Bedin with the stealth and suddenness of a cat to deflect Bobby Murdoch's cross-shot past Sarti.

'I had had enough of veering here and there, away from my position, and not really getting on the ball very much,' Chalmers says. 'I decided that the time was right for me to get back where I belonged. Maybe the last place the Italians expected me to pop up by then was in the heart of their penalty area. All afternoon I had been making runs to free up space for other people and now the favour had been returned beautifully.'

It remains, even now, so strange to consider that the Celtic forwards were ghostly presences at this feast of attacking football. Willie Wallace was used to feeling the heat both as a former foundry worker and as a footballer who liked to be where the tackles were warmest. So, as a maker and creator of goals, the 1967 European Cup final was the equivalent of providing an artist with a blank canvas but failing to supply them with paints. As with Stevie Chalmers and Bobby Lennox, his fellow forwards, Wallace was instructed by Jock Stein to push himself away from the heart of the action to its fringes. It was an unfussy role, one that demanded that Wallace subsume personal glory for the benefit of the team.

A lack of a supremely eye-catching appearance or style could make Wallace sometimes under-rated by the public. 'Well, he wasn't under-rated by us,' would be Billy McNeill's testy retort if confronted with such a suggestion.

The last of the Lisbon line-up to join Celtic, Wallace had also been closer than all of his teammates to missing out on the opportunity to perform for Jock Stein's grand new team. On the day before Celtic made their European Cup debut against

FC Zurich in September 1966, he had scored twice in a 7–2 Heart of Midlothian friendly win at Newcastle United and had Newcastle fans chanting his name – their club had been linked with him as a potential signing. His new home, he felt certain, would be somewhere in England: his restlessness – and that of several other Hearts players – had been long-advertised before Stein stepped in, in early December 1966, to pluck him away from Tynecastle and the Edinburgh club.

Upon signing for Celtic, Wallace stated that he had 'always wanted to play for either Celtic or Rangers. I don't believe in any of the fanatical nonsense about the two teams.' It was the comment of a true professional footballer. Once at Celtic Park, Wallace fitted in as seamlessly as if he had been at the club for years, his footballing intelligence allowing him to tune in, with digital precision, to the requirements of his teammates.

Always Wallace appeared to have an impish smile on his face when scoring goals and he was visibly relaxed at the Estádio Nacional. Wallace popped up here and there, now and then, throughout the match; a knock-down here, a flick-on there. Was he contributing next to nothing? No – when Auld veered left for the superb shot that slapped off the open face of the Inter crossbar in the first half, it had been Wallace who had dashed purposefully to his right to take Guarneri with him, clearing a path for Auld to go whooshing through and have a clear sight of goal.

And despite only glimpses of Wallace's skills being afforded to those watching, he was still involved in both Celtic goals. It was he who took the throw-in that led to Tommy Gemmell's equaliser and when Stevie Chalmers made one run to get on the end of Bobby Murdoch's cross-shot to score the winner, Wallace was making another run to take defenders out of Chalmers' path.

'Maybe I helped Stevie a bit,' Wallace says, 'by making a run to take a defender out of his way, but making decoy runs in the Celtic team of that time was done as part of our playing strategy. No matter who played in the team, we played for each other. That was our strength. It was nothing more than I would have done in many other games.'

It had been a brave strategy on the part of Jock Stein not only to attack a talented, confident and well-organised Internazionale team, but also to gamble through sacrificing his forwards in doing so. By the closing minutes, the stresses and strains of the entire enterprise had begun to tell on the Celtic manager. He was visibly tense and looked down at the ground beneath his feet, drawing patterns in the sandy gravel in front of the bench with the toes of his shoes. This contrasted with the ebullient figure who had gesticulated and instructed from the bench and who had looked fresh and confident at the beginning of the match, striding out on to the field of play, crisply dressed, wearing dark sunglasses and exuding the air of someone shaping his own destiny.

'When we lined up at 2–1 and we were all cheering,' Bobby Lennox says of the aftermath of the goal, 'big [Giacinto] Facchetti came up to centre-forward and you looked at the Italians and they looked exhausted. We were shouting to each other, "Just get the ball into the corners; we'll chase them into the corners." You thought, "They've gone. There is no way they are going to come back at us here." They had world-famous players – Mazzola, Facchetti, the wee outside-left [Domenghini] – but we played better on the day.'

From the restart, Facchetti gave the ball to Mazzola and he, at least, looked busy, eager as he took the ball into Celtic's half. Quickly his efforts at attacking were splintered, shattered against the flinty Celtic defence. Auld took the ball on and fed Chalmers and when he went coursing infield, he opted for a 25-yard shot that went just wide of Sarti's goal.

Again Inter sought to move forward but Guarneri's slack, slipshod pass aimed at Mauro Bicicli on the left was so poor that it drew a gesture of frustration from the midfielder. Corso, who appeared to become more lackadaisical than ever following Chalmers' goal, hooked a slothful pass, like something from the warm-up for a training game, from the left wing into the middle but only found a Celtic jersey. As Inter continued their desultory efforts to creep out of their own half, Bicicli lost the ball to Gemmell and Auld streaked away towards the penalty area, only to be upended by Tarcisio Burgnich. Auld rolled over three times, clutching his left thigh, to be dealt with by Neilly Mochan; treatment that required a full minute before Auld could regain his feet and tap the free-kick to Gemmell.

'Do you see that moat, twenty yards behind the goal?' Gemmell told Auld. 'This free-kick is going straight in there.' Subsequent to that, with time melting away, Auld expertly took the ball into the corner three times, suddenly looking static. When he finally conceded a goal-kick, Inter moved the ball forward through Gianfranco Bedin, who moved it up the wing for Cappellini but Craig and Auld converged on him just as Tschenscher's whistle signalled the end for Inter and the start of Celtic's celebrations.

At the final whistle, Lennox and Clark jumped into each other's arms, yelling, 'We've won! We've won!' Then Lennox, in a moment of mundanity, remembered that he had better retrieve his teeth from the back of the net. There was a real danger of several players attending the post-match reception in a toothless state as hundreds of supporters scaled the Estádio Nacional's moat and poured on to the pitch.

'Several of us had to run like crazy in the direction of Ronnie Simpson's net,' Billy McNeill recalled. 'Those with false teeth had left them in his cap for safe keeping so they could retrieve them swiftly for being pictured with the Cup, but Ronnie had forgotten about them in racing to celebrate with us. Fortunately, the teeth remained in his cap when we went to get them. It was amazing that his cap had not been taken away.' Amazing except that, on an exceptional afternoon, the highly unusual had become the norm.

CHAPTER 22

Dancing Class

It was fitting that Bertie Auld should be the final Celtic player to have possession of the ball during the European Cup final. It seemed as though he was rarely off it during the game. Not only that but there was something Italianate about Auld in the way he comported himself on a football field, which must have discomfited the footballers of Internazionale. Auld was an enormously refined player with a hard edge; swarthy; Latin in appearance; a snappy dresser off the field of play; and the pzazz with which he played the game must have left the Italians feeling as though they were looking at a mirror-image of themselves.

This was a player who danced with the ball as if he were its courtly suitor. Always available to give and to take a pass, he was matchless in Lisbon for sheer tailored style.

In one instance, early in the first half, he received the ball in the middle of the field, facing Mauro Bicicli, the opposing number 10. Bicicli, a few feet away, saw the opportunity to get in and harry Auld as the Celtic man was seemingly concentrating only on getting the ball under control as he received possession. Auld, who was taking the ball on his left foot, with Bicicli closing in fast, turned as if to hit the ball long with his left, as if he were entirely unaware of Bicicli's presence, but just as Bicicli went to block, Auld heeled it behind him, leaving the Italian helpless. This was a move that would one day become known as the Cruyff Turn. Maybe a 20-year-old Johan was watching with the rest of Europe, in Amsterdam that day in 1967?

Having executed that turn, Auld then had a great swathe of space in which to play and weigh up his options, almost at his leisure. Having looked around, he opted to take on a chastened Bicicli again, who now wished not to get too close to avoid further embarrassment. Auld, his new-found reputation creating a free path in front of him, glided forward, drew Armando Picchi out from defence and clipped a 25-yard left-footed shot goalwards, over the hands of the leaping Giuliano Sarti and only narrowly over the crossbar. It was one of a series of instances of Celtic giving Inter a shake that would, collectively, add up to a seismic rumble under the feet of the world's richest club.

'Johnstone is Celtic's best player,' Helenio Herrera, the Internazionale manager, had said after watching Celtic's 2–2 draw with Rangers on 6 May, 'but if I can put him out of my mind for a second – and it must be no more than a second – then Auld is a player who plays very well. The number 10 for Celtic is a formidable player.'

A hint that Auld meant to take the Italians on at their own game had arrived in the match's opening minutes. Inter had won a free-kick on their right and as Sandro Mazzola shaped to take it, Auld raced over to replace Tommy Gemmell and release the full-back into defence while Auld simply and boldly encroached on Mazzola. When Kurt Tschenscher, the referee, exhorted him to retreat, Auld made a conciliatory gesture but barely moved back any further. This was the type of gamesmanship at which Inter were expected to excel; not Celtic, not really.

Auld was a notably unenthusiastic trainer but on matchdays he provided Celtic with enormous vigour. Almost as notable as his efforts on goal was how expert he was at taking the ball for a walk. He would bring it under control and then put just enough pace on a touch to allow the ball to trundle alongside his beloved left boot on its own, no further touches required, keeping pace with him like a well-indulged pet trotting along beside its master. The level of control involved in doing this is notable but it also had a practical value as it enabled Auld to look up and around while utterly certain of where the ball was, knowing that it was there for him whenever he might need it.

'Each and every one of us was confident on the ball,' Auld says. 'The thing about Celtic Football Club in those days was that you had to have ability or you wouldn't have been there. The supporters were very knowledgeable when it came to football. Also, Jock Stein made you feel so important – he gave you alternatives all the time. We had experience where it matters and a solid backbone down the middle of the team.'

Another of Auld's tricks displayed on the day was a scissors dummy – going over the ball with one leg and then another on the run – and such moments, together with his natty free-kicks and enthusiastic persistence, helped gradually to pull Inter apart to such an extent that it is quite amazing that Auld was not particularly involved in either of Celtic's goals. He was also mighty unfortunate when, two minutes after Tommy Gemmell's equaliser, Auld confronted Bicicli at the corner of the Inter penalty area and shaped to move the ball to his right. Bicicli, by then, should have known better than to buy the dummy but Auld sold it to him anyway, shifting his weight slightly on to his left side before switching feet and prodding the ball past his Italian marker and along the white-marked perimeter of the penalty area. The flailing, disadvantaged Bicicli eased his body into Auld, who was clearly inside the box, and toppled the Scot, who, dumped on his rear, raised his arms in supplication to the referee, only a few yards away and with an uncluttered view of the incident. Bicicli turned his back on the game, seemingly resigned to having conceded a foul; the penalty claim would have been of a similar calibre to the one given against Jim Craig by Tschenscher. Bicicli's colleagues looked nervously on as the Celtic players appealed frantically to the official but Tschenscher, standing inside the penalty area, where Auld had been bowled over, raised his arm directly into the air to signal an indirect free-kick for obstruction rather than foul play.

'There was always laughter about with Jimmy and wee Bobby Lennox and Bertie, always fun,' John Clark says. 'Big Jock loved it as well.' An engaging, loquacious presence, Auld was the loudest of this Celtic team – and he had considerable competition. There was also a clever side to Auld and it was unsurprising to find him espousing the idea of education later in life.

Within a minute of Chalmers' goal, the relentless Auld was setting up the scorer for a left-footed shot at goal and in 88 minutes, when Auld was cut down by Tarcisio Burgnich, Auld lay prone for some time, to be attended to by Neilly Mochan, craftily frittering away a minute of time. After that, all that remained was for the streetwise Auld to take the ball into the corner three times to tick away some time before, finally, it actually was all over and Auld could go yelling to Stein insisting that he had been his best man on the day.

CHAPTER 23

Taking the Applause

The highly experienced Italians of Internazionale, who had been everywhere and done everything, had been enervated by the experience of facing this Celtic team. 'I have no strength left to talk,' Armando Picchi, the Inter captain, said at the end. A rhapsodic Tommy Gemmell, in contrast, enjoyed careering around the field for all of 45 minutes, cavorting cheerily with a mixed assortment of fans. He had been dehydrated by his throat-parching efforts and, bubbling along on the surface of a sea of jubilation, he spotted a mobile ice cream vendor and decided to make up for his loss of fluids. 'I'll have one of his ice lollies,' thought Gemmell, believing he would be allowed a 'freebie' given the occasion and his team's triumph. Instead, the vendor pursued Gemmell aggressively around the field of the Estádio Nacional for payment until a pressman handed over some money on behalf of the player.

Gemmell was not the only one seeking to capitalise on the chaos. Portuguese souvenir hunters had tried forcibly to remove the Celtic players' kit after invading the field with Scottish fans at the final whistle. Still seeking booty, they crammed into the dressing room, removing Celtic gear, as

Jim Craig entered in bare feet and John Clark with one boot missing.

'They were trying to pull your boots off as well and one of them did get one of the boots off,' Clark says of being simultaneously lifted on to the shoulders of Portuguese fans and relieved of his gear. 'There were a lot of Portuguese people there as well, a lot of Celtic supporters but a few Portuguese people on the field pulling away at people to get souvenirs. Big Jock saw it and tried to pull them away to give you a bit of space to get down.'

A planned post-match reception saw the day start to slow after so much intense action. The Inter players had arrived at the match in tracksuits and so had to go back to their hotel to change, making them arrive late and all the more like spectres at the feast. They smiled bravely through the hour-and-a-half-long reception. Herrera had been characterised in advance of the final as arrogant, blunt, gruff, disrespectful of opponents, but he was nothing less than sporting in the extreme following the final; indeed, he now proved statesmanlike and classy. 'There is no doubt about it,' he said. 'Celtic are worthy champions of Europe. They were terrific and all credit must go to Jock Stein. Now he is the master.'

Much would be made of the fine manner in which Celtic had played football in the final but, on the day, uppermost in the players' minds was the idea of winning and nothing else. 'I just wanted to win the European Cup,' Bobby Lennox says. 'I wouldn't have cared if it was an own goal or a deflection. I wouldn't have cared how we had won it. If [Giacinto] Facchetti had lobbed his own goalkeeper, I would have been quite pleased. It's nice to say we could have won 4–1 or 5–1. We won the European Cup. In big games, you just want to win; 2–1 was a great result.

'The only small regret is that we never got to parade the Cup because the supporters came on to the pitch. All the boys feel the same. Nobody would deny the supporters that – they had spent maybe a year's savings to be there – but it would have been nice to go on a lap of honour. That's the only thing that I'd have liked that didn't happen. I think, though, that, out of all the European Cup presentations, Billy going up to the top of that podium is the best of them. He really was like Caesar up there.

'People had come on to the field after the game and we had all tried to make for the dressing rooms. We had got down the stairs [from the pitch] when I swapped a jersey with one of the Italian boys in the tunnel. The changing rooms were strange – L-shaped, so some of us had to change in one section and the other five or six in the other. Afterwards, there were loads of people milling about and people didn't realise the Cup hadn't even arrived. Then Billy arrived with it. The thing is, you've beaten Inter Milan but I think it took weeks and weeks for it actually to register fully with us that we were the champions of Europe.'

For John Clark, 'the most disappointing thing ever was that you didn't get presented with your medals properly. We went to a restaurant with Inter Milan and they were later coming to it. You had the usual top table and, blah blah blah, all the speeches, and there was a box there from which you were to pick your own medal. That shows that UEFA let themselves down a wee bit that day.'

The evening had a dry end. The players collected their wives and girlfriends from a separate restaurant and then pushed through the crowds at the airport and back to Estoril, at 2am, to discover that the bar at the Hotel Palacio had closed. Half an hour later, the wives and girlfriends returned to the hotel – their flight had been badly delayed – and the players sat with them in the hotel lobby until around five in the morning. After an hour or two in bed, it was time to get up and back to Glasgow. 'People think you'd be painting the town red,' Bobby Lennox says, 'but it wasn't our best night. It happens.'

Jimmy Gordon's film would be the only one to preserve, in colour, the events of the 1967 European Cup final – and that it was to exist at all was a glorious fluke. An encounter with Robert Kelly, the Celtic chairman, had seen Gordon commissioned to make a film about Celtic but Kelly's intention was for the film to be a serious account of the club's earliest days. Instead, Gordon had been taken on a Technicolor ride all the way to the European Cup final to record a glorious present that had superseded a splendid past.

'There would be huge crowds for it at the cinema in Glasgow,' Gordon says, 'two shows a day and people queuing round the block. The interesting thing was that although everybody knows that Tommy Gemmell scored, three times a move goes down the wing and the ball doesn't go in and when, finally, the goal is scored, it was as though we were at the match [because of the jubilant reaction of the audience]. It took off. It was great fun doing it.

'Jock seemed to me to be thoroughly professional. I wasn't conscious of him relaxing but that was just a sign of his being a professional – he cared about what he did. At the end of it all, he said to me [of the filming], "You've done a good job."

'I said, "But, Jock, what a good job *you've* done."

'And he immediately said, "Aye but what do I do next season?" So he was immediately conscious of not being able to rest on his laurels. He was immediately conscious of the management of expectation, which nobody else was probably thinking about – so that is slightly revealing.'

The praise for Stein's players flowed like a river in spate. Kurt Tschenscher was effusive. 'Celtic were very easy to handle and are a credit to European football,' he said.

Around the world, there was delight and admiration for Celtic's doings. 'We wished them [Celtic] the win,' Vladimír Táborský, the Dukla Prague player, said, 'but it was still a surprise. Because Inter Milan were the team that garnered these trophies.' Josef Vacenovský, his teammate, adds, 'I wished them the win, because they beat us. So we actually ended up third.' Ivo Viktor, Dukla's thoughtful goalkeeper, was unsurprised by Celtic's win. 'Celtic rightfully won the final with Inter Milan,' he says, 'and was a top team at the time.'

Aberdeen were in the USA on tour when the news of Celtic's victory came through. 'We didn't get the game on television but when we heard that Celtic had won the European Cup we were very happy for them,' Bobby Clark says. 'They were a great team. I supported Clyde but Celtic Park was a place I could walk to when I was a boy. One of the Italian waiters at the Washington Hilton wasn't very pleased.'

Radivoj Radosav, out in Novi Sad, saw Inter capitulating to the type of game that had overwhelmed Vojvodina. 'Maybe we thought that Internazionale was a better team,' Radosav says, 'especially because we knew that Italians, with their style of play and very strong defence, will hardly concede a goal if they manage to take the lead. However, I think that, just like us, Internazionale also wasn't comfortable with the way Celtic played. Just like many other teams, they were unable to physically compare to Celtic.'

Sir Alf Ramsey, awaiting an international with England in Vienna, was warmed by Celtic's win. 'I got the impression that Celtic completely outclassed Inter,' he said. 'Celtic showed more determination, stamina, speed and enthusiasm. The England players were delighted and so was I.'

Celtic's victory was down to their combining the sophisticated ball skills and finesse of the southern European sides with the high work-rate and energy of the northern European – and specifically the British – game. This was an irresistible combination and it was the first time any side had done so to proper effect.

It helped that every one of the team fielded in Lisbon was of international class; and that, within that, more than half of those players were world-class. For those qualities to emerge, they had all required the clever, concerted effort on the part of a unique individual to make them click and whirr like the component parts of a graceful, smoothly-working machine.

'Without Jock,' Jim Craig says, 'none of it would have happened. You cannot be more clear than that. We just wouldn't have won the European Cup. Before he arrived, we were going nowhere. Even guys like Neilly Mochan, behind the scenes, were saying that the club was on a downhill slope.'

For Jimmy Johnstone, it was a unique scenario. 'That was a one-off, the team that won the Cup. They were superb. It is like somebody trying to copy somebody singing or something like that – they try but you've always got the original. You can't beat the original. That team were absolutely something else. It's just one of these things in a lifetime that happens and I don't think it will ever happen again. I don't think Celtic will ever again have a team as good as the 1967 one, especially with them all being homegrown, all Scottish, and all [from] within a radius of about thirty miles of each other.

'I've seen teams win the European Cup that have had maybe three or four great players who have excelled and who have carried the team, but I have never seen a team who had as much talent throughout the side. Everybody contributed in that game and at that time. Yes, I've seen some smashing teams. I'm talking about Ajax, with [Johan] Cruyff, [Johan] Neeskens and those tremendous players but there were maybe four or five of them who ran the team, who were the stars, who made it happen for them. The Celtic team in 1967 were eleven and all did their own bit and played their part.'

CHAPTER 24

A Tint of Gold

The European Cup trophy had sat beside Américo Tomás, the Portuguese president, awaiting the hands of Billy McNeill, who had to plough through crowds of supporters, wearily, exhaustedly, often looking in danger of being toppled over completely, sometimes appearing too drained to make it up the 120 steps but always with his eyes on the prize, determined finally to ascend the steps to the presentational podium.

The delay in McNeill's arrival meant that by the time he got there, a rare and special tinge of gold could be seen on the body of the trophy, a reflection of the sun sinking like a ship and creating some special Portuguese evening light. It was a sleek new trophy, a large pot with elongated arms, and it was being given a special tint – its own reflection of how Celtic had brought a new kind of colour to the final and to the competition. A worn McNeill tilted the European Cup in triumph as if it might be the last thing he would ever do.

This Celtic team had done it.

They had won it.

EPILOGUE

Tears and cheers characterised the return of the Celtic players to Glasgow on the day after their victory in Lisbon. Twenty-four hours after they had defeated Internazionale, their bus took them from the airport, close to Renfrew, and across Glasgow to Celtic Park. The players were overwhelmed by the number of people who were out on the streets to greet them enthusiastically.

'You have never seen so many people crying as there were on that bus,' Stevie Chalmers says. 'We knew there would be a reception for us at Celtic Park although Jock Stein tried to pretend that there was nothing arranged.' A Mr Stewart, who arranged maintenance work inside Celtic Park, had arranged for an open-backed lorry to transport the players, displaying the European Cup, around the running track that separated the terraces from the field of play. The welcome was tumultuous. Chalmers, a quiet man, slipped away afterwards to be home with his family in Bishopbriggs. For the extrovert Tommy Gemmell, in contrast, the return to Glasgow signalled the start of a weekend-long party back home in Craigneuk, a follow-on from his crazy evening in Lisbon when he had been the only member of Stein's team to have hit the nightclubs of the Portuguese city in celebration.

'We celebrated all summer,' recalls Jim Craig, 'and eventually I had to disappear to Ireland because it was getting to the stage where you couldn't walk along the road. Liz and I went to Donegal and although there were people talking to us there as well, there were not as many as in Glasgow.'

For the restless Stein, consumed by football, the question was how to maintain the momentum that had brought Celtic the European Cup. His answer was to get the players back on the training field as soon as possible. One week after Lisbon, on 1 June, the day the Beatles released the epochal *Sgt Pepper's Lonely Hearts Club Band*, his players were back in training, with Stein also seeking to define a new era in his own sphere. Celtic were due to face Real Madrid in Alfredo Di Stéfano's testimonial on 7 June and Stein was determined that they would give a good account of themselves. Chalmers was out in front, light and lean, on the training runs, one week after scoring the most important goal in Celtic's history.

The game would begin a new phase for Stein's team. Never again, the Celtic manager knew, could a Celtic team play as they had done in Lisbon, with the forwards sacrificed for the general good of the team. Nor could the full-backs be expected to play every match hurtling relentlessly up and down the field. The element of surprise in all that had gone and it had demanded a level of commitment that had taken each player to the very limit of his capacity. So Stein began experimenting with a new style. Willie O'Neill was brought in at left-half and John Clark played at right-half to offer better cover for Jim Craig and Gemmell when upfield, lessening the necessity of their having to race back to cover. That meant sacrificing a forward against Real and it proved to be no less a person than Chalmers. Reputations, no matter how fresh or how well-earned, meant nothing to Jock Stein.

'We are at the top but we won't stay there by standing still,' Stein said. 'The game keeps moving and we will move with it but I am determined that we will move forward with attack in mind and not defence. We plan now to stay on the crest.'

The torrent of triumphs continued with a 1–0 victory over Real in front of 120,000 inside the Bernabéu. The Spanish spectators were the latest set of enthralled admirers of Celtic that year, giving the 'Olé' to some of Celtic's better moves as the game progressed, and joining the 18 million people in Britain who had been captivated when watching the European Cup final being broadcast live on television on 25 May. Stein suggested that his players had been the highest paid in Britain over the 1966–67 season and the Celtic directors happily decided to pocket £1,200 each from the £25,068 profit that the club made over the season. Stein announced that, now that he had achieved his initial ambition of whipping the first team into shape, he would attend to the rest of the club and that summer he set up a thorough restructuring of the youth development system.

It was difficult to see what could go wrong for Celtic with Stein at the helm and, over the next decade, the success continued, with Celtic reaching one European Cup final and two semi-finals, losing in cruel and unfair fashion in the last four, on each of the latter two occasions. By the mid-1970s, though, the growing gulf in financial strength between the Scottish and English game meant that Stein could not retain the talented players who would come through his new youth system and, in the years since, that gulf has grown immensely. Yet there remains an undying enthusiasm for football among the Celtic support, who remain sustained by Lisbon even if they were not born to see or hear of it at the time. It shows what can be done through application, energy, enthusiasm and skill.

It was appropriate that on Wednesday 28 September 2016, exactly fifty years to the day since Celtic had participated in their first European Cup tie, they would celebrate with their first home Champions League group-stage match of the 2016–17 season. Back in 1966, Celtic had welcomed FC Zurich, a collection of accomplished but happy-go-lucky part-timers. Five decades on, Celtic hosted Manchester City, the brashest example of the twenty-first century's many mega-rich football clubs. Zurich had been the champions of Switzerland and had slowly built up a respectable reputation in European football. City, in contrast, had been transformed overnight through a combination of immensely wealthy Middle-Eastern owner-ship and the lucrative contracts with which Sky Television has fattened the clubs in the FA Premier League since 1992. City had finished a mere fourth in the Premier League in the spring of 2016 and so were not even the champions of their country, but details such as that were almost an irrelevance to the UEFA Champions League, itself a monetised version of the European Cup in which Celtic triumphed.

City, unlike Celtic, had never won the European Cup or the Champions League, the tournament into which it had meta-morphosed. They had barely come near it. They had, though, the previous season, triumphed in a contest that was now almost as important – they had been the club that took the greatest amount of money from the tournament. Real Madrid won gold by defeating Atlético Madrid in the final; City, who tumbled out in the semi-finals, quite happily raked in the silver, earning approximately £65 million from the Champions League in the 2015–16 season. City's squad, drawn from top-class inter-national nations all over the world, was valued at £500 million; Celtic had assembled theirs at a cost of around £20 million.

During the quarter-century of the Champions League's exist-ence, the gap between those clubs in the continent's largest and smallest countries had grown steadily, most notably through Champions League television revenue being distributed to

UEFA's clubs in relation to the size of the television audience in their country. For Celtic, from a nation of five million or so, this was a real restriction and, combined with their being in the Scottish League, which was largely unattractive to television companies, Celtic and other clubs from smaller leagues were put at a greater financial disadvantage with every passing year.

A new proposal for 2018 would see UEFA allocate sixteen of the thirty-two Champions League group stage places to clubs from England, Germany, Italy and Spain. Around the time this was mooted, in the autumn of 2016, Mesut Özil and Alexis Sánchez of Arsenal were each seeking a new wage of around £250,000 per week. Yet Arsenal, for all their wealth, had never won Europe's top trophy either – their money could only go so far. The ultimate fear, though, was that in the near future the influence of the clubs in the larger leagues might lead to the Champions League becoming a closed shop.

It all makes the days of 1967 look quaint in comparison, when Celtic surprised the continent by triumphing in the European Cup through ingenuity and invention.

'I felt the city was stunned,' Len Murray, a notable Glasgow lawyer, says of enjoying the aftermath of Celtic's victory. 'I honestly don't think the footballing world in the city had expected that they would win. It gave Glasgow a bit of pride, it really did, and it brought tremendous credit not just to the city but to Scotland. Inter Milan, kings of Europe; we had brought them down. I think the great majority of the people in Glasgow welcomed it and were very pleased and proud about it – apart from the "nuts"; and we can't do anything about them . . .

'These [the Celtic players] were guys that the city could relate to. They weren't foreigners, they didn't regard themselves as being other than you and I, would chat to fans when they came across them, would go to supporters' "dos" without any hesitation, would relate to the support in the way that modern teams don't. They weren't living in different worlds. That feeling lasted way beyond and into the rest of the Stein era and into the seventies and eighties, into Billy McNeill's time as manager [which ended in 1991].'

Those who had rolled up to see Celtic face Zurich in 1966 would have felt their club was in with a sporting chance of going some distance in the European Cup. Only the most wildly optimistic would have expected their first tilt in the tournament to end in victory but, on the other hand, few fans would have discounted it entirely. The lesson of the Champions League is that the chances of a club such as Celtic winning have been almost systematically reduced to the point at which such a hope has been all but extinguished. That had been emphasised a fortnight earlier when Celtic had gone to Barcelona in fine fettle after a 5–1 defeat of Rangers and with Brendan Rodgers, an inspirational new manager, buoying the club, only to suffer their record European defeat, losing 7–0. It meant that the occasion of the club's first meeting with City induced trepidation rather than anticipation. Trundling up to the ground that evening, Celtic fans would have settled for a respectable performance rather than demanding victory, as had always been the case in the Stein era. A tournament that had once, for their club, been all about glory and achievement, was now about perspective and realism. A lively 3–3 draw with City proved highly satisfactory. Despite high ticket prices, the stadium would be sold out for all three of Celtic's home European ties in the group stage of the tournament. The appetite remained among the fans to see the major names in European football and the flicker of hope that a Celtic team might one day emulate their 1967 predecessors remained alive.

There remained one constant from fifty years earlier: the electrifying power of the Celtic Park crowd, renowned across the continent. Borussia Moenchengladbach had been drawn in the same group and the reaction of some of their players, on hearing the draw, was to state that this was the tie – not the one in the Camp Nou against Barcelona – to which they were really looking forward. Perhaps this, in itself, should provide hope for Celtic because it must be clear to everyone who knows football that if clubs such as Celtic and Ajax Amsterdam and Anderlecht and all the other major clubs in minor leagues, who have heritage, passionate supporters and special stadiums, are pushed even further to the fringes of European football, the game will lose something irreplaceable.

Celtic's run to the 1967 final was almost perfectly structured, providing them with testing opponents in each round but holding in store the biggest contemporary name of all for the final, when Celtic were expected to fall victim to Internazionale's technique, cunning and experience. This was the richest club in the world but Celtic toppled them. Now, there is a whole collection of super-rich clubs blocking the way to the trophy, clubs who rotate among themselves the places in the semi-finals year after year: Barcelona, Real Madrid, Atlético Madrid, Chelsea, Manchester United, Bayern Munich, Manchester City, Juventus, Borussia Dortmund and others. The last time a club from one of the smaller nations, such as Celtic, won the tournament was Porto, in 2004, managed by José Mourinho, who had used his club's victory over Celtic in the 2003 UEFA Cup final as a springboard to victory. It showed that an innovative and determined manager could still make the difference, even in the age of fabulous footballing wealth. With a Mourinho at the helm, might a Celtic team featuring Henrik Larsson have made the same leap?

If there is to be a kernel of hope that the feat of the Lisbon Lions might be repeated, it is that, confronted by this mountain of money that they can barely ascend, Celtic should fall back upon their own resources, just as Porto did. Scottish football seemed to be in abject condition as the fiftieth anniversary of the Lions' achievement came around. The quality of Scottish Premiership football by the 2016–17 season had become unexceptional, with Celtic streaking away from their competitors almost from the moment the league competition began. Too many dull and functional teams – and managers – populate the Scottish game.

There remains a lack of professionalism among Scottish footballers that can only be reined in by a manager as strong as Stein. The author recalls telephoning one twenty-first-century Celtic player who saw nothing wrong, at nine o'clock in the evening, with being on his way out for a night in town, even with training in the morning. Too many Scottish players reach too easily, too unthinkingly, for a burger or for a beer.

Yet there is playing talent in abundance in Scotland at youth level. The passion among the young for the game remains high and the interest in football is almost at its zenith, thanks, ironically, to the televising of competitions such as the Champions League. Anyone watching youngsters perform on a Saturday morning can see an appetite and ability and yet a disconnect happens somewhere that means that that has almost dissipated by the time they might be ready to perform at senior level. It is clear that this talent is not being refined and channelled properly. The Lisbon Lions joined Celtic once they were in their mid- to late teens, or even their early twenties, and were largely self-taught through playing endlessly with a football. Now, the most obviously talented boys are snatched away to join 'pro-youth' schemes at Scotland's professional clubs while still at primary school, train four nights a week and sit on buses like professionals to travel across the land for matches when their time should be spent simply enjoying the game. Stevie Chalmers, who scored the winner in Lisbon and did not play professionally until he was 23, would not be considered by any club nowadays. Tommy Gemmell, the other goalscorer, was working as an apprentice electrician in a giant steelworks when he signed for Celtic. Breathing space is required to allow boys to develop their game and to grow as players and as people.

Saturday morning 'coaches' yell from the touchline at tiny players despite SFA instructions for them not to do so; they extend a stiff, straight arm to get their back three into line – in a four-a-side game on a tiny pitch – just as they have seen it done on *Match of the Day*. They participate in practice games with frightened, tiny children – specifically against SFA guidelines. The SFA have done much to improve the game at youth level, reducing the sizes of pitches and introducing small-sized goals, and wisely abolishing league tables and trophies, but then, at the age of twelve, young players move to full-blown, full-pitch competitive football. What happens? Boneheaded coaches start to emphasise physical fitness and stamina in training, squeezing the joy out of the game for the young. For whom do such methods have the greatest appeal? To the most boneheaded boy footballers. Boneheaded coaches beget boneheaded football. The SFA have put in place good ideas as to how the game should be organised; the next stage is for them to get their people out there and police closely youth-team coaches to make sure they adhere to their carefully prepared guidelines.

A lack of resources produced the gems that were the Lisbon Lions. They were hungry for success and the lesson from that for the modern era is that football teams can be coached – but only so far. Even on the exalted stage of the European Cup final, Celtic players carried out actions that showed they were thinking for themselves: Tommy Gemmell bursting into attack to score when he should really have been defending; Ronnie Simpson backheeling the ball in an exposed position; Stevie Chalmers, showing initiative and casting aside his pre-match instructions. Modern young players should also be allowed to show initiative within an organised framework. Yet go along to watch young players of a Saturday morning and you will see coaches shouting deadening instructions from the touchline.

The Lisbon Lions were a reflection of the society that made them, when working-class people were employed in tight-knit communities, when technological entertainment consisted of minuscule black-and-white televisions. They rarely travelled beyond the boundaries of their own locale and most of them had not been in an aeroplane or abroad until they joined Celtic. This was not restrictive – through remaining local, they got to know themselves better, felt more secure, more rooted and fitted in well with each other once they had become part of the professional football club. Kicking a ball around was the most colourful escape from grey surroundings. When the weather became too wet, boys in the 1950s would move inside, often to a tenement close to practise their skills by knocking the ball off the walls because the interior of a tenement or other 1950s home was not always a more cosy environment than being outside. Society has gone too far to go back to all that, but boys will still play football long and lustily if given the chance. Now that living standards have increased, the old reliance on hungry, working-class boys must also be scrutinised. Germany won the 2014 World Cup with a team shot through with middle-class, highly educated footballers who could drink in the sophisticated tactical and lifestyle demands of the modern game. Yet where are the middle-class Scottish footballers? The game in this country sets its face against the middle class, jettisoning a whole swathe of potential players that we cannot afford to lose. The choice between education and football is too stark.

Could the achievement of the Lisbon Lions happen again? Not in exactly the same fashion, but the encouraging thing is that it almost certainly would have to be carried out in at least a very similar fashion. Celtic cannot compete in the transfer market or in wages with the thin sliver of elite clubs in Europe. Producing a team heavily featuring players developed by the club must be a priority.

Celtic have the crowds, the ability to attract a manager of ingenuity and, as Leicester City showed in winning the FA Premier League and progressing well in the Champions League, if you have committed players performing consistently well for a knowledgeable and flexible manager, it can be an irresistible combination. Local players are essential to providing the club with a connection to the supporters and strengthening the commitment of all in and around a football club.

'I felt we were well below the level required for that type of football' Stevie Chalmers said of facing Valencia, the Inter-Cities Fairs Cup holders, on Celtic's European debut in 1962. Celtic were, Chalmers suggests, the 'apprentices while the Spanish team's players were the master craftsmen'. Look how quickly Jock Stein's team turned all that on its head. If it could happen then, we have to believe it can happen again.

A YEAR AND A DAY

25 May 1966
Friendly, McMaster University Playing Fields, Hamilton, Ontario
Hamilton Primos 0, Celtic 11
Celtic: Murdoch 3, Lennox 4, McBride 2, Clark (pen), Gemmell
  Bobby Murdoch opened the scoring in the sixth minute and Celtic scored eight more goals before half-time for the biggest win of their close-season North American tour.

27 May 1966
Friendly, Roosevelt Stadium, Jersey City, New York
Bologna 0, Celtic 0
  A lively friendly saw both sides committed to contesting the game fiercely but neither could make the breakthrough on an unsatisfactory pitch.

29 May 1966
Friendly, Roosevelt High School Stadium, St Louis
St Louis All Stars 1, Celtic 6
St Louis All Stars: Knox
Celtic: McBride 2, Lennox, Auld, Hughes, Chalmers
  Bertie Auld was fielded at centre-forward in a match played on a fine pitch. A total of 32 players were used – 18 by the All Stars and 14 by Celtic.

1 June 1966
Friendly, Kezar Stadium, San Francisco

Celtic 2, Tottenham Hotspur 1

Celtic: Auld, Lennox

Tottenham Hotspur: Mackay

A vibrant game saw Bertie Auld put Celtic ahead with a 25-yard shot in the 25th minute. One minute later, Dave Mackay scored from the rebound of his own penalty-kick to equalise for Spurs. An outstanding team goal saw Bobby Lennox notch the winner in the 59th minute in front of a 12,000 crowd.

4 June 1966
Friendly, Empire Stadium, Vancouver

Celtic 1, Tottenham Hotspur 1

Celtic: Lennox

Tottenham Hotspur: Venables

Bobby Lennox scored his 18th goal of Celtic's North American tour to give Celtic a 19th-minute lead in front of a near 20,000 crowd. Five minutes from time, Terry Venables equalised and the goal stood despite Celtic protests that Billy McNeill had been pushed off the ball. Jimmy Johnstone was dismissed for the strength of his protests but when he refused to leave the field, the referee relented and allowed him to remain.

9 June 1966
Friendly, Kezar Stadium, San Francisco

Bayern Munich 2, Celtic 2

Bayern Munich: Ohlhauser 2

Celtic: Lennox, McBride

Two very well-taken goals by Rainer Ohlhauser, the Bayern striker, gave the West German side a lead that was undeserved on the balance of play. Bobby Lennox got one back in the 75th minute before a brawl erupted among the players. Once the game had settled down again, Joe McBride got the equaliser close to the end.

12 June 1966
Friendly, Los Angeles Memorial Coliseum

Atlas 0, Celtic 1

Celtic: Gallagher

A match played in intense humidity saw Celtic match the highly technical Mexican league runners-up for creativity and two minutes from time, Charlie Gallagher scored the only goal of the game.

6 August 1966
Friendly, Celtic Park

Celtic 4, Manchester United 1

Celtic: Lennox 7, Murdoch 10, McBride 15, Foulkes 61 (og)
Manchester United: Sadler 12

United fielded ten internationals, including Bobby Charlton and Nobby Stiles of England, who, one week previously, had beaten West Germany to win the World Cup at Wembley Stadium. John Connelly, the winger, had played his part in the group stages. Bobby Lennox had half-a-dozen efforts on goal, including the shot for the opening goal that Harry Gregg, the Irishman in United's goal, got his fingers to but could not stop. For the second, Stevie Chalmers' through-ball to Jimmy Johnstone saw the winger jink into space to cross and Joe McBride dummy the ball to leave Bobby Murdoch with the goal gaping in front of him thanks to the movement of his teammates. Joe McBride got the third and a Bill Foulkes own goal made it 4–1. Lennox and Chalmers had been used through the middle to confront directly Nobby Stiles and Foulkes, the United centre-half. 'I was marking Bobby Lennox and he ran the legs off me,' Nobby Stiles said.

Attendance: 60,000

13 August 1966
Scottish League Cup Group Stage, Tynecastle Stadium, Edinburgh

Heart of Midlothian 0, Celtic 2

Celtic: McBride 19 (pen), 89

A useful Hearts side played a lot of good football but created few chances. They still made Celtic wait until late to be sure of the win but the away team were sharper, faster and quicker-thinking throughout. Again Jock Stein showed that he was ahead of his time in using a lone striker in the first half – Bobby Lennox – before switching to a partnership – Lennox and Stevie Chalmers – for the second period. It was still a low-key beginning to the season, a functional rather than fancy 2–0 win achieved in windy, rainy conditions.

Attendance: 29,000

17 August 1966
Scottish League Cup Group Stage, Celtic Park

Celtic 6, Clyde 0

Celtic: Lennox 5, 60, 63, McBride 30 (pen), 44, Chalmers 83

Clyde were helpless in the face of Celtic's attacking power, with Jimmy Johnstone to the fore. John Wright and Stan Anderson, the Clyde centre-halves, struggled to stop Celtic's attackers all evening.

Attendance: 30,000

20 August 1966
Scottish League Cup Group Stage, Celtic Park

Celtic 8, St Mirren 2

Celtic: Lennox 10, 72, McBride 24 (pen), 26, 44, 46, Auld 58, Chalmers 86

St Mirren: Treacy 78, 82

An efficient and stylish demolition of part-time St Mirren, for whom Jim Thorburn, the goalkeeper, made a series of fine saves to make it a respectable thrashing.

Attendance: 32,000

23 August 1966
Glasgow Cup quarter-final, Ibrox Park

Rangers 0, Celtic 4

Celtic: McNeill 8, Lennox 31, 67, 84

Stein opted to leave John Hughes out for the fourth successive game of the new season and Celtic swept eagerly into the match on a notable night in the history of Old Firm fixtures, one on which Rangers would pay a heavy price for Jim Forrest and Willie Johnston missing good chances in the first five minutes. Celtic allowed the home side generous dollops of possession but Dave Smith and Alex Smith, their expensive new signings, each looked impotent in the face of Celtic's cover, organisation and efficient defending. It was an even match for all of eight minutes – when Bertie Auld's free-kick found Charlie Gallagher to cross in the direction of Billy McNeill. Ron McKinnon, the Rangers centre-half, made a wonky attempt at a clearance and the ball fell neatly for McNeill who clipped it through the legs of Billy Ritchie, the goalkeeper.

Bobby Lennox began his hat-trick with a shot from the edge of the box that he clipped past Ritchie via the underside of the crossbar. For his second, Lennox collected John Greig's half-clearance then confronted Ritchie before pinging the ball past him. The final goal saw Lennox use his pace to fly past McKinnon and Davie Provan before screwing a shot past Ritchie that narrowly evaded the goalkeeper, diving low to his right.

After a bright start from Rangers, the home side looked slow in comparison with their opponents and they were thoroughly outmanoeuvred tactically and technically.

Attendance: 76,456

27 August 1966
Scottish League Cup Group Stage, Celtic Park

Celtic 3, Heart of Midlothian 0

Celtic: McBride, 54, 73 (pen), Chalmers 69

Hearts packed their defence but still created enough opportunities for Willie Wallace, the Hearts forward, to miss a hat-trick of sterling chances before Celtic settled to a steady win.

Attendance: 46,000

31 August 1966
Scottish League Cup Group Stage, Shawfield Stadium

Clyde 1, Celtic 3

Clyde: Gilroy 35

Celtic: McBride 16, 38 (pen), Gemmell 86

An ultra-defensive Clyde sat back and invited Celtic to attack. McBride scored for the fifth successive game. John Clark was the stand-out in an unfussy Celtic victory, the most ordinary performance in a season in which they had been glittering.

Attendance: 18,000

3 September 1966
Scottish League Cup Group Stage, St Mirren Park, Love Street, Paisley

St Mirren 0, Celtic 1

Celtic: Murdoch 53

St Mirren packed their defence, the latest Scottish club to do so in the face of Celtic's force, but attacked enough for fine saves from Ronnie Simpson to pave the way for the only goal, which came from a Jimmy Johnstone cutback for Bobby Murdoch, inside the penalty area, to knock a shot into the net, off a post.

Attendance: 20,000

10 September 1966
Scottish League First Division, Shawfield Stadium
Clyde 0, Celtic 3
Celtic: Chalmers 10, McBride 18, Hughes 75

An easy sidefoot from Stevie Chalmers opened the scoring on a day on which Celtic's superiority could have brought them a pile of goals. Celtic were crisp and competent from back to front and barely troubled by their Glasgow neighbours who had now conceded 12 goals to Celtic in the opening month of the season.

Attendance: 16,500

14 September 1966
Scottish League Cup quarter-final first leg, Celtic Park
Celtic 6, Dunfermline Athletic 3
Celtic: McNeill 1, Hughes 4, Auld, 11, 70, McBride 20 (pen), Johnstone 23
Dunfermline Athletic: Ferguson 18, 85, Hunter 62

Bobby Murdoch failed to score but ran the match with consummate authority while Celtic, overall, were irresistible in taking a 5–1 lead only midway through the first half, sparked by a McNeill header from a Johnstone corner inside the opening minute. Bertie Auld whacked in a fine long-range shot with, unusually, his right foot and then waggled that leg in front of Stein – a gesture few others in the team would have embraced. Stein had spoken carefully of the need to secure a two-goal lead over Dunfermline before the second leg of this quarter-final but Celtic made a mockery of their manager's caution. Alex Ferguson, the Dunfermline forward, had, injured, watched Celtic defeat Clyde but even the scouting report of their budding coach could do nothing to prevent the East End Park side wilting in the face of the furnace-like heat of Celtic's attacking play on the night.

Attendance: 36,000

17 September 1966
Scottish League First Division, Celtic Park
Celtic 2, Rangers 0
Celtic: Auld 1, Murdoch 3

Auld masterminded this victory, scoring after 50 seconds, controlling the game from midfield and exploiting slowness in a Rangers side that was second-best in every aspect of the game. The opening goal saw Celtic pierce Rangers' fragile defence at the first attempt. Bobby Lennox flew past Ron McKinnon, the Rangers centre-half, to cross. Joe McBride miskicked but Auld swept the ball into the corner of the Rangers net. Two minutes later, Bobby Murdoch spooned the ball into the same corner from just outside the penalty area. Having seized the initiative with those early goals, Celtic paced their way through the remainder of the game and the defence stood firm in the face of Rangers' blunt, route-one attempts at bullying their way to an equaliser. Celtic could have sought – and scored – further goals but instead showed some sophistication through opting to contain Rangers confidently.

Attendance: 70,000

21 September 1966

Scottish League Cup quarter-final second leg, East End Park

Dunfermline Athletic 1, Celtic 3

Dunfermline: Fleming 70
Celtic: McNeill 33, Chalmers 42, 54

Dunfermline Athletic assaulted Celtic in every sense during the opening half an hour, throwing everything at the visiting team, but once Billy McNeill had headed in a Jimmy Johnstone cross in the 33rd minute and Stevie Chalmers had added two smoothly taken goals, the contest was over and Celtic were in the semis. In eight League Cup ties, Celtic had averaged four goals a game.

Attendance: 20,000

24 September 1966

Scottish League First Division, Dens Park

Dundee 1, Celtic 2

Dundee: Penman 28
Celtic: Lennox 32, Chalmers 77

In a match that took place six weeks into the competitive season, Andy Penman put Celtic behind for the first time with a fine 25-yard shot. Stung, Celtic quickly found the antidote. Billy McNeill advanced into the Dundee penalty area and used his aerial power to head a Johnstone free-kick to Lennox for the forward to equalise. Stevie Chalmers notched the winner, after having replaced Joe McBride, suffering from a thigh strain, at half-time – the first time that Celtic had used a substitution in a league game; the substitution rule had been introduced for the 1966–67 season. Chalmers detested the distinction – as a true competitor, he wished always to be in the starting line-up. Billy McNeill (for dissent) became the first Celtic player booked in the 1966–67 season.

Celtic's visit to Dens Park had also produced an interesting cameo, when Willie Morrison, one of the linesmen, was forced to leave the field after feeling ill. It was agreed that he would be replaced by Alex Kinninmouth, one of the Dundee substitutes, and as Kinninmouth made his way across the pitch, scrutinised by Jock Stein, standing at the edge of the field of play, Bertie Auld told the Dundee man, 'Remember that there are two teams on the pitch.' Before Kinninmouth could swing into action, though, John Dearie, a spectator, had volunteered to stand in for the stricken official. Kinninmouth returned to the bench but he was on his feet again, four minutes later, when he replaced Bobby Wilson, the injured Dundee player. It was an amusing sideshow on a day when Celtic won 2–1.

Attendance: 28,000

28 September 1966
European Cup first round first leg, Celtic Park

Celtic 2, FC Zurich 0

Celtic: Gemmell 64, McBride 69

A defensive, rugged Zurich held out until midway through the second half when Tommy Gemmell put Celtic ahead with a spectacular long-range shot. Zurich defenders stood off the full-back as he advanced, seemingly confident that they could thwart another Celtic attempt at threading the ball through a highly efficient and competent Swiss defence. Instead, Gemmell fairly whacked a near-unstoppable shot high into the net. Joe McBride added a second five minutes later with a low shot that appeared to be deflected. McBride had the ball in the net again, not so much in the dying seconds but in the dead seconds of the match. Fred Hansen, the Danish referee, had blown for full-time just as McBride was midway through the process of putting the ball in the net.

Attendance: 47,604

1 October 1966

Scottish League First Division, Celtic Park

Celtic 6, St Johnstone 1

Celtic: Johnstone 11, 51, Lennox 37, 60, McBride 66, 70.

St Johnstone: Kilgannon 54

Wing power, in the shape of Jimmy Johnstone and John Hughes, drove Celtic to the win, with Hughes helping to construct three of the six goals.

Attendance: 24,000

5 October 1966

European Cup first round second leg, Letzigrund

FC Zurich, 0 Celtic 3

Celtic: Gemmell 22, 48 (pen), Chalmers 38

An early, spirited flurry from the Swiss proved to be the only trouble for Celtic as they went on to exert complete control over the match and to cruise to an efficient and impressive victory. Notably, Tommy Gemmell scored another fine, long-range goal to open the scoring, almost a finely detailed copy of his goal in the first leg. Clever positioning and sharp reflexes from Stevie Chalmers put Celtic two ahead and Gemmell made sure the Glasgow club was out of sight with a penalty shortly after the half-time interval.

Attendance: 20,236

8 October 1966

Scottish League First Division, Easter Road

Hibernian 3, Celtic 5

Hibernian: Cormack 10, Davis 37 (pen), McGraw 90

Celtic: McBride 14, 41, 43, 73, Chalmers 30

An eagerly anticipated Edinburgh–Glasgow clash had ensured the Easter Road stand was sold out a week in advance of the match. Hibernian had been challenging Celtic at the top of the league in the early weeks of the season but they were outclassed in some style as Jock Stein made a return to the club he had managed before taking over at Celtic.

Attendance: 43,256

11 October 1966
Glasgow Cup semi-final, Celtic Park

Celtic 4, Queen's Park 0

Celtic: McBride 7, 88, Lennox 28, Gallagher 48

Bent Martin, the goalkeeper, made his first-team debut and Ian Young appeared for the first time in the season but Celtic were untroubled throughout an easy victory.

Attendance: 17,000

15 October 1966
Scottish League First Division, Celtic Park

Celtic 3, Airdrieonians 0

Celtic: McBride 64, Lennox 68, 87

A straightforward win for Celtic, even without Bobby Murdoch, unwell, and Bertie Auld, rested for the Monday evening League Cup semi against the same opponents. Jimmy Johnstone too was absent. Bobby Lennox, Ian Young and Charlie Gallagher were brought in as their replacements but seamlessly Celtic took apart another set of opponents.

Attendance: 41,000

17 October 1966
Scottish League Cup semi-final, Hampden Park

Celtic 2, Airdrieonians 0

Celtic: Murdoch 63, McBride 77

A policy of mass defence on Airdrie's part kept the game goalless for more than an hour, with Roddy Mackenzie, the goalkeeper, excelling. Once Bobby Murdoch had put Celtic ahead with a powerful, long-range shot, the victory was almost assured and Joe McBride's goal made certain of it.

Attendance: 36,936

24 October 1966
Scottish League First Division, Celtic Park

Celtic 5, Ayr United 1

Celtic: Lennox 2, Hughes 45, Johnstone 57, 88, Gemmell 69
Ayr United: Black 40

A comprehensive clattering of Ayr, bottom of the First Division, took Celtic five points clear of Rangers, Kilmarnock and Hibernian at the top of the First Division after their 21st consecutive victory. Despite scoring goals both early and late in the first half, Celtic had been ordinary and Stein offered an understated explanation of how he had given his players a friendly jolt. 'At half-time I just had a quiet word here and a quiet word there with certain players. We got what we wanted.'

Attendance: 21,000

29 October 1966

Scottish League Cup final, Hampden Park

Celtic 1, Rangers 0

Celtic: Lennox 19

This was Celtic's 36th match without defeat since losing the replay of the Scottish Cup final to Rangers in the spring of 1966. The only goal of the game was a piece of precise perfection. Bertie Auld's pass found Joe McBride, who headed it down for Bobby Lennox, in clear green space inside the penalty area, to take the ball on the half-volley and whip it instantaneously behind Norrie Martin in the Rangers goal. Stevie Chalmers became the first substitute to be used in a League Cup final when he replaced John Hughes, who had suffered a knee injury, early in the second half. Chalmers insisted on giving his medal to Hughes, which, Hughes said, 'was a very nice thing to do'. The Scottish League made arrangements to issue Chalmers with a replacement.

Attendance: 94,532

2 November 1966

Scottish League First Division, Celtic Park

Celtic 7, Stirling Albion 3

Celtic: Johnstone 6, McBride 12, 41, 48, Chalmers 19, 42, Auld 25
Stirling Albion: McGuinness 43, Reid 65, Kerray 87

Stirling Albion, in February 1966, had, surprisingly, been the last team to defeat Celtic in the Scottish League but this was more to form – another pummelling of a club struggling at the foot of the First Division meant that Celtic had now enjoyed a run of 28 consecutive, competitive home wins and were undefeated at home in 35 matches. Jimmy Johnstone headed the opening goal and Joe McBride notched a hat-trick. Billy McNeill, the Celtic centre-half, recalled that Jim Kerray, the Albion centre-forward, gave him an especially difficult evening, so much so that McNeill would rate him a more difficult opponent than some of the continentals Celtic faced in the European Cup.

Attendance: 21,000

5 November 1966
Scottish League First Division, Celtic Park

Celtic 1, St Mirren 1

Celtic: Gemmell 47
St Mirren: Treacy 54

An unusual day at Celtic Park saw Celtic take the field in an all-green change strip with numbers on the backs of the shirts and Tommy Gemmell fielded at centre-half in place of Billy McNeill, suffering from a heavy cold. After a concerted and constructive opening 20 minutes, Celtic's teamwork unravelled and, in the 82nd minute, Bobby Murdoch became the first Celtic player to be dismissed in the 1966–67 season. He was booked for comments made to a linesman after a throw-in had been given to St Mirren, and when, seconds later, further comment was made to Bert Henderson, the referee, Murdoch was given a second booking and sent from the field. Jock Stein intervened to try to prevent photographers taking pictures of the Celtic player. Dennis Connachan, the St Mirren goalkeeper, a former Celtic provisional signing, performed impressively on his debut for the Paisley club, and Celtic's attackers were askew with their shooting against a team that was second-bottom of the First Division. Gemmell scored with a shot from distance but he and Jim Craig looked uncertain of one another when Frank Treacy equalised.

Attendance: 24,000

7 November 1966
Glasgow Cup final, Celtic Park

Celtic 4, Partick Thistle 0

Celtic: Chalmers 11, Lennox 24, 26, 43

This was as simple a cup-final victory as Celtic might have hoped to experience. Celtic had won, on the toss of a coin, the right to host the match and superb finishing from Stevie Chalmers and Bobby Lennox, with a hat-trick, had Partick swept away by half-time after the Firhill side had begun the match by attempting to sit deep and absorb pressure.

Attendance: 31,000

12 November 1966
Scottish League First Division, Brockville Park

Falkirk 0, Celtic 3

Celtic: McBride 3, 43 (pen), Auld 63

Bertie Auld was in imperious form to control a match that Celtic dominated from first to last. Auld supplied the cross-ball that Bobby McDonald, the Falkirk goalkeeper, dropped for Joe McBride to score in the opening minutes and it was from Auld's pass that Johnny Markie handled to concede the penalty that McBride converted shortly before half-time. An Auld header concluded the scoring.

Attendance: 12,000

19 November 1966
Scottish League First Division, East End Park

Dunfermline Athletic 4, Celtic 5

Dunfermline Athletic: Robertson 32, Ferguson 34, 48, Paton 39
Celtic: Murdoch 35, Johnstone 44, Auld 67, McBride 69, 89 (pen)

Willie Cunningham, the Dunfermline manager, had insisted beforehand that his team could win and make a greater contest of the title. His players were almost as good as his word. With Alex Ferguson, the centre-forward, rampant, they went ahead shortly before half-time and suffered defeat only when Roy Barry, the centre-half, was adjudged to have handled the ball and given away a penalty in the final seconds, from which McBride scored the winner. It was the first time the Celtic defence had conceded more than three goals in the 1966–67 season and the only time they would be behind by two goals. The late winner ensured that Celtic ended an icy afternoon three points ahead of Rangers at the top of the First Division.

Attendance: 21,500

26 November 1966
Scottish League First Division, Celtic Park

Celtic 3, Heart of Midlothian 0

Celtic: Miller 12 (og), McBride 76, 88 (pen)

Hearts roared into this match promising revenge for their two earlier defeats in the season and limped home with a 3–0 defeat. Alan Anderson, the Hearts captain, had suggested that Celtic had been 'lucky' to beat his team on the two previous encounters that season. Well, they were pretty lucky once again. Only some fine goalkeeping from Jim Cruickshank, the Hearts goalkeeper, prevented Celtic scoring more.

Attendance: 40,000

30 November 1966
European Cup second round first leg, Stade Marcel-Saupin

Nantes 1, Celtic 3

Nantes: Magny 16
Celtic: McBride 24, Lennox 50, Chalmers 67

An early Johnstone header from a Willie O'Neill cross bounced off the underside of the crossbar as Celtic sought to notch the opening goal but the visiting team were caught out with too many players upfield when Gabriel De Michèle, the Nantes left-back, raced down the left wing and provided a pass for Francis Magny, who got the better of Billy McNeill to open the scoring in the 16th minute. That early setback served to concentrate Celtic minds and a Bobby Lennox cross enabled Joe McBride to sidestep De Michele and whip home the equaliser in style. An even better goal put Celtic ahead. Murdoch prodded the ball through the middle and Lennox fended off two challengers, drew the goalkeeper, and, from the edge of the six-yard box, lashed the ball home. Stevie Chalmers made it three, anticipating a Bertie Auld cross that went weaving through the Nantes defence for Chalmers to crack the ball high into the net. Jock Stein was effusive in his praise for his team. 'This was the best result we could have hoped for,' he said. 'It was a wonderful team effort.'

Attendance: 15,464

3 December 1966
Scottish League First Division, Rugby Park

Kilmarnock 0, Celtic 0

Rugby Park had long been a difficult venue for Celtic to visit in the 1960s and Kilmarnock, a team hefty in size and determined in intent, going well in the Fairs Cup, were a powerful outfit. A sizeable crowd, drawn to the potential spectacle, put so much pressure on creaking old Rugby Park that crush barriers gave way several times, leading to supporters spilling on to the pitch. This was the first time Celtic had been involved in a goalless game in the 1966–67 season but the draw was a welcome result from a game played just three days after a wearying and pressurised visit to France in the European Cup. Stein expressed himself unworried by the outcome. Bobby Ferguson, the Kilmarnock goalkeeper, performed exceptionally well to keep Celtic out and on the only occasion he was beaten, Andy King, the Kilmarnock right-back, hooked a McNeill header off the line. Celtic were largely ineffective in attack throughout and so too were Kilmarnock, leading to an anodyne afternoon of football.

Attendance: 27,000

7 December 1966

European Cup second round second leg, Celtic Park

Celtic 3, Nantes 1

Celtic: Johnstone 13, Chalmers 56, Lennox 78
Nantes: Georgin 36

Nantes had intended to 'plan a surprise' for Celtic and Robert Budzynski, the captain, had insisted, 'We'll show the Scottish people how the game of football should be played.' Their best-laid plans soon went awry when Jimmy Johnstone darted into the Nantes penalty area and angled a shot from right to left that flew past the outstretched right-hand of André Castel, the Nantes goalkeeper, and into the far corner of the goal to put the tie just about out of reach for the French champions. 'You never know in football,' Jock Stein had said as he had anticipated the second leg of the tie with Nantes, which Celtic were expected to complete easily. 'Nantes aren't too bad on the break. A quick goal and they might be back in the tie. We must be watchful.' The Celtic manager's canny ability to foretell how a football match might go looked as accurate as ever when, shortly after Johnstone's goal, Francis Magny went close and a Vladica Kovačević shot struck the inside of the post. Johnstone was still the main attraction, holding on to the ball, hogging it sometimes, on the back of his reputation-enhancing evening in Nantes, but shortly before half-time Gérard Géorgin slipped Bernard Blanchet's cross past Simpson for the equaliser, making Nantes only the second club, after Barcelona, to have scored at Celtic Park in European competition. Magny almost got a second a couple of minutes later but Simpson saved the Frenchman's first attempt and his effort at putting the rebound away. Swirling wind and rain impeded both sets of players but Johnstone, for all his showmanship, set up the final two goals: a fine, rising header from Stevie Chalmers that swept over Castel's left shoulder and a close-in shot from Lennox, on the stretch.

Attendance: 39,120

10 December 1966
Scottish League First Division, Celtic Park

Celtic 4, Motherwell 2

Celtic: Chalmers 30, 41, 82 Murdoch 67
Motherwell: Murray 78, Lindsay 83

This match provided a debut for Willie Wallace but Joe McBride was an absentee for the second successive match through a knee injury that Jock Stein insisted had cleared up fully, leaving the player entirely fit. Rumour would suggest that Wallace might have been bought to replace Stevie Chalmers but Chalmers showed he was far from finished, scoring three snappily taken goals. It was impossible to imagine that Jock Stein saw him as being easily replaceable. Wallace was involved in the build-up in three of the four goals. 'If I did have three "assists",' he said, 'I was just doing my job. All the goals were real team efforts. It was a match that I really enjoyed.' A long-range Bobby Murdoch shot provided Celtic's other goal on a day on which they were diligently dominant. John 'Dixie' Deans, the Motherwell striker, was sent off in the second half for a foul on Jimmy Johnstone.

Attendance: 40,000

17 December 1966
Scottish League First Division, Celtic Park

Celtic 6, Partick Thistle 2

Celtic: Wallace 2, 24, Chalmers 15, 74, Murdoch 32, McBride 57
Partick Thistle: Duncan 36, Gibb 65

Willie Wallace did his utmost to justify Jock Stein's claim that in his person he had signed an entire forward line. His first goal was set up by McBride heading across the face of goal for Wallace to steer the ball over the line with his own head. A splendid half-volley from Wallace made it 3–0 midway through the first half after Stevie Chalmers had slipped home Celtic's second. A long-range Bobby Murdoch shot and a goal from McBride, looking offside, brought the fourth and fifth and Wallace concluded a productive afternoon by setting up Chalmers for Celtic's sixth goal.

Attendance: 25,000

24 December 1966
Scottish League First Division, Pittodrie Stadium

Aberdeen 1, Celtic 1
Aberdeen: Melrose 30
Celtic: Lennox 23

Pittodrie proved a vital ally for Aberdeen, the hard ground and the icy conditions making it testing for the away side in their attempts to play their usual seamlessly stylish football. They were still the slicker, smoother side. Aberdeen worked assiduously to bridge the chasm in class and, on the day, succeeded to some degree, forcing Ronnie Simpson into a series of impressive saves. Bobby Lennox scored when Tommy McMillan, the Aberdeen centre-half, miscontrolled a ball. Simpson's accomplished save from Frank Munro in the final minute meant that this was Celtic's 33rd competitive match without defeat of the 1966–67 season in four competitions. It also left them five points ahead of second-placed Rangers as Christmas Day arrived and ten months unbeaten in the Scottish League.

Attendance: 31,000

31 December 1966
Scottish League First Division, Tannadice Park

Dundee United 3, Celtic 2
Dundee United: Døssing 23, Gillespie 73, Mitchell 75
Celtic: Lennox 13, Wallace 24

On the final day of the year, Celtic lost for the first time in the 1966–67 season and for the first time in the league for ten months. United, a team laced with useful Scandinavian players, were lively from the start and maintained a high level of energy despite going behind to a Bobby Lennox goal early in the match. When United equalised through Finn Døssing, it took only a minute for Celtic to regain the lead, through Willie Wallace, but this was a United team of stern character, one that had defeated Barcelona home and away already that season, in the Inter Cities Fairs Cup. They continued to match Celtic for attacking flair, equalising through Dennis Gillespie when he knocked in a powerful shot from 25 yards. With 15 minutes remaining, Ian Mitchell, who had scored the second against Barcelona in their 2–0 Tannadice victory in October 1966, took the ball round Ronnie Simpson, who had played in the shadow of Tannadice on annual holidays staying with his Dundonian granny. Mitchell slipped it into the empty net for the goal that proved to be the winner.

Attendance: 22,000

7 January 1967

Scottish League First Division, Celtic Park

Celtic 5, Dundee 1

Celtic: Wilson 2 (og), Wallace 4, 88, Johnstone 20, Gallagher 28
Dundee: Cameron 52

It was vital for Celtic to get back into action after their matches at New Year with Clyde and Rangers having been postponed because of inclement weather. That inactivity, coupled with the defeat at Dundee United on Hogmanay, had whittled away their lead at the top to a mere two points, over Aberdeen. They were back on form against the team from the other side of Dundee's Tannadice Street, going forward with pace and control from the opening minute and creating a bevy of scoring opportunities, four of which were taken to put them out of sight after only half an hour. Only magnificent goalkeeping from John Arrol, in the Dundee goal, prevented Celtic's coming close to emulating the club's record 11–0 scoreline, against Dundee, in the 1890s.

Attendance: 37,000

11 January 1967

Scottish League First Division, Celtic Park

Celtic 5, Clyde 1

Celtic: Chalmers 12, 72, Gallagher 54, Gemmell 74, Lennox 75
Clyde: Gilroy 32

Clyde performed exceptionally well, bucking the trend of their earlier encounters with Celtic by taking the game to the home side often and sometimes with considerable verve. The result did, though, reflect very well the ability of Celtic to tough out a tricky match and then devastate plucky opponents through their superior finishing ability. Stevie Chalmers had put Celtic ahead after the home side had begun the match in dominant fashion but Joe Gilroy had rewarded his teammates for their initiative with an equaliser shortly after the half-hour. Chalmers set up Charlie Gallagher for the goal that put Celtic ahead again and then, in a four minute spell, goals from Chalmers, Tommy Gemmell, with a 30-yard shot, and Bobby Lennox, with a neat header, put the game completely beyond Clyde.

Attendance: 38,000

14 January 1967

Scottish League First Division, Muirton Park

St Johnstone 0, Celtic 4

Celtic: Johnstone 63, 69, Chalmers 86, Lennox 90

For the first time this team of players took to the field together: Ronnie Simpson, Jim Craig, Tommy Gemmell, Bobby Murdoch, Billy McNeill, John Clark, Jimmy Johnstone, Willie Wallace, Stevie Chalmers, Bertie Auld and Bobby Lennox. The team creaked only slowly into action in this game but once they clicked, St Johnstone were left to rue their failure to make more of having had a good deal of the play early on in the match.

Attendance: 19,000

21 January 1967

Scottish League First Division, Celtic Park

Celtic 2, Hibernian 0

Celtic: Wallace 12, Chalmers 38

On a day of grey, low-hanging sky at Celtic Park, and on a heavy pitch, Celtic rose above the oppressive conditions as they overwhelmed a good Hibernian side through an unwavering commitment to attacking football. Willie Wallace and Stevie Chalmers had each had attempts that rebounded off a goalpost before Wallace, in 12 minutes, pelted the ball past Thomson Allan in the Hibernian goal. A corner-kick, taken by Jimmy Johnstone in the 38th minute, was headed across goal by Bertie Auld and Stevie Chalmers finished it off to make it 2–0.

Attendance: 41,000

28 January 1967

Scottish Cup first round, Celtic Park

Celtic 4, Arbroath 0

Celtic: Murdoch 13, Gemmell 19, Chalmers 33, Auld 81

After a midweek break at Seamill, where the players relaxed through golfing, Celtic faced an Arbroath side going well in the Second Division and on course for promotion. Jimmy Johnstone was absent with an ear infection, but Jock Stein promised he would field his 'strongest possible side' and that there would be 'no experiments' for the type of tie that filled him with greater apprehension than those against more illustrious opponents. Arbroath had stayed overnight at a hotel in Largs and had trained for an hour at the Inverclyde Recreation Centre on the morning of the match, but none of that was to any avail as an efficient Celtic performance, with goals contributed from all parts of the team, saw the home side ease into the next round with little trouble.

Attendance: 31,000

4 February 1967

Scottish League First Division, Broomfield Park

Airdrieonians 0, Celtic 3

Celtic: Johnstone 12, Chalmers 47, Auld 70

As with so many of their predecessors this season, Airdrie discovered that performing creditably against Celtic counted for nothing at all once the Glasgow side turned on the turbo-chargers.

Attendance: 22,000

7 February 1967

Friendly, Celtic Park

Celtic 0, Dinamo Zagreb 1

Dinamo Zagreb: Zambata 89

'I hope to see the new Celtic born,' Stein said of a friendly on which he set great store. 'It will be attack, attack against Dinamo Zagreb. We don't care if we lose four or five goals as long as we can score six.' As an experiment to find a new style of play, it failed, and the goals failed to flow too, Celtic succumbing to their first home defeat since Dundee had won at Celtic Park in August 1965. Yet the experimental 3-4-3 formation did yield chances, with Tommy Gemmell, Bobby Lennox, Stevie Chalmers, Bobby Murdoch and Jimmy Johnstone passing up good opportunities. Slaven Zambata, the Zagreb centre-forward, scored from close range in the final moments of an intriguing match.

Attendance: 46,000

11 February 1967

Scottish League First Division, Somerset Park

Ayr United 0, Celtic 5

Celtic: Johnstone 42, Chalmers 57, 62, 82, Hughes 59

An unusual kick-off time of one o'clock ushered in an unusually subdued first-half performance from Celtic but they offered full recompense for that by pulling Ayr apart during the second period. 'Our players are conditioned mentally and physically to a three o'clock start and every Saturday morning is carefully worked out,' Stein said. 'But here we were kicking off when players are used to having lunch.' Once Celtic did tap in to some good form, John Hughes, on the left wing, and Jimmy Johnstone, on the right, made it a memorable afternoon for those who had followed Celtic to Somerset Park and a forgettable one for the home supporters.

Attendance: 19,000

18 February 1967
Scottish Cup second round, Celtic Park

Celtic 7, Elgin City 0

Celtic: Chalmers 43, Lennox 44, 45, 70, Hughes 62, Wallace 83, 89

'Who would dare forecast the result?' Jimmy Ross, the Elgin City secretary, said of this Cup tie with Celtic after the Highland League side had defeated Ayr United of the First Division. Ross may have been showing a humorous touch or have been inspired by Berwick Rangers' defeat of Rangers, but nevertheless Stein was taking the tie seriously. 'You cannot afford to relax for a minute, especially in a Cup tie,' he said 'Be sure we will not treat Elgin City lightly.' Still, he had been relaxed enough not to travel north to see which of Elgin or Ayr would emerge from their postponed fixture to be Celtic's opponents. Celtic did relax at Seamill in advance of the tie, with golf, swimming and steam baths before slipping seven goals past their opponents for their biggest win of the season.

Attendance: 34,000

25 February 1967
Scottish League First Division, Annfield Stadium

Stirling Albion 1, Celtic 1

Stirling Albion: Peebles 23

Celtic: Hughes 52

'Our defeat there last season is warning enough for our players,' Jock Stein said in advance of the match with Stirling Albion, which, coming almost exactly a year after that loss, brought back unwelcome memories, with Celtic only three points ahead of Rangers in the First Division. The warning was not emphatic enough as Celtic, at a muddy Annfield, struggled to a draw with a side toiling in the First Division's valley of ashes. The doughty players of Stirling were determined to defend with desperation and Willie Murray, the goalkeeper, performed excellently as Celtic swamped their unheralded opponents. For all that, victory was denied Celtic when, in the final minute, Billy McNeill rose in the Stirling Albion penalty area and planted a header past Murray. Ian Foote, the referee, ruled it out as a goal for no discernible reason.

Attendance: 16,000

1 March 1967

European Cup quarter-final first leg, Vojvodina Stadium

Vojvodina Novi Sad 1, Celtic 0

Vojvodina: Stanić 69

Fireworks were sent soaring into the Serbian night air after this victory for the home side, whose impressive football had Celtic pinned down for much of the match. Yet, for all their clever, intricate play, Vojvodina lacked a punchy finish and only rarely was Ronnie Simpson directly troubled. Indeed, the visitors might have escaped with a 0–0 draw but for an error on the part of Tommy Gemmell. Vojvodina flew at Celtic from the outset and slick early moves saw both Svemir Đorđić and Vladimir Rakić narrowly miss the target. The game continued in the same vein, with Celtic attacking only sporadically and unprofitably. Then, with 69 minutes played, Tommy Gemmell lost the ball slackly to Đorđić and he moved it on swiftly to Milan Stanić, who clipped it with alacrity past Ronnie Simpson to the exuberant acclaim of the home crowd.

Attendance: 24,000

4 March 1967

Scottish League First Division, St Mirren Park, Love Street

St Mirren 0, Celtic 5

Celtic: Wallace 31, 88, Lennox 48, Hughes 53, Gemmell 82 (pen)

On a pitch that resembled the swamp from a B-movie horror film, the svelte Celts still managed to flit across the surface swiftly and efficiently in dealing dutifully with the flimsy threat of St Mirren, a side that had held them to a turbulent draw earlier in the season. 'This was an excellent result for us,' Jock Stein said. 'There could have been a setback because of our midweek trip abroad, injuries and the pitch but we came through it all very well.' Notably, Stein had fielded John Hughes, habitually the outside-left, on the right wing and the player had looked thoroughly comfortable in that role.

Attendance: 18,000

8 March 1967

European Cup quarter-final second leg, Celtic Park

Celtic 2, Vojvodina Novi Sad 0

Celtic: Chalmers 61, McNeill 90

'We have to go for goals,' Jock Stein said in advance of a match that proved a similar entity to the one in Serbia, this time with Vojvodina massing in defence and Celtic doggedly seeking to create a hole in the dyke. Stevie Chalmers had been nursing a shoulder injury that he had collected in the first leg and had missed the league match at St Mirren on the Saturday – he was a player that Vojvodina feared because of his pace and his assiduous devotion to hard work. With Joe McBride injured and Willie Wallace ineligible, Chalmers' presence was vital. Dobrivoje Trivić and Vasa Pušibrk were back on the left wing for Vojvodina after suspension. Pušibrk missed a good chance to open the scoring for Vojvodina after five minutes and Vojvodina more than held their own until half-time, leaving Celtic Park anxious and tense. The equaliser arrived when Ilija Pantelić, the goalkeeper, failed to cut out a Tommy Gemmell cross and Chalmers clipped the ball home. With seconds remaining, and Vojvodina still composed, Billy McNeill met a Charlie Gallagher corner to head the winner. It was one of only three goals that McNeill would score that season. This was the first time in European competition that Celtic had recovered to win a tie after having lost the first leg.

Attendance: 75,000

11 March 1967

Scottish Cup quarter-final, Celtic Park

Celtic 5, Queen's Park 3

Celtic: Gemmell 7 (pen), Chalmers 23, Wallace 33, Murdoch 38, Lennox 84

Queen's Park: Gemmell 1 (og), Hopper 31, 46

'This tie is no less important than the one against Vojvodina,' Jock Stein bluffed in advance of the encounter with the Glasgow amateurs, the enormous noise from the European Cup quarter-final crowd three days earlier seemingly only just dying down as the spectators ambled into Celtic Park for this domestic quarter-final that promised a wild contrast with that night of drama. A thread had run through Celtic's season of players who had blundered coming good and making amends. Gemmell's short backpass had given Vojvodina the lead in Novi Sad but it had been Gemmell whose pounding run and cross had set up Stevie Chalmers to score, crucially, in the return match. Gemmell now scored a first-minute own goal against Queen's Park but quickly equalised through a penalty. Queen's Park were managed by Harold Davis, the hearty former Rangers player, who placed the accent on his team's physical fitness. 'Even when Celtic beat us 4–0 earlier in the season, we were still running with them at the end,' he said, revealing the aspect of football that was closest to his heart. 'We are not going like lambs to the slaughter.' His players afforded Celtic a lively game until Bobby Lennox sealed Celtic's place in the semis.

Attendance: 34,000

18 March 1967
Scottish League First Division, Celtic Park

Celtic 3, Dunfermline Athletic 2

Celtic: Chalmers 3, Gemmell 21 (pen), Wallace 42
Dunfermline Athletic: Ferguson 19, 87

A solid victory over Dunfermline was notable for Alex Ferguson becoming the player to score most often against Celtic over the season, with his fourth and fifth goals against them.

Attendance: 41,000

20 March 1967
Scottish League First Division
Celtic Park

Celtic 5, Falkirk 0

Celtic: Chalmers 25, 74, Auld 28, Hughes 67, Gemmell 68 (pen)

'I would hope that goal-average won't be needed at the end of the day,' Jock Stein had said in advance of a match that saw his team do much to fulfil his wish. Celtic regained the lead at the top of the league, at Rangers' expense, going two points ahead on a Monday evening on which they used up their game in hand. A stuffy Falkirk side were eviscerated by some excellent play on the part of John Hughes and Stevie Chalmers. Jimmy Johnstone returned after suspension and was fouled by Doug Baillie in the penalty area to concede the penalty from which Tommy Gemmell scored. Sweet strikes from Chalmers, Bertie Auld and Hughes put Celtic fully in control, while the fifth was a mere tap-in from Chalmers after Auld's shot had struck a post.

Attendance: 25,000

25 March 1967
Scottish League First Division, Tynecastle Stadium

Heart of Midlothian 0, Celtic 3

Celtic: Auld 42, Wallace 62, Gemmell 85 (pen)

Celtic had not won a league match at Tynecastle since the 1954–55 season, when Jock Stein was the team captain, but they cruised to the victory here despite Bobby Murdoch being carried off the field with damaged ankle ligaments two minutes into the match and then forced to leave it altogether with quarter of an hour remaining, replaced by Bobby Lennox. The victory was built, as so often, on Ronnie Simpson keeping out the opposition when the score was 0–0. Danny Ferguson, the Hearts midfield player, had a superb scoring opportunity repulsed by Simpson stopping his shot after nine minutes. Bertie Auld put Celtic ahead with a volley, Willie Wallace added to that with a powerful free-kick and Tommy Gemmell made it three with a penalty – his fourth in consecutive games – after Jimmy Johnstone had been felled inside the area.

Attendance: 25,000

27 March 1967
Scottish League First Division, Firhill Stadium

Partick Thistle 1, Celtic 4

Partick Thistle: Flanagan 52

Celtic: Lennox 41, Chalmers 59, 86, Wallace 67

Celtic's 100th league goal of the season was a fine one, Bobby Lennox meeting Jimmy Johnstone's low corner with a powerful, angled shot that flew from the edge of the penalty area into the roof of the net. Arriving shortly before half-time, the goal was utterly deserved after a first half in which Celtic had frequently pinned down Partick in their penalty area with a host of shots and headers that Georgie Niven, the goalkeeper, his defence and his goal-frame had repelled. A Celtic goal in such circumstances tended to signal a subsequent flood, once the dam had broken, but instead John Flanagan, the Partick forward, equalised shortly after the break, with a fine 30-yard shot. A Stevie Chalmers header from Johnstone's cross put Celtic in front again, then Johnstone set up Willie Wallace, playing in midfield in the absence of the injured Bobby Murdoch, for Celtic's third before Chalmers scored the final goal with a header from a Tommy Gemmell cross.

Attendance: 30,000

1 April 1967

Scottish Cup semi-final, Hampden Park

Celtic 0, Clyde 0

Clyde had conceded 17 goals in four games against Celtic and were a part-time team but, under the management of Davie White, had had an excellent season. A representative of Dukla Prague, Celtic's European Cup semi-final opponents, plonked himself down in the main stand at Hampden but saw a poor performance from the Scottish champions. 'We struggled a bit in midfield and never really got going as we can,' Stein admitted, 'but Clyde played very well and we cannot grudge them a draw.' The Celtic manager had knocked on the Clyde dressing room door after the match to congratulate his opponents on their performance.

Attendance: 56,704

5 April 1967

Scottish Cup semi-final replay, Hampden Park

Celtic 2, Clyde 0

Celtic: Lennox 2, Auld 24

The speed, directness and decisiveness of Bobby Lennox and Stevie Chalmers proved key to the win that sent Celtic into the Scottish Cup final. Both forwards were involved in the opening goal, which arrived after only two minutes, as a Celtic team chastised by Stein for their performance in the first game with Clyde set out to make amends. Chalmers' close-range shot was blocked by Tommy McCulloch, the Clyde goalkeeper, and Lennox, following in, slipped the rebound smartly past him. Bertie Auld zipped on to a headed flick from Chalmers midway through the first half and sent a shot high into the net to make it 2–0 and after that Celtic motored serenely through the remainder of the match, easing into their third successive Scottish Cup final.

Attendance: 55,138

8 April 1967

Scottish League First Division, Fir Park

Motherwell 0, Celtic 2

Celtic: Wallace 58, Gemmell 79 (pen)

'We will have to plan with Dukla in mind,' Jock Stein said of a match at Fir Park that suddenly took on a dun hue in comparison to the European Cup semi-final to be staged at Celtic Park four days later. Stein, as good as his word, left out Bobby Murdoch, back in training after injury, but needed badly for the game with the Czechs. Jimmy Johnstone also missed the match, supposedly to allow him to recover fully from influenza. Two early saves from Ronnie Simpson kept Celtic level as they started stutteringly but the team had righted itself by the beginning of the second half, when Willie Wallace controlled a loose clearance on the turn and rotated rapidly to rifle a 25-yard shot high into the Motherwell net. Yet another Tommy Gemmell penalty, late in the game, completed a routine win made special only by Wallace's exceptional goal.

Attendance: 21,000

12 April 1967

European Cup semi-final first leg, Celtic Park

Celtic 3, Dukla Prague 1

Celtic: Johnstone 27, Wallace 59, 65
Dukla Prague: Štrunc 44

Dukla Prague set Celtic a tremendous test of composure and kno-whow, using all their *mittel*-European wiles to frustrate Celtic's efforts to pep up the pace of the match. It was the Czechs who came clos-est to opening the scoring early in the match when Stanislav Štrunc broke through but Ronnie Simpson raced from goal to force Štrunc into shooting quickly – and Simpson stopped his hasty shot. Stevie Chalmers, for Celtic, appeared to have scored a legitimate goal when heading home a Jimmy Johnstone cross but it was disallowed by referee Joaquim Fernandes Campos, a Portuguese. The opening goal came from Johnstone himself, who hurtled on to a rebound that he nicked over Ivo Viktor as the gigantic goalkeeper hurtled out towards him. Dukla's equaliser moments before half-time owed as much to lassitude in the Celtic defence as to their own creative play; a series of slack attempts at clearances led to the grounded Josef Nedorost supplying Štrunc with the pass that the crafty winger angled past Simpson. With almost an hour gone of a tense, stop–start game, Tommy Gemmell advanced on the left and sent a high ball forward that Willie Wallace, with a first-time shot, volleyed past Viktor. Wallace, on his European debut for Celtic, made it 3–1 when Bertie Auld cleverly leaned over the ball at a free-kick, as if to steady it, only to nudge it sideways to Wallace who sharply struck it past Viktor.

Attendance: 74,406

19 April 1967

Scottish League First Division, Celtic Park

Celtic 0, Aberdeen 0

Aberdeen had generously agreed to bring this match forward by three days to allow Celtic extra time to prepare for their vital European Cup second leg with Dukla Prague on 25 April – although it did also provide the Pittodrie side with a full ten days of uncluttered preparation in advance of their Scottish Cup final with Celtic at Hampden Park. 'We did not play well,' Stein said of a flat occasion for both sides. Aberdeen had by now drifted away from the top of the league but this dour draw, Stein felt, did much to prepare Celtic for the Scottish Cup final. It meant, he said, that his team 'were completely confident that we could raise our game by 500 per cent'. It also left Celtic three points ahead of Rangers in the league, with each team having three games left to play.

Attendance: 33,000

25 April 1967

European Cup semi-final second leg, Stadion Juliska

Dukla Prague 0, Celtic 0

On a chilly central European day, in the heart of Prague, Celtic were pinned back almost from the moment the game began. Celtic barely mustered a scoring opportunity worthy of the name and Stevie Chalmers, the lone striker, was isolated, but received a huge hug from Stein afterwards for his bravery and commitment in keeping the Dukla defence occupied and hindering the Czechs' attempts at building up play from the back. It was the only time in his career that Chalmers would be singled out for such personal praise from the manager. The defence performed in exemplary fashion to thwart a Dukla side that held possession with some style but who lacked the ability to quicken the game in and around the penalty area, thus failing to get under Celtic's blanket defence. Billy McNeill was outstanding both in organising the Celtic defence and in heading away magnificently anything that came to him in the air. A sporting home crowd applauded him off the field at the conclusion of a match that ended in dull disappointment for the Czechs and delight for the Scots.

Attendance: 19,157

29 April 1967

Scottish Cup final, Hampden Park

Celtic 2, Aberdeen 0

Celtic: Wallace 42, 50

'We can compare with Celtic in all aspects of the game,' Eddie Turnbull, the Aberdeen manager, said two days before the Scottish Cup final. 'We are their equals in team strength, teamwork, in any position and in individual skill.' Strange, then, that Aberdeen were finishing fourth in the First Division, 16 points behind Celtic despite being without the demands and distractions of European football. Turnbull, unfortunately, would be taken ill shortly before kick-off and so would not see his team taken apart quite ruthlessly by Celtic on the day, going behind to two astutely taken goals from Willie Wallace, both resulting from sharp cutbacks from the goal-line. Aberdeen did revive and rally and one Ronnie Simpson save, from Jens Petersen, the centre-half, was exceptional for its improvisation, the goalkeeper scrambling across his line to boot the ball away just as the Dane looked to have given Aberdeen a glimmer of hope. Celtic, though, had been in charge throughout and had shown themselves superior to Aberdeen in every way: slick, sleek, professional and tidy in harvesting the best chances from a good crop. 'Everything worked out perfectly,' Stein said. 'Stevie Chalmers, who got a real buffeting in Prague, got a much easier game on the wing than he would have had in the middle ... yet he put in a power of work in the job he was given to do. Our boys are so versatile, so willing to do the job they get. They play for each other and for the club.'

Attendance: 126,000

3 May 1967

Scottish League First Division, Celtic Park

Celtic 2, Dundee United 3

Celtic: Gemmell 27 (pen), Wallace 61

Dundee United: Hainey 55, Gillespie 68, Graham 71

Celtic paraded the Scottish Cup at half-time, at which point they led Dundee United through a Tommy Gemmell penalty and further celebrations were planned for full-time, with a lap of honour promised if Celtic secured the league title, for which they required only a single point. The players would, instead, remain inside the dressing room after United, firmly rooted in mid-table, bettered their own home victory over Celtic at New Year with Celtic's sole home defeat of the season. John Hughes replaced Stevie Chalmers, still smarting from the blows he had received against Dukla, but the forward flopped as Celtic fell to their first competitive defeat at Celtic Park for 21 months. The clinching of the league title had looked a formality when Dennis Gillespie tripped Bobby Lennox inside the penalty area and Tommy Gemmell lashed home the resultant penalty-kick. Billy Hainey, who had scored against Barcelona with a 35-yard shot, equalised after half-time with a swerving chip over Ronnie Simpson. Willie Wallace put Celtic ahead again but again United equalised, Gillespie heading in an Orjan Persson corner. Three minutes after that, Gemmell was short with a pass back and Jackie Graham nipped in to replicate the scoreline when United had won on New Year's Eve.

Attendance: 44,000

6 May 1967
Scottish League First Division, Ibrox Park

Rangers 2, Celtic 2
Rangers: Jardine 40, Hynd 81
Celtic: Johnstone 41, 74

Celtic got the point they needed to clinch the 1966–67 league title on an afternoon of near-incessant rain at Ibrox, but the dull conditions could not take the shine off a pristine performance on a muddy, difficult surface. Celtic's freedom of movement was rather restricted in the first half as Rangers pushed to retain their interest in taking the title. Billy McNeill found Roger Hynd a handful but Hynd was isolated in a fashion that Stein would never have allowed with regard to one of his own players in such a match. Hynd, a centre-half, had been selected to lead the forward line by John Lawrence, the interfering Rangers chairman, to Hynd's embarrassment as the the player felt there were forwards who should have played ahead of him. Sandy Jardine opened the scoring for Rangers with a fine long-range shot but within a minute, Jimmy Johnstone had equalised, cleverly anticipating the rebound after Bobby Lennox's shot had struck the post and tipping the ball over the line from close range. During the second half, with Johnstone revelling in being given a free role, he topped his performance with a stunning effort, veering inside on to his left foot and curling a shot into the top corner of the Rangers net from 25 yards out. A late equaliser from Hynd gave Rangers a draw but Celtic the championship.

Attendance: 78,000

15 May 1967

Scottish League First Division, Celtic Park

Celtic 2, Kilmarnock 0

Celtic: Lennox 24, Wallace 76

Jock Stein was carried shoulder-high on to the pitch at the end of a match that was the only competitive fixture in Celtic's season not to have any serious significance in terms of the result. The three national domestic trophies, plus the Reserve League Cup and the Glasgow Cup, were transported around the perimeter of the pitch at half-time, on the roof of a car decorated in green and white. Although there were no trophies at stake, Stein took the match seriously enough to field 'as strong a side as I've turned out all season and it will be near enough the team that will play in Lisbon. There will be no question of anyone taking it easy. That is how a player gets hurt.' For all such bluster, Stein fielded John Fallon in goal for the first time in 20 months, resting Ronnie Simpson, and John Cushley at centre-half to allow Ron Greenwood, the watching West Ham United manager, to get a look at the player in competitive action, with a view to his subsequent transfer to Upton Park. It was Cushley's only appearance of the season. An effervescent Celtic easily defeated Kilmarnock. Bobby Lennox, midway through the first half, flipped the ball over Bobby Ferguson in the Kilmarnock goal to open the scoring. Willie Wallace made it 2–0 with a powerful left-foot shot.

Attendance: 22,000

25 May 1967

European Cup final, Estádio Nacional, Lisbon, Portugal

Celtic 2, Internazionale 1

Celtic: Gemmell 63, Chalmers 85

Internazionale: Mazzola 7 (pen)

'This is the biggest occasion Celtic have faced,' Jock Stein said, 'the biggest any club can face. The players know how much it means in every way.' They showed that Stein's words, as ever, were pointedly correct. On a firm, flinty pitch, Celtic, as was their wont in Europe over the season, worked their way into the match gradually, to a point at which they were entirely dominant by the time the second half began. Jock Stein had expressed himself uninterested in the team that Internazionale would field except to say, 'My own personal wish is that Herrera is able to field his best team.' Stein was confident that his players could take the game to the Italians and they did so in exquisite style. He treated his players, he said, not as a team but as a family. 'I reckon that the dividends have been reaped because I was able to gain their complete confidence.' That mutual confidence was reflected in Stein's team playing as they had never done before and would never do again, with players constantly interchanging positions selflessly for the benefit of the team effort. It was the summation of all that Stein had learned, absorbed and imparted in all his years as a footballer and as a football manager, and it made for greatness. Stein, the day before the final, had promised the Portuguese, 'We will attack and entertain.' They did. Sandro Mazzola's early penalty was levelled by a 22-yard Tommy Gemmell shot and Stevie Chalmers nicked the winner at the end.

'It was a great occasion,' Jimmy Johnstone said. 'Inter must have seen us and said, 'What a beauty! Here we go!' But after the first 20 minutes we were saying, "Hey, are these [the Italians] kidding us on? When are they going to start to play?" We were running them ragged, so we were. See when you look at that game, could you believe how many chances we made? We could have beaten them 10 . . . we could have beaten them 10–1 with the chances. Sarti had a game that was unbelievable – out of this world. That was it. And the heat – it was hot enough for it to have burned a hole in your head!'

There could have, should have, been more goals for Celtic but sometimes less really is more.

Attendance: 45,000

BIBLIOGRAPHY

Newspapers

Evening Citizen, Evening Times, Daily Express, Glasgow Herald, Observer, Sunday Express, Mail on Sunday, Sunday Times

Books

Celtic: Pride and Passion (Mainstream Publishing 2014) by Jim Craig and Pat Woods

The Head Bhoys (Mainstream Publishing 2002, 2003) by Graham McColl

Lion Heart (Virgin Books, 2004, 2005) by Tommy Gemmell with Graham McColl

The Official Biography of Celtic (Headline Books, 2008) by Graham McColl

The Official History of Celtic (Hamlyn Books, 1995, 1996, 1998) by Graham McColl

Thirty Miles from Paradise (Headline Books, 2007, 2008) by Bobby Lennox

The Winning Touch (Headline Books, 2012) by Stevie Chalmers with Graham McColl

ACKNOWLEDGEMENTS

This book began to take shape in the mid-1990s, when I first interviewed Jimmy Johnstone, and over the years I have been privileged to interview, in depth, others of the Lisbon Lions to glean their tremendous insights into that 1966–67 season and Celtic's ultimate triumph, in Lisbon. I am grateful to them all: Bertie Auld, Stevie Chalmers, John Clark, Jim Craig, the late Tommy Gemmell, the late Jimmy Johnstone, Bobby Lennox, Billy McNeill and Willie Wallace.

I would also like to thank the following, whose help was invaluable: Tom Cairns, Bobby Clark, Luigi Crippa at FC Internazionale, Sandy Davie, Charlie Gallagher, Joe Gilroy, Jimmy Gordon – Lord Gordon of Strathblane, Billy Hainey, Uli Hesse, John Hughes, Othmar 'Omi' Iten, Kristyna Kratochvílová at FK Dukla Prague, Jakob 'Kobi' Kuhn, Patrick Lienhart, the late Joe McBride, Richard Mills at the University of East Anglia, Len Murray, Vasa Pusibrk, Radivoj Radosav, Yannick Rappan at the Swiss Football Association, Benny Rooney, Milos Subotin, Website Editor and Social Media Manager of Vojvodina Football Club, Finn Sulzer at FC Zurich, Vladimir Taborsky, Josef Vacenovsky and Ivo Viktor.

Special thanks to Ian Marshall at Simon & Schuster for commissioning this book and for assiduous, helpful and creative editing, and to Kevin Pocklington at Jenny Brown Associates who was instrumental in bringing the idea to life and then taking it forward. Thanks also to Harriet Dobson at Simon & Schuster.